Hol

KT-502-449

The Good Research Guide

Healthcare Library H05
Tom Rudd Unit
Moorgreen Hospital
Southampton SO30 3JB
Tel: 023 8047 5154
www.hantshealthcarelibrary.nhs.uk
library.moorgreen@southernhealth.nhs.uk

This book is due for return on or before the last date shown below

- 7 APR 2010

5 NOV 10

17 FEB 2014

2 1 DEC 2016

1 3 MAR 2017

withdrawn

The Good Research Guide

for small-scale social research projects

Third Edition

Martyn Denscombe

HEALTHCARE LIBRARY
ROYAL SOUTH HANTS HOSPITAL
BRINTONS TERRACE
SOUTHAMPTON
SO14 0YG

Open University Press

Open University Press
McGraw-Hill Education
McGraw-Hill House
Shoppenhangers Road
Maidenhead
Berkshire
England
SL6 2QL

email: enquiries@openup.co.uk
world wide web: www.openup.co.uk

and Two Penn Plaza, New York, NY 10121-2289, USA

First published 1998
Reprinted 1998, 1999, 2000, 2001
Second edition printed 2003
Reprinted 2005 (twice), 2006
This third edition printed 2007
Reprinted 2008

Copyright © Martyn Denscombe 2007

All rights reserved. Except for the quotation of short passages for the
purposes of criticism and review, no part of this publication may be
reproduced, stored in a retrieval system, or transmitted, in any form,
or by any means, electronic, mechanical, photocopying, recording or
otherwise, without the prior written permission of the publisher or a
licence from the Copyright Licensing Agency Limited. Details of such
licences (for reprographic reproduction) may be obtained from the
Copyright Licensing Agency Ltd of Saffron House, 6–10 Kirby Street,
London, EC1N 8TS

A catalogue record of this book is available from the British Library

ISBN-13: 978 0 03 522022 9 (pb)
ISBN-10: 0 03 522022 3 (pb)

Library of Congress Cataloging-in-Publication Data
CIP data applied for

Typeset by RefineCatch Limited, Bungay, Suffolk
Printed in Finland by WS Bookwell, Finland 2008

The *McGraw·Hill* Companies

Contents

List of figures

Acknowledgements

There are those close to home who contribute to the completion of a book by putting the author in a position to start, sustain and finish the book. For this reason, and many others, I would like to dedicate this book to my family. Thanks especially to Viv – this book is for you. Friends and colleagues have also played their part. David Field and Derek Layder, in particular, have provided support and encouragement over the years. Colleagues at De Montfort University also deserve my thanks for being good to work with.

Martyn Denscombe
Leicester

Introduction

A book for 'project researchers'

Social research is no longer the concern of the small elite of professionals and full-time researchers. It has become the concern of a far greater number of people who are faced with the prospect of undertaking small-scale research projects as part of an academic course or as part of their professional development. It is these people who provide the main audience for this book.

The aim of the book is to present these *project researchers* with practical guidance and a vision of the key issues involved in social research. It attempts to provide project researchers with vital information that is easily accessible and which gets to the heart of the matter quickly and concisely. In doing this, the book is based on three premises:

1 Most of what needs to be known and done in relation to the production of competent social research can be stated in *straightforward language*.
2 The foundations of good social research depend on paying attention to *certain elementary factors*. If such factors are ignored or overlooked, the research will be open to criticism and serious questions may be raised about the quality of the findings. Good research depends on addressing those key points. The answers may vary from topic to topic, researcher to researcher. There may be no one 'right' answer, but the biggest possible guarantee of poor research is to ignore the issues.
3 Project researchers can safeguard against making elementary errors in the design and execution of their research by using a *checklist approach*, in which they assure themselves that they have attended to the 'minimum' requirements and have not overlooked crucial factors associated with the production of good research

Part I

Strategies for social research

The process of putting together a piece of good research is not something that can be done by slavishly following a set of rules about what is right and wrong. In practice, the *social researcher is faced with a variety of options and alternatives and has to make strategic decisions about which to choose*. Each choice brings with it a set of assumptions about the social world it investigates. Each choice brings with it a set of advantages and disadvantages. Gains in one direction will bring with them losses in another, and the social researcher has to live with this.

There is no 'one right' direction to take. There are, though, some strategies that are better suited than others for tackling specific issues. In practice, good social research is a matter of 'horses for courses', where approaches are selected because they are *appropriate* for specific types of investigation and specific kinds of problems. They are chosen as 'fit for purpose'. *The crucial thing for good research is that the choices are reasonable and that they are made explicit as part of any research report.*

Horses for courses

- Approaches are selected because they are appropriate for specific types of investigation and specific kinds of problems.
- 'Strategic' decisions aim at putting the social researcher in the best possible position to gain the best outcome from the research.
- In good research the choices are (a) reasonable and (b) made explicit as part of any research report.

Key decisions about the strategy and methods to be used are usually taken right at the start of a project. When you have embarked on a particular approach it is not easy to do a U-turn. Particularly for small-scale research, there tend to be tight constraints on time and money, which mean that the researcher does not have the luxury of thinking, 'Well, I'll try this approach and see how it goes and, if it doesn't work, I'll start again with a different approach . . . put Plan B into operation.' In the real world, research projects are normally one-off investigations where, if you do not get it right first time, the research fails.

To avoid starting on a path that ultimately gets nowhere there are some things which can be taken into consideration right at the outset as the researcher contemplates which approach to choose. In effect, the checklist on the following page can be used by the project researcher to gauge if what he or she has in mind is a 'starter' or a 'non-starter' as a proposition. If the researcher is able to score well in the sense of meeting the points in the checklist – not all, but a good majority – then he or she can feel fairly confident that the research is starting from a solid foundation and that it should not be necessary to back-track and start again once the project has got under way.

Key decisions about social research

When undertaking research you should feel confident about answering 'yes' to the following questions: ☑

Issue	Factors to be considered	
Relevance Does it really matter whether the research takes place?	• Does the research have significance in relation to some practical or theoretical issue?	☐
	• Will the research build upon existing knowledge about the topic?	☐
Feasibility Can it be done?	• Is there sufficient time for the design of the research, collection of data and analysis of results?	☐
	• Will the resources be available to cover the costs of the research (e.g. travel, printing)?	☐
	• Will it be possible and practical to gain access to necessary data (people, events, documents)?	☐
Coverage Are the right things included?	• Will an adequate number and suitable diversity of people, events, etc. be included?	☐
	• Will it be reasonable to make generalizations on the basis of the data collected?	☐
	• Is it likely that there will be an adequate response rate?	☐
Accuracy Will the research produce true and honest findings?	• Will the data be precise and detailed?	☐
	• Are respondents likely to give full and honest answers?	☐
	• Will the investigation manage to focus on the most vital issues?	☐
Objectivity What chance is there that the research will provide a fair and balanced picture?	• Can I avoid being biased because of my personal values, beliefs and background?	☐
	• Will the research be approached with an open mind about what the findings might show?	☐
	• Am I prepared to recognize the limitations of the research approach that is adopted?	☐
Ethics What about the rights and feelings of those affected by the research?	• Can I avoid any deception or misrepresentation in my dealings with the research subjects?	☐
	• Will the identities and the interests of those involved be protected?	☐
	• Can I guarantee the confidentiality of the information given to me during the research?	☐

© M. Denscombe, *The Good Research Guide*. Open University Press.

1

Surveys

What is a survey?

In one sense, the word 'survey' means 'to view comprehensively and in detail'. In another sense it refers specifically to the act of 'obtaining data for mapping'. These aspects of the definition of a survey, of course, derive from the classic versions of geographical surveys and ordnance surveys which map out the landscape or the built environment of roads and buildings. The principles, though, have been used to good effect on mapping out the social world as well as the physical world and, indeed, surveys have emerged in recent times as one of the most popular and commonplace approaches to social research. Such *social* surveys share with their physical counterparts some crucial characteristics.

- *Wide and inclusive coverage.* Implicit in the notion of 'survey' is the idea that the research should have a wide coverage – a breadth of view. A survey, in principle, should take a panoramic view and 'take it all in'.
- *At a specific point in time.* The purpose of mapping surveys is generally to 'bring things up to date', and so it is with the notion of social surveys. Surveys usually relate to the present state of affairs and involve an attempt to provide a snapshot of how things are at the specific time at which the data are collected. Though there might be occasions when researchers will wish to do a retrospective study to show how things used to be, these remain more an exception than the rule.

- *Empirical research.* In the sense that 'to survey' carries with it the meaning 'to look', survey work inevitably brings with it the idea of empirical research. It involves the idea of getting out of the chair, going out of the office and purposefully seeking the necessary information 'out there'. The researcher who adopts a survey approach tends to buy in to a tradition of research which emphasizes the quest for details of tangible things – things that can be measured and recorded.

> **Key point**
>
> **The survey approach is a research strategy, not a research method. Many methods can be incorporated in the use of a social survey.**

These three characteristics of the survey approach involve no mention of specific research methods. It is important to recognize this point. The survey approach is a research *strategy*, not a method. Researchers who adopt the strategy are able to use a whole range of methods within the strategy: questionnaires, interviews, documents and observation. What is distinctive about the survey approach is its combination of a commitment to a breadth of study, a focus on the snapshot at a given point in time and a dependence on empirical data. That is not to deny that there are certain methods which are popularly associated with the use of surveys, nor that there are certain methods which sit more comfortably with the use of the strategy than others. This is true for each of the main research strategies outlined in the book. However, in essence, surveys are about a particular approach – not the methods – an approach in which there is empirical research pertaining to a given point in time which aims to incorporate as wide and as inclusive data as possible.

Types of survey

Surveys come in a wide variety of forms, and are used by researchers who can have very different aims and discipline backgrounds. A brief listing can never include all the possibilities, but it can help to establish the most common types of survey and give some indication about their application.

Postal questionnaires

Probably the best known kind of survey is that which involves sending 'self-completion' questionnaires through the post. This generally involves a large-scale mailing covering a wide geographical area.

Postal questionnaires are usually, though not always, received 'cold' by the respondent. This means that there is not usually any personal contact between the researcher and the respondent, and the respondent receives no prior notification of the arrival of the questionnaire.

Link up with **Response rates, pp. 22–5**

The proportion of people who respond as requested to such 'cold' postal questionnaires is quite low. The actual proportion will depend on the nature of the topic(s) and the length of the questionnaire. As a rough guide, any social researcher will be lucky to get as many as 20 per cent of the questionnaires returned. As a result, this form of postal questionnaire tends to be used only with very large mailings, where a low response will still provide sufficient data for analysis. The small proportion that respond is unlikely to represent a true cross-section of those being surveyed in terms of age, sex, social class, etc. Some types of people are more likely to fill in and return their questionnaires than others. However, the results can be 'weighted' according to what is already known about the composition of the people being surveyed (in terms of age, sex, social class, etc.), so that the data which eventually get analysed are based on the actual proportions among those surveyed rather than the proportions that were returned to the researchers via the post.

Internet surveys

The Internet survey provides a fast and cheap alternative to postal surveys, telephone surveys and face-to-face clipboard questionnaires when it comes to collecting survey data (Couper, 2000; Dillman, 2007). Using the Internet, the survey can be conducted in one of three main ways:

- *An email questionnaire.* The questions are sent as part of the email itself.
- A questionnaire sent with an email as *an attachment.*
- *A web-based questionnaire.* The questionnaire can be designed as a web page and located on a host site, waiting for people who visit the site to complete it.

Link up with **Internet questionnaires, pp. 160–1**

As with other forms of survey, the response rate from Internet surveys is influenced by the visual appeal of the questionnaire and the ease with which it can be answered and returned. Likewise, the response rate is boosted where potential respondents are contacted in advance, especially where the contact involves a personalized form of message in which people are greeted by name. And a planned follow-up of non-responses enhances the response rate just as it does with a postal survey (Dillman, 2007). Internet surveys do not appear to have any significant distorting impact on the nature of the information that is provided by respondents. Although there is not a great deal of research evidence on this point, where researchers have compared findings from web-based and paper-based questionnaires the evidence would suggest that there is, in fact, little or no difference between the modes of delivery (Denscombe, 2006; McCabe, 2004).

Sampling frames, however, are less readily available in relation to Internet research than for postal surveys. Given the nature of email addresses and website addresses it is more difficult than with postal addresses to direct the survey towards respondents who fit specific required categories. This is particularly the case if the survey involves a web-based questionnaire where the respondents comprise those who self-select by choosing to visit a particular website. Internet surveys, though, can use ready-made email lists, where these exist, in order to contact a sample of appropriate people, e.g. a company's list of employees' email addresses or a discussion group on the web.

Face-to-face interviews

As the name suggests, the face-to-face survey involves direct contact between the researcher and the respondent. This contact can arise through approaches made by the researcher 'in the street'. The sight of the market researcher with her clipboard and smile is familiar in town centres. Or the contact can be made by calling at people's homes. Sometimes these will be 'on spec' to see if the householder is willing and able to spare the time to help with the research. On other occasions, contact will be made in advance by letter or phone.

The face-to-face interview is a more expensive way of conducting the survey than the use of the post, Internet or telephones to collect information. Interviewer time and interviewer travel costs are considerable. Weighed against this, researchers might expect the data obtained to be more detailed and rich, and the face-to-face contact offers some immediate means of validating the data. The researcher can sense if she is being given false information in the face-to-face context in a way that is not possible with questionnaires and less feasible with telephone surveys.

The response rate will be better than with other survey approaches. Part of the researcher's skill is to engage the potential respondent and quickly manoeuvre the person to get his or her co-operation. An armlock is not called for here; something a little more subtle. The point is, though, that the face-to-face contact allows the researcher the opportunity to 'sell' the thing to the potential respondent in a way that the use of questionnaires and telephones does not.

Face-to-face contact also allows researchers to select carefully their potential respondents so that they get responses from just those people needed to fill necessary quotas. A required number of males and females can be ensured. A suitable balance of age bands can be guaranteed. Appropriate numbers of ethnic groups and earnings categories can be incorporated with a minimum prospect of redundant material. There is an efficiency built into this form of data collection despite its expensive nature.

Link up with **Quota sampling, p. 15**

Telephone interviews

Telephone surveys used to be considered a rather suspect research method, principally because it was felt that contacting people by phone led to a biased sample. In the past there was a strong probability that the kind of people who could be contacted by phone were not representative of the wider population; they tended to be the financially better off. However, telephone surveys are now in widespread use in social research, and there are three main reasons for this.

1 *Telephone interviewing is cheaper and quicker than face-to-face interviewing.* Researchers do not have to travel to all parts of the country to conduct the interviews – they only have to pick up a phone. This has always been recognized as an advantage but, until recently, there have been doubts about the reliability of the data gathered by telephone. Social researchers have not been willing to sacrifice the quality of data for the economies that telephone interviewing can bring.
2 *People are as honest in telephone interviews as they are with face-to-face type interviews.* Question marks are now being placed against any assumption that face-to-face interviews produce better, more accurate, data.
3 *There is the prospect of contacting a representative sample when conducting surveys by phone.* Most people aged over 18 years can be contacted directly by telephone. Developments in technology have boosted the attractiveness of telephone surveying because it has become easier to contact a *random sample* of the population using a 'random-digit dialling' technique. Researchers can select the area they wish to survey and identify the relevant dialling code for that area. They can then contact phone numbers at random within that area using random-digit dialling, where the final digits of the phone numbers are produced by computer technology which automatically generates numbers at random.

Telephone contact brings with it some of the immediate one-to-one interaction associated with face-to-face interviews. Although it forfeits the visual contact of face-to-face interviewing, it retains the 'personal' element and the two-way interaction between the researcher and the respondent. It gives the researcher some brief opportunity to explain the purpose of the phone call and to cajole the respondent into providing the required information: 'Or perhaps I can call back at a later time if that is more convenient.' On the other hand, the telephone contact is more intrusive than the postal questionnaire, intruding on people's quality time at home in a way that a postal questionnaire does not. But, perhaps, more than this, it confronts the problem of having to contend with the 'double-glazing' sales pitch which comes over the phone in the guise of research. *The methods of genuine research can be used and abused to sell products rather than collect information.*

Caution

Cell phones pose something of a problem for telephone surveys. Increasingly, 'mobiles' are being used instead of – not just in addition to – conventional land-line phones and it is likely that, as things progress, more people will come to rely exclusively on their cell phone and cease to use a household land-line number. As a consequence, telephone surveys will face a new challenge in terms of reaching a representative sample of the population. Principally, this is because cell phone numbers are not allocated by geographical location (in the UK). This means that the researcher can know very little about the likely social background of any cell phone user included in a survey.

Documents

All too often in writing about social surveys, attention is focused solely on surveys of people. Yet, in practice, the strategy of the survey can be applied to documents as well as living people. The social researcher can undertake empirical research based on documents which incorporates as wide and as inclusive data as possible, and which aims to 'bring things up to date'. Newspapers, company reports, and committee minutes are just some of the possible sources that can be surveyed.

Observations

Classic social surveys involved observations of things like poverty and living conditions. Such observation followed the tradition of geographical and ordnance surveys, with their emphasis on looking at the landscape. Although the practice of conducting a survey through observing events and conditions is less common as a feature of social research in the twenty-first century, it serves to remind us that the survey strategy can use a range of specific methods to collect data and that we should not get hung up on the idea of a social survey as meaning the same thing as a postal questionnaire survey. As well as asking people what they do and what they think, surveys can also *look* at what they actually do.

Surveys and sampling

Social researchers are frequently faced with the fact that they cannot collect data from everyone who is in the category being researched. As a result, they rely on getting evidence from a portion of the whole in the expectation and hope that what is found in that portion applies equally to the rest of the 'population'.

It is not good enough, though, to *assume* that findings for the sample will be replicated in the rest of the population. The sample in the first place needs to be carefully selected if there is to be any confidence that the findings from the sample are similar to those found among the rest of the population being investigated.

Basically, there are two kinds of sampling techniques that can be used by social researchers. The first is known as 'probability' sampling, the second as 'non-probability' sampling. Probability sampling, as the name suggests, is based on the idea that the people or events that are chosen as the sample are chosen because the researcher has some notion of the probability that these will be a representative cross-section of people or events in the whole population being studied. Non-probability sampling is conducted without such knowledge about whether those included in the sample are representative of the overall population.

FIGURE 1 Population and samples

Probability sampling

Random sampling

This approach to sampling involves the selection of people or events literally 'at random'. Behind the use of random sampling lies the assumption that,

- if there are a sufficiently large number of examples selected and
- if their selection has genuinely been 'at random',

then the resulting sample is likely to provide a *representative* cross-section of the whole. To illustrate the idea, with a random sampling approach the researcher might decide to select a sample from the electoral register. The researcher might use a random set of digits (produced specifically for the purpose) to choose the page and line of the register to select a person for inclusion in the sample. The list of random digits ensures the choice is genuinely 'random'.

Link up with **Sampling frame, pp. 19–21**

Systematic sampling

Systematic sampling is a variant of random sampling. It operates on the same principles but introduces some system into the selection of people or events. With the systematic sampling approach, the researcher's choice of people from the electoral register is based on choosing every '*n*th' case. This could be every hundredth person listed in the register, for instance.

If the researcher knows that there are something like 100,000 people listed in the register and he or she wants to identify about 1,000 people for the sample, it is easy to work out that by choosing every hundreth entry in the register this number can be reached quite accurately.

Stratified sampling

A stratified sample can be defined as one in which every member of the population has an equal chance of being selected *in relation to their proportion within the total population*. In the first instance, then, stratified sampling continues to adhere to the underlying principle of randomness. However, it adds some boundaries to the process of selection and applies the principle of randomness *within* these boundaries. It is something of a mixture of random selection and selecting on the basis of specific identity or purpose.

To illustrate the point, a researcher who wishes to collect information about voting behaviour will know in advance, from demographic data, that the population of voters from whom data are to be collected will include a given proportion of males and females, and will include given proportions of different age bands from 18 years up. The researcher should also realize from a review of the literature that sex and age are factors linked with voting behaviour. When constructing the sample, then, the researcher could wisely choose to adopt a stratified sampling approach in which:

- *all relevant categories* of sex and age are included;
- the numbers included for each category are *directly in proportion* to those in the wider population (all voters).

In this way, the voting intentions displayed by the sample are likely to correspond with the voting intentions in the wider population of voters.

The significant advantage of stratified sampling over pure random sampling is that the social researcher can assert some control over the selection of the sample in order to guarantee that crucial people or crucial factors are covered by it, and in proportion to the way they exist in the wider population. This obviously helps the researcher when it comes to generalizing from the findings of the research.

Quota sampling

Quota sampling is widely used in market research. It operates on very similar principles to stratified sampling. It establishes certain categories (or strata) which are considered to be vital for inclusion in the sample, and also seeks to fill these categories in proportion to their existence in the population. There is, though, one distinctive difference between stratified and quota sampling. With quota sampling, the method of choosing the people or events that make up the required number within each category is not a matter of strict random selection. In effect, it is left up to the researcher to choose who fills the quota. It might be on a 'first to hand' basis – as when market researchers stop people in the street. The people might be appropriate but were chosen because they just happened to be there, not as part of a random selection from a known population. The technical difference here excites statisticians but need not trouble the project researcher too much. The crucial point is that, like stratified sampling, it has the advantage of ensuring the representation of all crucial categories in the sample in proportion to their existence in the wider population. It does so without waste. Because the quotas are set in advance, no people or events that subsequently become 'surplus to requirements' are incorporated into the research. Quota sampling, then, has particular advantages when it comes to costs – especially when used with face-to-face interviewing. Its main *disadvantage* is that the numbers needed in each category in order to be in proportion with the wider population can turn out to be quite small – small enough indeed to put a question mark against their use for statistical analysis. The more strata that are used – age, sex, ethnicity, social class, area of residence, etc. – the more likely it is that the quotas for specific categories will be small.

Link up with **Face-to-face interviews, pp. 10–11**

Cluster sampling

The question of resources needs to be taken seriously when it comes to the selection of samples. Identifying units to be included, contacting relevant respondents and travelling to locations can all entail considerable time and expense. The virtues of a purely random selection, then, can be weighed against the savings to be made by using alternative approaches which, while they retain some commitment to the principles of random selection and the laws of probability, try to do so in cost-effective ways.

Cluster sampling is a typical example of this. The logic behind it is that, in reality, it is possible to get a good enough sample by focusing on naturally occurring clusters of the particular thing that the researcher wishes to study. By focusing on such clusters, the researcher can save a great deal of time and money that would otherwise have been spent on travelling to and fro visiting research sites scattered throughout the length and breadth of the land. The selection of clusters as appropriate sites for research follows the principles of probability sampling outlined above. The underlying aim is to get a representative cluster, and the means for getting it rely on random choice or stratified sampling.

A good example of a naturally occurring cluster is a school. If the researcher wishes to study young people aged between 11 and 16 years, then secondary schools offer the possibility of using cluster sampling because they contain a concentration of such people on one site. The researcher does not need to organize the grouping of all the young people on one site – they are there anyway – and it is in this sense that the school offers a naturally occurring cluster.

Multi-stage sampling

Multi-stage sampling, as the name suggests, involves selecting samples from samples, each sample being drawn from within the previously selected sample. For example, from a 'population' of 5,000 schools researchers might select a quota sample of 200 schools for inclusion in their study. Within these 200 schools they might then proceed to conduct a survey with a randomly selected sample of 1,000 students. Subsequently, a small sample of 100 students might be selected for further study. In principle, multi-stage sampling can go on through any number of levels, each level involving a sample drawn from the previous level.

Non-probability sampling

There are often occasions when researchers find it difficult or undesirable to choose their sample on the basis of probability sampling. The reasons for this are varied but, in the main, will be because:

- The researcher feels it is not feasible to include a sufficiently large number of examples in the study.
- The researcher does not have sufficient information about the *population* to undertake probability sampling. The researcher may not know who, or how many people or events, make up the *population*.
- It may prove exceedingly difficult to contact a sample selected through

conventional probability sampling techniques. For example, research on drug addicts or the homeless would not lend itself to normal forms of probability sampling.

Under such circumstances, the social researcher can turn to forms of non-probability sampling as the basis for selecting the sample. When one does so, there is a departure from the principle which underlies probability sampling: that each member of the research population stands an equal chance of being included in the sample. With non-probability sampling this is certainly not the case. A different set of criteria come into play, in terms of how and why people or events get included in the study. The crucial and defining characteristic of non-probability sampling, whatever form it takes, is that the choice of people or events to be included in the sample is definitely *not* a random selection.

Purposive sampling

With *purposive sampling* the sample is 'hand picked' for the research. The term is applied to those situations where the researcher already knows something about the specific people or events and deliberately selects particular ones because they are seen as instances that are likely to produce the most valuable data. In effect, they are selected with a specific purpose in mind, and that purpose reflects the particular qualities of the people or events chosen and their relevance to the topic of the investigation. From the researcher's point of view, the question to ask is this: 'Given what I already know about the research topic and about the range of people or events being studied, who or what is likely to provide the best information?'

The advantage of purposive sampling is that it allows the researcher to home in on people or events which there are good grounds for believing will be critical for the research. Instead of going for the typical instances, a cross-section or a balanced choice, the researcher can concentrate on instances which will display a wide variety – possibly even a focus on extreme cases – to illuminate the research question at hand. In this sense it might not only be economical but might also be informative in a way that conventional probability sampling cannot be.

Snowball sampling

With *snowballing*, the sample emerges through a process of reference from one person to the next. At the start, the research might involve, for example, just a few people. Each can be asked to nominate two other people who would be relevant for the purposes of the research. These nominations are then contacted and, it is hoped, included in the sample. The sample thus snowballs in size as each of the nominees is asked, in turn, to nominate two or more further persons who might be included in the sample.

Snowballing is an effective technique for building up a reasonable-sized sample, especially when used as part of a small-scale research project. One advantage is that the accumulation of numbers is quite quick, using the multiplier effect of one person nominating two or more others. Added to this, the researcher can approach each new person, having been, in a sense, sponsored by the person who had named him or her. The researcher can use the nominator as some kind of reference to enhance his or her *bona fides* and credibility, rather than approach the new person cold. And, of course, the snowball technique is completely compatible with purposive sampling. People can be asked to nominate others who meet certain criteria for choice, certain conditions related to the research project and certain characteristics such as age, sex, ethnicity, qualifications, residence, state of health or leisure pursuits. In a nutshell, snowballing can be very useful for developing the numbers involved in the sample and the issues linked to the research.

Theoretical sampling

With theoretical sampling, the selection of instances follows a route of discovery based on the development of a theory which is 'grounded' in evidence. At each stage, new evidence is used to modify or confirm a 'theory', which then points to an appropriate choice of instances for research in the next phase.

Link up with **Grounded theory, Chapter 6**

Convenience sampling

Convenience sampling is built upon selections which suit the convenience of the researcher and which are 'first to hand'. Now some words of caution are needed in relation to this. To be honest, an element of convenience is likely to enter into sampling procedures of most research. Because researchers have limited money and limited time at their disposal, it is quite reasonable that where there is scope for choice between two or more equally valid possibilities for inclusion in the sample, the researcher should choose the most convenient. As Stake makes the point, 'Our time and access for fieldwork are almost always limited. If we can, we need to pick cases which are easy to get to and hospitable to our inquiry' (Stake, 1995: 4). If two or more clusters are equally suitable as research sites, it would be crazy to opt for ones that were the furthest away without some good reason to do so.

 Caution

Convenience itself offers nothing by way of justification for the inclusion of people or events in the sample. It might be a reasonable practical criterion to apply when faced with equally viable alternatives but, in its own right, is not a factor that should be used by researchers to select the sample. Choosing things on the basis of convenience runs counter to the rigour of scientific research. It suggests a lazy approach to the work. Good research selects its items for study not on the basis that they are the *easiest* to obtain but for specific reasons linked to the subject matter of the research and the requirements of the investigation. For this reason, *the practice of convenience sampling is hard to equate with good research.*

The sampling frame

The use of a sampling frame is very important. A sampling frame is an objective list of 'the population' from which the researcher can make his or her selections.

A sampling frame should ideally contain a complete, up-to-date list of all those that comprise the population for research. As far as surveys of people are concerned, various registers are the most usual basis for the sampling frame. Examples of a sampling frame would be the voting register, the telephone directory or a school attendance list. These supply a list of the residents or school children. The researcher could then either select the required sample size purely at random, or do it more systematically by choosing every tenth, hundredth or whatever case.

Constructing a sampling frame

Researchers wishing to conduct a survey will need to search for a suitable sampling frame. However, it is quite possible that there may not be one that actually meets the needs of the researcher. In this case, he or she will have to produce one. When constructing a sampling frame, it is worth bearing in mind that there are specialist companies supplying lists of addresses. Some companies are able to supply *private addresses* within given postcode or zip-code areas. Usually, they will extract sections from a huge national database which contains 98 per cent of all private addresses in the country. It is also possible to obtain precise address lists of businesses, schools, hospitals, charities and other organizations. Researchers can obtain mailing lists which can be all-encompassing (e.g. all schools in Australia, all hospitals in California), or companies will supply much smaller lists for particular purposes. There is no need to buy a list of all schools, for instance, because the researcher can specify just those kinds of school relevant for research – possibly just secondary schools in the London area, or just primary schools in Wales. Such specific lists tend to suit the needs of small-scale research projects, not least because they can be supplied at relatively low cost. The lists supplied can come in the form of gummed labels for posting, or the researcher can purchase the addresses in the form of a computer database that can be reused as many times as needed for mailing purposes. Generally, mailing lists supplied by commercial companies are kept up-to-date and are as complete as it is reasonably possible to be.

Bias in sampling frames

There is a danger with the use of any sampling frame that it might be incomplete or out of date. A list of private addresses will not lead the researcher to those who are homeless and live on the streets. An electoral register will not include those under 18 years of age or those who, for whatever reason, have not registered to vote. Things omitted might well be different in some important respects from the things which actually exist on the list, and overlooking them as part of the research can lead to a biased sample. Just as damaging for the purposes of research, registers can include certain items that should not be there. They can contain names of people who have passed on – in either a geographical or a mortal sense. People move home, people die, and unless the register is regularly and carefully updated on a routine basis there is the likelihood that it will be out of date and include items it should not. Either way, the impact can be significant as far as research is concerned. If the sampling frame systematically excludes things that should be in, or systematically includes things which should be out, the sample will almost inevitably be biased. So it is vital that the researcher should check on the completeness and up-to-dateness of any sample frame that is considered for use.

 Caution

Since it is unlikely that any sampling frame will be perfect, deficiencies ought to be acknowledged. Good research does not depend on trying to hide limitations in matters like this. It is far better to recognize any ways in which the sampling frame might be less than perfect and to discuss the possible impact on the nature of the sample and the results obtained by the research. There needs to be a brief discussion as part of the research methodology about who is likely to have been missed from the frame and what impact this might have. Any measure taken to compensate for missing items should be explained.

A good sampling frame

A good sampling frame should be:

- *Relevant:* it should contain things directly linked to the research topic.
- *Complete:* it should cover all relevant items.
- *Precise:* it should exclude all the items that are not relevant.
- *Up-to-date:* it should incorporate recent additions and changes, and have redundant items cleansed from the list.

Internet research and sampling frames

The principle that samples should not be biased is one that applies as much to Internet research as it does to other research methodologies. Internet research, though, faces some distinct problems in terms of ensuring that its data are based on a representative group or a cross-section of the population. Not least, this is because addresses, identities and contact points on the Internet are very different from postal addresses and phone numbers in the 'real' world. In cyberspace, an address and an identity can be very temporary and give us precious little background information. In any case, contact lists of email addresses for members of the public and organizations do not exist in anything approaching the likes of an electoral register, postcode address file or telephone directory.

There are, though, some lists that can be useful. There are, for example, distribution lists (provided by Google, Yahoo!, Hotmail and others) that are predominantly based on special interest groups. These do not represent a cross-section of the population that could be used as a frame for the random selection of a sample, but they do provide a list of people that can be used by a researcher who wants a purposive sample based on the particular subject matter around which the interest group revolves. Also, email lists of employees within an organization are likely to be reasonably complete and up-to-date (Stanton and Rogelberg, 2001). Intranets in work organizations tend to serve known populations and can prove a valuable resource for surveys of employees.

Access to such lists, whether based on a special interest group or an organization's employees, will probably require authorization. It is important that such authorization from the moderator of a distribution list or an appropriate person within the organization is obtained in advance of any contact with those on the lists.

Response rates

When surveys are based on responses from people or organizations there is the likelihood that some of those who are contacted with requests for information will not co-operate. The aim of good research is to keep such non-responses to a minimum and to achieve the highest response rate that is possible in relation to the kind of research being conducted.

The willingness of people to go along with the research is affected principally by the following factors.

- *Nature of respondents* (age, sex, disability, literacy, employment status, etc.). Certain kinds of people are less inclined than others to spare the time and make the effort to comply with requests to help with research. Busy people can ill afford the time. Others with more time on their hands, those who are retired for instance, might be more inclined to get involved. People with communication disadvantages, those with reading or hearing difficulties, are less likely than others to get involved unless there is special attention devoted to their needs.
- *Subject of research* (sex, race, religion, politics, income). Certain subjects are taboo and others are sensitive. If the investigation touches on intimate matters or embarrassing topics, there is every likelihood that the response rate will be low. To a lesser extent, where research delves into matters of religion, politics and income there tends to be a lower response rate.
- *Interviewer appearance* (age, sex, social class, ethnicity, clothes, accent). Where the research involves face-to-face contact between the researcher and the respondent, physical appearance has an effect on the response rate. The general adage is that respondents need to feel 'comfortable' with the presence of the researcher. Such comfort, of course, depends on the topic being investigated and the prejudices of the respondent. Within that context, however, the researcher needs to avoid, as far as is possible, presenting himself or herself in a way that will be perceived as threatening or unwholesome by the potential respondent.

Link up with **The interviewer effect, pp. 184–6**

- *Social climate* (free speech). The right to free speech is obviously a factor that will influence people's willingness to collaborate with research and to supply honest and full answers. But this is not simply a matter of legal rights in a democratic society. There are situations in organizations and other social settings where potential respondents may not *feel* free to speak their thoughts. A threatening climate, wherever it exists and whatever its cause, can reduce the response rate.

Bias from non-responses

The main problem with a high non-response rate is that the researcher has little way of knowing whether those who did not respond were in some way different from those who did respond. If the non-respondents are indeed different from the respondents in some significant and relevant way (e.g. in terms of age, sex, gender, social class, religion) the data available to the researcher will be biased, because they systematically overlook facts or opinions from the non-response group. This potential bias arising from non-responses is critical.

There are two types of non-response, both of which can lead to bias in the sample. First, there is *non-response through refusal*. As we have already made the point, if there are grounds for believing that those who refuse are consistently of a different type from those who tend to provide responses, and this difference is relevant to the matter at hand for the research, then there is the likelihood of a bias in the results. Second, there is *non-response stemming from non-contact*. If the sampling frame is used to identify a number of people, items or locations for inclusion in the sample, the researcher needs to be sure that these are indeed contacted and included. Or, perhaps more pertinently, the researcher needs to be sure that any non-contact with those identified through the frame is more or less a random occurrence. If there is any element of a *systematic non-contact* the researcher faces the prospect of having a biased sample. If, for example, the sample is based on household addresses, researchers calling at these addresses between 9 a.m. and 5 p.m. will tend to miss contact with those who are at work. To avoid this they would need to make contact in the evenings as well as during the day.

Response rates will vary markedly within social research depending on the methods being used, the nature of the respondents and the type of issues being investigated. So there is no hard and fast rule about what constitutes an acceptable response rate. With large-scale postal questionnaire surveys, for instance, it will not be uncommon to get a response rate as low as 10–15 per cent. Interviews, arranged by personal contact between the researcher and the interviewees, are the kind of approach at the other end of the spectrum where very high response rates can be expected – possibly even 100 per cent. Rather than look for a figure above which a response rate is acceptable and below which the results become suspect, it is *more productive to evaluate the response rate that is actually achieved in terms of the following questions.*

- *Is the level of response reasonable and in line with comparable surveys?* The researcher can look to similar studies as a way of gauging whether the response rate is acceptable. The methods, the target group, the topic of research, the sponsor of the research and the use of prior contact are all important factors here. Each has a bearing on the level of response. The benchmark, then, needs to be set by the experience of *similar* surveys.
- *Have appropriate measures been adopted to minimize the likelihood of*

non-responses, and have suitable steps been taken to follow up non-respondents to encourage them to collaborate with the research? With any style of research there are practical measures which can be taken to reduce to a minimum the things that deter people from participating in research. These, obviously, will depend on the methods being used and the people being targeted. It is with large-scale questionnaire-type surveys that the measures are generally associated. In such surveys, the research should always build in some tactics for capturing those who do not respond at the initial contact. After a tactful delay, such people should be reminded, and possibly even cajoled into responding.

- Most importantly, *do the non-respondents differ in any systematic and relevant fashion from those who have responded?* Of course, to answer this question the researcher needs to have some information about those who have been targeted but not responded. This may prove difficult. None the less, it is good practice to endeavour to get some data about the non-respondents and to assess whether they are different from the respondents in any way that will have a bearing on the representativeness of the findings.

Response bias and Internet research

In terms of response rates and refusals to participate, fears have been voiced in connection with the use of Internet surveys and questionnaires. It has been suggested that if people feel ill at ease using computers or the Internet the chances are that they will be reluctant to participate in online research. It would appear, however, that such anxieties are largely unfounded. The evidence would point to the fact that postal surveys and Internet-based questionnaires produce similar response rates and, if anything, there are indications that online research might actually be preferred where either is an option (Dillman, 2007, Truell *et al.*, 2002).

Response bias might also arise if people respond differently when using Internet-based data collection methods, if they provide different kinds of answer or supply different amounts of information as a consequence of the online data collection method. On this point, again, the evidence would suggest that there is no particular 'mode effect' associated with Internet research. The quality of responses obtained through Internet survey research is much the same as that of responses produced by more traditional methods (Denscombe, 2006).

Bias through non-contact, however, remains a significant issue for Internet research. Internet research that relies on responses from visitors to websites has the problem that it cannot presume that those who visit the site constitute a cross-section of the population. The issue relates to the use of chat rooms, news groups and online interviews as well. The concern is that those who are contacted and who respond might be representative not of the general public but just of those who are online and interested in a particular subject.

There is also the matter of *Internet connectivity*. Although it is often written that the Internet eliminates the boundaries of space and opens up the prospect of data collection on a global scale, the reality is that certain regions of the world are more likely to be included than others when it comes to research. Since the vast majority of Internet users live in the USA, Europe or Asia Pacific rim countries, those who live in poorer parts of the world are less likely to be included. And, although a large and increasing proportion of the population in developed countries is online, there are still demographic differences that need to be taken into consideration when it comes to who *uses* the Internet the most. The situation could well change rapidly and might vary from country to country but, in the UK in the early years of the new millennium:

- access to the Internet tends to correlate with social class, with wealthier groups being more likely to have access than poorer groups;
- men are more likely to use the Internet than women;
- the elderly are less likely to have access to the Internet than other groups.

For all these reasons, Internet research is better suited to coverage that is deliberately targeted at specific groups. It is better suited to non-probability sampling techniques.

Size of the sample

In order to generalize from the findings of a survey, the sample needs to be of an adequate size. This, of course, begs the question 'What is an adequate size for a sample?' – a straightforward and perfectly reasonable question. However, it is a question which does not lend itself to a correspondingly straightforward answer. The answer, in fact, depends on a number of factors connected with the research which need to be borne in mind and weighed up by the researcher in the process of reaching a decision about the necessary size of the sample.

Big is beautiful(?)

The 'big is beautiful' stance on survey size is based on the principle that the more instances that are covered the less likely it is that the findings will be biased. With a large sample, the researcher is more assured that:

- *all aspects of relevance to the research* question will have been covered and included in the findings;
- there will be some balance between the proportions within the sample and the proportions which occur in the overall population being investigated.

Both factors enhance the representativeness of the sample and, in turn, this allows greater confidence about making generalizations based on findings from the sample.

However, while this provides a good starting point for judging an adequate sample size, it still side-steps the issue of exactly what number of people or events needs to be included in the sample in order for it to be 'adequate'. The researcher still needs to know 'how many'. And for this, statisticians point out that the following points need to be considered.

The accuracy of the results

Any sample, by its very nature, might produce results which are different from the 'true' results based on a survey of the total population. Inevitably, there is an element of luck in terms of who gets included in the sample and who gets excluded, and this can affect the accuracy of the findings which emerge from the sample. Two different samples of 100 people, chosen from the same population and using the same basic method, will produce results that are likely to be slightly different. This is not so much a fault with the sample as a built-in feature of sampling. It is known as the *sampling error*.

To achieve greater accuracy, the researcher might need to increase the size of the sample. Statistical procedures can be used to calculate what specific sample size will be necessary in order to achieve a given level of accuracy. However, there is an interesting point that springs from statistical estimates and sample size. It is that there is relatively little advantage to be gained in terms of accuracy once a sample has reached a given size. There are diminishing returns to increases in the size of samples. In effect, this means that *the crucial factor to be considered in relation to sample size is not the proportion of the population which gets included in the survey, but the absolute size of the sample*. This runs contrary to common sense, which would probably say to us that the degree of accuracy of results would depend on what proportion of the population is included in the sample. Common sense might say that a sample of 25 per cent of cases will produce better results than a sample of 10 per cent. Statistics would say that where the population size is large, there is hardly any increase in accuracy to be obtained by incorporating another 15 per cent.

The absolute size of the sample will depend on the complexity of the population and the research questions being investigated. But, to give an illustration, market research companies will often limit their national samples to around 2,000 to give accurate enough results, and opinion polls in Britain tend to be based on stratified samples of something over 1,000 people. Adding another 5,000 to the sample would not appreciably increase the accuracy of the findings, which are used to generalize about the opinions of over 50 million people.

The number of subdivisions likely to be made within the data

When calculating the number of people or events to include in the sample the researcher needs to take into consideration the complexity of the data that are likely to emerge. A sample size which initially looks quite large might produce only very small returns in relation to specific subdivisions. So, for example, a sample of 100 people used to investigate earnings and occupational status might need to be subdivided according to the age, sex, ethnicity, marital status and qualifications of the people, and according to whether they are full-time, part-time, unemployed, child-rearing or retired. This simple investigation would need a cross-tabulation of five personal factors by five occupational factors, i.e. 25 subdivisions of the data. If the data were equally distributed, this means that there would be only four cases in each of the subdivisions, which is hardly an adequate basis for making generalizations.

In practice, of course, we know that the data would not be evenly distributed and that many of the subdivisions would end up with no cases in them at all. The researcher therefore needs to think ahead when planning the size of the sample to ensure that the subdivisions entailed in the analysis are adequately catered for.

The likely response rate

A survey rarely achieves a response from every contact. Especially when using postal questionnaires and the like, the rate of response from those contacted is likely to be pretty low. As far as sample size is concerned, though, the important thing for the researcher to consider is that the number in the original sample may not equal the number of responses that are finally obtained which can be used in the research. The researcher needs to predict the kind of response rate he or she is likely to achieve, based on the kind of survey being done, and build into the sample size an allowance for non-responses. If the researcher wants to use a sample of some 100 people for research and is using a postal questionnaire survey for which a response rate of 30 per cent is anticipated, the original sample size needs to be 334.

Resources available

Research in the real world does not take place with infinite time and resources. In practice, social research is tailored to meet the constraints of the time and money available for it. Commercial research companies actually advise potential customers that for a given sum of money they can be supplied with results within a given level of accuracy; a greater level of accuracy will cost more. The customer and the commercial researcher need to agree about whether results will be accurate *enough* in relation to the money available to do the research and, in terms of survey research, much of the cost will reflect the chosen size of the sample. This means that *there is a general tendency to choose the minimum sample size that is feasible in light of the level of accuracy demanded of the findings.*

> **Key point: sample size**
>
> 'In practice, the complexity of the competing factors of resources and accuracy means that the decision on sample size tends to be based on experience and good judgement rather than relying on a strict mathematical formula.' (Hoinville *et al.*, 1985: 73)

Sample size and small-scale research

The use of surveys in social research does not necessarily have to involve samples of 1,000 or 2,000 people or events. Whatever the theoretical issues, the simple fact is that surveys and sampling are frequently used in small-scale research involving *between 30 and 250* cases. However, four points need to be stressed in relation to the use of smaller sample sizes.

- Extra attention needs to be paid to the issue of how representative the sample is and special caution is needed about the extent to which generalizations can be made on the basis of the research findings. Provided that the limitations are acknowledged and taken into account, the limited size of the sample need not invalidate the findings.
- The smaller the sample, the simpler the analysis should be, in the sense that the data should be subjected to fewer subdivisions. Keeping the analysis down to four factors, for instance, greatly increases the prospect of having a reasonable number of cases in each category.
- Samples should not involve fewer than 30 people or events. Certainly, it is a mistake to use statistical analyses on samples of fewer than 30 without exceptional care about the procedures involved. Further, it is not acceptable to present the findings of small surveys as percentages without specifying the actual numbers involved. To write that 10 per cent of respondents held a particular opinion when commenting on a survey of 30 people is to attempt to disguise the very low number (i.e. three) on which the comment is based. At best this is naive; at worst it is deceptive.
- In the case of qualitative research there is a different logic for the size of the sample and the selection of cases to be included. A small sample size is quite in keeping with the nature of qualitative data.

Sampling and qualitative research

Traditionally, it is probability sampling which has set the standard for social research. It follows statistical laws and is well suited to the selection of samples in large-scale surveys designed to produce quantitative data. However, researchers who conduct small-scale research, especially qualitative researchers, find it difficult to adhere to the principles and procedures of probability sampling for selecting their people or events. Either it is not possible to include all types to be found in the population within a small sample, or not enough is known about the characteristics of the population to decide which people or events are suitable for inclusion in the sample. Some researchers have even attacked the principles of probability sampling as altogether inappropriate for smaller-scale, qualitative research. For these researchers, the selection of people or events for inclusion in the sample tends to be based on non-probability sampling.

The word 'tends' is quite important here. There is no absolute reason why qualitative research cannot use principles of randomness, or operate with large numbers. There are, however, some sound theoretical reasons why most qualitative research uses *non-probability sampling techniques* and good practical reasons why qualitative research deals with *small numbers* of instances to be researched.

One justification for non-probability sampling techniques stems from the idea that the research process is one of *'discovery'* rather than the testing of hypotheses. This approach was popularized by Glaser and Strauss (1967) and, in various reformulations, provides a foundation for the distinct approach to sampling which characterizes qualitative research. In this approach, the selection of people, texts or events to include in the research follows a path of discovery in which the sample emerges as a sequence of decisions based on the outcomes of earlier stages of the research. It is a strategy which Lincoln and Guba (1985) describe as 'emergent and sequential'. Almost like a detective, the researcher follows a trail of clues. As each clue is followed up it points the researcher in a particular direction and throws up new questions that need to be answered. Sometimes the clues can lead the researcher up blind alleys. Ultimately, though, the researcher should pursue his or her investigation until the questions have been answered and things can be explained.

Link up with **Grounded theory, Chapter 6**

This process can be exciting. It can also prove frustrating. Certainly, it tends to be *time-consuming* in a way that the snapshot survey approach is not. The research necessarily takes place over a period of time as the sequence of 'clues' is investigated. And the process also confounds efforts to specify at the beginning of a research project exactly what the sample to be studied will entail. To the horror of those who are committed to conventional survey approaches, *the size and composition of the sample is not completely predictable at the outset*. This does not mean that the qualitative researcher has no idea of which or how many people, texts or events will be included. A shrewd look at the time and resources available, and some reading of similar studies, will help to give a reasonable indication before the research starts. However, such an estimate of which and how many must remain exactly that – an estimate. It cannot be treated as a rigid and inflexible part of the research design if the qualitative research is to adhere to the 'discovery' route.

Another difference between the sampling which tends to be associated with quantitative research and the sampling which tends to be associated with qualitative research concerns the issue of 'representativeness'. With qualitative research, people, texts or events are not necessarily selected as being representative or normal instances. It is more likely than is the case with quantitative approaches that the selection will try to include *special instances* – ones that are extreme, unusual, best or worse. This allows the qualitative researcher to get 'maximum variation' in the data that are collected, a broad spectrum rather than a narrowly focused source of information. This, of course, accords with the spirit of qualitative research and its quest for explanations which encompass complexity, subtlety and even contradictions. It also allows a check on the findings based on the 'mainstream'. Miles and Huberman (1994) call these special instances 'outliers', and commend their inclusion in the process of discovery as a check which explores rival possible explanations and tests any explanation based on mainstream findings, by seeing if they can work with instances which are distinctly *not* mainstream. As they argue:

> Outliers are not only people; they can be discrepant *cases*, atypical *settings*, unique *treatments*, or unusual *events* . . .
> But the *outlier is your friend*. A good look at the exceptions, or the ends of a distribution, can test and strengthen the basic finding. It not only tests the generality of the finding but also protects you against self-selecting biases, and may help you build a better explanation.
> (Miles and Huberman, 1994: 269, original emphasis)

Qualitative research, then, tends to adopt an approach to sampling which is based on *sequential discovery* of instances to be studied and which emphasizes the inclusion of *special instances* more than is generally the case with quantitative research. These two features tend to lead qualitative researchers towards non-probability sampling strategies such as 'purposive sampling', 'snowballing' and 'theoretical sampling', rather than strategies based on principles of randomness and probability. And, *the sample size will be relatively small*.

Advantages of surveys

- *Empirical data.* As an approach to social research, the emphasis tends to be on producing data based on real-world observations. The very notion of a survey suggests that the research has involved an active attempt by the researcher to go out and look and to search. Surveys are associated with getting information 'straight from the horse's mouth'. And, more than this, the search is purposeful and structured. As a consequence, survey research tends to *focus on data more than theory* – although, of course, good survey research is not entirely devoid of theory. It is a matter of emphasis.
- *Wide and inclusive coverage.* The notion of a survey involves the idea of a span of vision which is wide and inclusive. Here lies the key to a major advantage of the survey approach. Its breadth of coverage means that it is more likely than some other approaches to get data based on a representative sample. This, in turn, means that the findings from good survey research score well when it comes to generalizability. If the coverage is suitably wide and inclusive it gives credibility to generalized statements made on the basis of the research. Internet surveys can be particularly valuable in this respect. They can allow access to people and situations that would not otherwise be possible. They can enable contact with groups who, for social or physical reasons, the researcher might not otherwise be able to meet. For practical reasons, non-mobile groups (e.g. the disabled, those who are hospitalized, those in prison), various subcultures (e.g. drug dealers, jet-setters) and those living in dangerous places (e.g. war zones) could be more available via the Internet than they would be using more conventional means of contact.
- *Surveys lend themselves to quantitative data.* Researchers who find that quantitative data will suit their needs will find themselves drawn to the survey approach. The survey approach lends itself to being used with particular methods, such as the postal questionnaire, which can generate large volumes of quantitative data that can be subject to statistical analysis. There is nothing which inherently excludes the use of surveys with qualitative research, as we have seen, but it can prove particularly attractive for the researcher wishing to use quantitative data.
- *Costs and time.* Surveys are not necessarily cheap but, relative to strategies such as experiments and ethnography, they can produce a mountain of data in a short time for a fairly low cost. The *costs are perhaps more predictable* than is the case with other strategies. Added to this, the results, though they are not instant, can be obtained over a fairly short period of time. The researcher can set a finite time-span for this, which is very useful when it comes to planning the research and delivering the end-product. Internet surveys, in particular, help with reducing the turnaround time between sending out a questionnaire and receiving a completed response.

he researcher gets the replies more quickly not just because of the delivery
me but also because people get round to answering the questions sooner
an with conventional surveys. Also Internet surveys can reduce the costs
undertaking research. In terms of the collection of data there is no travel,
venue needed and no specialist equipment required. The data supplied
the Internet, as a bonus, arrive in a format that is ready for analysis.
ere is no need for the transcription of audio tapes, and data from some
es of Internet questionnaire can be automatically entered to spread-
sheets, databases or statistics packages. There are potentially no data entry
costs.

Disadvantages of surveys

- *Tendency to empiricism.* There is nothing inevitable about this, but there is
  none the less a danger that a user of the survey approach, with its focus
  on producing data based on a wide and inclusive coverage, can become
  obsessed with the data to the exclusion of an adequate account of the implications of those data for relevant issues, problems or theories. There is a
  danger that the 'data are left to speak for themselves'. The *significance* of the
  data can become neglected.
- *Detail and depth of the data.* To the extent that the survey approach gets
  associated with large-scale research using methods such as the postal questionnaire, the data that are produced are likely to lack much by way of detail
  or depth on the topic being investigated. This is almost inevitable. If the
  researcher wants detail and depth, then the case study approach might be
  more beneficial. This should not blind us to the point that surveys tend
  to forfeit depth in favour of breadth when it comes to the data that are
  produced.
- *Accuracy and honesty of responses.* The survey approach has advantages
  when it comes to the representativeness of the data that it can produce, but
  the other side of the coin is that the emphasis on wide and inclusive coverage limits the degree to which the researcher can check on the accuracy of
  the responses. Again, the use of the survey approach, as such, does not
  prevent researchers checking on the accuracy or honesty of the responses,
  but resourcing generally places severe constraints on the prospects of doing
  so. Most vividly, this is illustrated by the use of postal questionnaires with a
  survey approach.
- *Sample bias with Internet surveys.* Although an increasing proportion of
  the population in the developed world has access to the Internet, it would
  be premature to say that everyone is online. Official statistics and market
  research show that certain groups and certain regions are more likely to be
  connected than are others. Being connected, in this sense, means having

the equipment to use the Internet. It does not say anything about how enthusiastic different groups might be about its use – how frequently and for what purpose. There is the obvious danger, then, that surveys conducted via the Internet might involve sample bias, and produce results not based on a representative sample.

- *Easily ignored.* Response rates from surveys are often quite low and getting a reasonable response rate can be quite a challenge for the researcher. Partly, this is because it is easy to ignore a researcher's request for help that comes through the post or via email. Internet surveys, in particular, suffer in this respect. It is extremely quick and very easy to delete requests for co-operation. They can be 'binned' at the touch of a button.

Checklist for surveys and sampling

When undertaking survey research you should feel confident about answering 'yes' to the following questions: ☑

1 Will data be collected from a cross-section of relevant people or events? ☐

2 Is it clear which sampling technique(s) is being used in the research?
   - random sampling ☐
   - systematic sampling ☐
   - stratified sampling ☐ } quantitative research
   - quota sampling ☐
   - cluster sampling ☐
   - multi-stage sampling ☐
   - purposive sampling ☐
   - snowball sampling ☐ } qualitative research
   - theoretical sampling ☐

3 When choosing the sample size have I taken account of . . .
   - the desired level of accuracy? ☐
   - the likely non-response rate? ☐
   - the sub-divisions in the data? ☐

4 Is the sample size larger than 30? ☐

   If not, have the implications of this for statistical analysis been recognized in the research? ☐

5 Have I assessed the sampling frame in terms of how far it is
   - complete and inclusive? ☐
   - up-to-date? ☐
   - relevant for the research topic? ☐

   Have any deficiencies been acknowledged and their implications taken into account? ☐

6 Is the response rate comparable with that obtained by other similar surveys? ☐

7 Have efforts been made to see if there are significant differences between the respondents and the non-respondents? ☐

8 Where appropriate, has consideration been given to the impact of Internet research in terms of potential bias in sampling? ☐

© M. Denscombe, *The Good Research Guide*. Open University Press.

2

Case studies

What is the case study approach? • When is it appropriate to use a case study approach? • The relevance of the case study • The selection of cases • Can you generalize from a case study? • Boundaries to case studies • Advantages of the case study approach • Disadvantages of the case study approach • Checklist for the case study approach

Case studies focus on one (or just a few) instances of a particular phenomenon with a view to providing an in-depth account of events, relationships, experiences or processes occurring in that particular instance. The use of case studies has become extremely widespread in social research, particularly with small-scale research. When researchers opt for a case study approach they buy into a set of related ideas and preferences which, when combined, give the approach its distinctive character. True, many of the features associated with the case study approach can be found elsewhere and are not necessarily unique to this strategy. However, when brought together they form a broad approach to social research, with an underlying rationale for the direction and planning of an investigation that separates it from the rationale for survey research or the rationale for experimental research.

What is the case study approach?

Spotlight on one instance

The starting point and arguably the defining characteristic of the case study approach is its *focus on just one instance of the thing that is to be investigated.*

Occasionally, researchers use two or more instances but, in principle, the idea of a case study is that a spotlight is focused on individual instances rather than a wide spectrum. The case study approach, then, is quite the opposite of any mass study. The logic behind concentrating efforts on one case rather than many is that there may be insights to be gained from looking at the individual case that can have wider implications and, importantly, that would not have come to light through the use of a research strategy that tried to cover a large number of instances – a survey approach. The aim is to illuminate the general by looking at the particular.

In-depth study

The prospects of getting some valuable and unique insight depends on being able to investigate things in a way that is different from, and in some senses better than, what is possible using other approaches. What a case study can do that a survey normally cannot is to study things in detail. When a researcher takes the strategic decision to devote all his or her efforts to researching just one instance, there is obviously far greater opportunity to delve into things in more detail and discover things that might not have become apparent through more superficial research.

Focus on relationships and processes

Relationships and processes within social settings tend to be interconnected and interrelated. To understand one thing it is necessary to understand many others and, crucially, how the various parts are linked. The case study approach works well here because it offers more chance than the survey approach of going into sufficient detail to unravel the complexities of a given situation. It can deal with the case as a whole, in its entirety, and thus have some chance of being able to discover how the many parts affect one another. In this respect, *case studies tend to be 'holistic' rather than deal with 'isolated factors'*. It follows from this that within case studies there is a tendency to emphasize the detailed workings of the relationships and social processes, rather than to restrict attention to the outcomes from these. Quite rightly, *a good case study plays to its strengths*. End-products, outcomes and results all remain of interest to the case study researcher, but if attention were not given to the processes which led to those outcomes then the value of the case study would be lost. The real value of a case study is that it offers the opportunity to explain *why* certain outcomes might happen – more than just find out what those outcomes are. For example, when one is looking at the turnover of labour in an organization, the strength of a case study approach would be that it could investigate the processes that explain the actual level of turnover – the intricate details of the recruitment policy, staff development, nature of the work, levels of pay, background of the workers, etc., and how all these are interrelated – all this over and above giving a detailed description of what the facts of the situation are with respect to labour turnover (the outcome).

Natural setting

'The case' that forms the basis of the investigation is normally something that already exists. It is not a situation that is artificially generated specifically for the purposes of the research. It is not like an experiment where the research design is dedicated to imposing controls on variables so that the impact of a specific ingredient can be measured. As Yin (1994) stresses, the case is a 'naturally occurring' phenomenon. It exists prior to the research project and, it is hoped, continues to exist once the research has finished.

Multiple sources and multiple methods

One of the strengths of the case study approach is that it allows the researcher to use a variety of sources, a variety of types of data and a variety of research methods as part of the investigation. It not only allows this, it actually invites and encourages the researcher to do so. Observations of events within the case study setting can be combined with the collection of documents from official meetings and informal interviews with people involved. Questionnaires might be used to provide information on a particular point of interest. Whatever is appropriate can be used for investigating the relationships and processes that are of interest.

> **Key point: the case study strategy**
>
> The decision to use a case study approach is a strategic decision that relates to the scale and scope of an investigation, and it does not, at least in principle, dictate which method or methods must be used. Indeed, a strength of the case study approach is that it allows for the use of a variety of methods depending on the circumstances and the specific needs of the situation.

Case study research characteristically emphasizes		
Depth of study	rather than	Breadth of study
The particular	rather than	The general
Relationships/processes	rather than	Outcomes and end-products
Holistic view	rather than	Isolated factors
Natural settings	rather than	Artificial situations
Multiple sources	rather than	One research method

When is it appropriate to use the case study approach?

The case study approach works best when the researcher wants to investigate an issue in depth and provide an explanation that can cope with the complexity and subtlety of real life situations. In particular, it lends itself to the study of processes and relationships within a setting. The use of more than one research method sits comfortably with the case study approach although, in practice, the use of the case study approach has been aligned with qualitative research far more than it has with quantitative research.

Case studies have been used for a wide range of purposes within social research. Predominantly, they have been used in relation to the discovery of information (following an inductive logic). Less commonly, they have been used in relation to the testing of theory (following a deductive logic). It is quite possible, in practice, for any particular case study to incorporate elements of both. The following table, then, depicts the possible ways in which case studies might be used but does not imply that any particular case study must be restricted to just the goals associated with just one category.

The uses of a case study	
Discovery led	
Description	Describes what is happening in a case study setting (e.g. events, processes and relationships).
Exploration	Explores the key issues affecting those in a case study setting (e.g. problems or opportunities).
Comparison	Compares settings to learn from the similarities and differences between them.
Theory led	
Explanation	Explains the causes of events, processes or relationships within a setting.
Illustration	Uses a case study as an illustration of how a particular theory applies in a real life setting.
Experiment	Uses a case study as a test-bed for experimenting with changes to specific factors (or variables).

The relevance of a case study

The case study approach generally calls for the researcher to make choices from among a number of possible events, people, organizations, etc. The researcher needs to pick out one example (or just a few) from a wider range of examples of the class of thing that is being investigated: the choice of one school for a case study from among the thousands that could have been chosen; the choice of one sexually transmitted disease (STD) clinic from among the many in hospitals across the country; the focus on one bus company from among the hundreds throughout the nation which provide local public transport services. Whatever the subject matter, the case study normally depends on a conscious and deliberate choice about which case to select from among a large number of possibilities. Two points follow from this.

First, cases are not randomly selected; they are selected on the basis of known attributes. As a distinct alternative to the randomization principle associated with classic experiments and large-scale surveys, instances selected for a case study are chosen on the basis of their distinctive features. Instances selected for an experiment or a large-scale survey are chosen on a random basis to ensure as far as possible that they do *not* represent any specific factors relating to the variable that is being studied, but quite the opposite is true when it comes to case study research.

Second, the criteria used for the selection of cases need to be made explicit and need to be justified as an essential part of the methodology. Initially, this involves identifying the key features of the case and providing relevant information about that feature. For example, if the research topic was 'small firms in the automotive industry' the criterion for the selection of any particular organization as the basis for a case study would be 'size'. If size is defined in terms of the number of employees, then details would need to be given about the number of employees in the selected firm and how this compares with (a) definitions of small firms (the theory) and (b) a profile of the size of other firms throughout the automotive industry. Such details are vital because they justify the choice of the particular firm as a suitable example of the broader category of the thing being studied (small firms) and they form the basis for any generalizations that can be made from the case study findings (see below).

> **Key point**
> A case study should be chosen deliberately on the basis of specific attributes to be found in the case – attributes that are particularly significant in terms of the practical problem or theoretical issue that the researcher wants to investigate.

The selection of cases

All case studies need to be chosen on the basis of their relevance to the practical problems or theoretical issues being researched. But, having established this, the selection of the specific case will also reflect a range of other considerations as well. These other factors concern the way the case study is to be used and the amount of flexibility the researcher is able to exercise in the selection of the specific case.

The way the case will be used

Typical instance

The most common justification to be offered for the selection of a particular case is that it is typical. The logic being invoked here is that the particular case is similar in crucial respects with the others that might have been chosen, and that the findings from the case study are therefore likely to apply elsewhere. Because the case study is like most of the rest, the findings can be generalized to the whole class of thing.

Extreme instance

A case might be selected on the grounds that, far from being typical, it provides something of a contrast with the norm. An illustration of this would be the selection of an organization which is notably smaller or notably larger than usual. Among local authorities in the country, a very small one might be chosen for a case study, and the logic for doing so would be that this would allow the influence of the factor (size) to be more easily seen than it would be in the average size authority. In an extreme instance, a specified factor is seen in relief – highlighted in its effect.

Test-site for theory

The logic for the selection of a particular case can be based on the relevance of the case for previous theory. This is a point Yin (1994) stresses. Case studies can be used for the purposes of 'theory-testing' as well as 'theory-building', to use Layder's (1993) distinction. The rationale for choosing a specific case, then, can be that it contains crucial elements that are especially significant, and that the researcher should be able to predict certain outcomes if the theory holds true.

Least likely instance

Following the idea of test-sites for theory, a case might be selected to test the validity of 'theory' by seeing if it occurs in an instance where it might be least expected. So, for example, a researcher who wants to test the 'theory' that school teachers place a high value on their autonomy could deliberately select a situation where such autonomy would seem to be least valued: a school with team teaching in open plan classrooms. If there is evidence supporting the 'theory' even under such 'least likely' conditions, then the 'theory' has all the more credibility.

Practical considerations

Although researchers should never rely on practical reasons as the principal or the sole criterion for selecting a case, it would be naive to ignore the fact that, in the real world of research, such factors do have a bearing on the selection of cases.

A matter of convenience

In the practical world of research, with its limits to time and resources, the selection of cases is quite likely to include a consideration of convenience. Faced with alternatives which are equally suitable, it is reasonable for the researcher to select the one(s) which involves the least travel, the least expense and the least difficulty when it comes to gaining access. The crucial point here, though, is that convenience should only come into play when deciding between equally suitable alternatives. Selection on the basis of 'the first to hand', 'the easiest' or 'the cheapest' is not a criterion in its own right which can be used to justify the selection of cases. If used on its own, in fact, it would almost certainly be a symptom of poor social research. Used properly, it is subordinate to the other criteria.

Intrinsically interesting

If a case is intrinsically interesting then it can prove an attractive proposition. The findings are likely to reach a wider audience and the research itself is likely to be a more exciting experience. There are even some experts in the field who would go as far as to argue that selection on the basis of being intrinsically interesting is a sufficient justification in its own right (Stake, 1995). This hits at the heart of the debate about whether cases are studied 'in their own right', as Stake would maintain, or for what they reveal about others of the kind, and, in light of its controversial nature, it would be rather foolhardy for the newcomer or project researcher to use this as the sole criterion for selecting a case. The vast majority of social researchers would not see it as a justification for selection in its own right. It might work for journalism, but social research by most definitions calls for more than just this (Ragin, 1994). It is far wiser, therefore, to regard any intrinsic interest of the case as a criterion to be used when deciding between instances that in all other crucial respects are equally suitable, and as a bonus.

No real choice

On some occasions, researchers do not really have a great deal of choice when it comes to the selection of suitable cases for inclusion in the investigation. The choice is more or less dictated by circumstances beyond their control. This happens in the following two circumstances.

The study is part of commissioned research

Commissioned research might leave the researcher with little leeway in the selection of cases. The funder is quite likely to stipulate that the research must be linked to a specified organization or activity, leaving no discretion on the matter to the researchers themselves. Under such circumstances, there is no real choice in the selection of cases.

There are unique opportunities

There are times when events occur which provide the researcher with unique opportunities. The events themselves, of course, will not be unique; they will be instances of a class of such events. The opportunity to study such events, however, may be unique. Situations which could not be planned or created present themselves as 'one-off chances'. At one level, this could take the form of social catastrophes, such as war, famine or natural disaster. At a more mundane level, the unique opportunities could reflect the unpredictable or rare nature of the events. Strikes, for example, might be the kind of class of events that could be illuminated through the depth study of individual cases. Researchers, though, will have little choice over which instances they select as their cases and will necessarily find themselves homing in on such events as and when they occur. As a consequence, there is no real element of choice in the selection of the cases.

Can you generalize from a case study?

The value of a case study approach is that it has the potential to deal with the subtleties and intricacies of complex social situations. This potential comes from the strategic decision to restrict the range of the study to just one or a few cases. When opting for this approach, however, the social researcher is likely to confront scepticism about the findings – scepticism which arises from doubts about how far it is reasonable to generalize from the findings of one case. The researcher will probably find people asking questions such as:

• How *representative* is the case?

- Isn't it possible that the findings, though interesting, are *unique* to the particular circumstances of the case?
- How can you *generalize* on the basis of research into one instance?

These are reasonable questions. They reflect the key issue of generalization in social research and need to be addressed by anyone who decides to adopt a case study approach. They should not be ignored in the hope that readers of the research report will overlook the point. Indeed, it is good practice for any researcher who decides to choose a case study approach to pre-empt possible criticism by addressing the issue head-on. There should be an explicit defence against the allegation that you cannot generalize from case study findings, and this can use the following three arguments.

1. Although each case is in some respects unique, it is also a single example of a broader class of things. If, for example, the study is based on a small primary school this is to be treated as an instance of other schools which are small and which are in the primary sector. It is one of a type (Hammersley, 1992; Ragin and Becker, 1992; Yin, 1994).

2. The extent to which findings from the case study can be generalized to other examples in the class depends on how far the case study example is similar to others of its type. To pursue the example of the small primary school, the applicability of the findings from the case study to other small primary schools will depend on how far the case study example shares with other schools in the class (small size, primary sector) features which are significant as far as the operation of such schools are concerned. Its catchment area, the ethnic origins of the pupils and the amount of staff turnover might be regarded as vital factors. If so, the generalizability of the findings from the particular case study school to small primary schools in general will depend on the extent to which its profile on these factors is typical of those found elsewhere. Equally, the case study researcher might wish to stress the extent to which the particular example being investigated is unusual, and thus emphasize the limits to how far the findings should be generalized to others in the class.

Either way, the crucial tasks for the case study researcher are:

- to identify significant features on which comparison with others in the class can be made; and
- to show how the case study compares with others in the class in terms of these significant features.

With the example of the small primary school, this means that the researcher must obtain data on the significant features (catchment area, the ethnic origins of the pupils and the amount of staff turnover) for primary schools in general, and then demonstrate where the case study example fits in relation to the overall picture.

3. Reports based on the case study include sufficient detail about how the case compares with others in the class for the reader to make an informed judgement about how far the findings have relevance to other instances. When it comes to making generalizations on the basis of case studies some of the responsibility falls to the reader. The *reader* of the findings will use the information to make some assessment of how far the findings have implications across the board for all others of the type, or how far they are restricted to just the case study example. The reader, though, must be provided with the necessary information on which to make an informed judgement on this matter.

Comparing a case with others of its type

Comparison might call for the inclusion of details on the following factors.

Physical location	geographical area, town, building, room, furniture, decor
Historical location	developments and changes
Social location	catchment area, ethnic grouping, social class, age, sex and other background information about the participants
Institutional location	type of organization, size of organization, official policies and procedures

Boundaries to case studies

The use of a case study approach assumes that the researcher is able to separate some aspect of social life so that it is distinct from other things of the same kind and distinct from its social context. Without some notion of a *boundary*, it becomes impossible to state what the case is. If the case has no end-point, no outside, then it bleeds into other social phenomena and ceases to have any distinct identity. The notion of a 'case', then, must carry with it some idea of a boundary which is sufficiently clear and obvious to allow the researcher to see what is contained within the case (and to be incorporated into the investigation) and what is outside the case (and therefore to be excluded from the focus of the study). In principle,

- a 'case' needs to be a fairly *self-contained entity*;
- a 'case' needs to have fairly *distinct boundaries*.

It follows that *good case study research needs to contain a clear vision of the boundaries to the case and provide an explicit account of what they are.* This may sound basic and rather obvious. However, in practice, the identification of clear and consistent boundaries can pose quite a hard task for the social researcher. It is just not as easy as it seems.

Advantages of the case study approach

- The main benefit of using a case study approach is that the focus on one or a few instances allows the researcher to *deal with the subtleties and intricacies* of complex social situations. In particular, it enables the researcher to grapple with relationships and social processes in a way that is denied to the survey approach. The analysis is holistic rather than based on isolated factors.
- The case study approach allows the use of a variety of research methods. More than this, it more or less encourages the use of *multiple methods* in order to capture the complex reality under scrutiny.

Link up with **Mixed methods, Chapter 7**

- In parallel with the use of multiple methods, the case study approach fosters the use of *multiple sources* of data. This, in turn, facilitates the validation of data through *triangulation*.
- The case study approach is particularly suitable where the researcher has little control over events. Because the approach is concerned with investigating phenomena as they naturally occur, there is *no pressure on the researcher to impose controls* or to change circumstances.
- The case study approach can fit in well with the needs of small-scale research through *concentrating effort on one research site* (or just a few sites).
- Theory-building and theory-testing research can both use the case study approach to good effect.

Disadvantages of the case study approach

- The point at which the case study approach is most vulnerable to criticism is in relation to the *credibility of generalizations* made from its findings. The case study researcher needs to be particularly careful to allay suspicions and to demonstrate the extent to which the case is similar to, or contrasts with, others of its type.
- Unwarranted though it may be, case studies are often *perceived as producing 'soft' data*. The approach gets accused of lacking the degree of rigour expected of social science research. This tends to go alongside the view of

case study research as focusing on processes rather than measurable end-products, as relying on qualitative data and interpretive methods rather than quantitative data and statistical procedures. Often, case studies are regarded as all right in terms of providing descriptive accounts of the situation but rather ill-suited to analyses or evaluations. None of this is necessarily justified, but it is a preconception which the case study researcher needs to be aware of, and one which needs to be challenged by careful attention to detail and rigour in the use of the approach.

- On the technical side, the *boundaries* of the case can prove difficult to define in an absolute and clear-cut fashion. This poses difficulties in terms of deciding what sources of data to incorporate in the case study and which to exclude.
- *Negotiating access* to case study settings can be a demanding part of the research process. Research can flounder if permission is withheld or withdrawn. In case studies, access to documents, people and settings can generate ethical problems in terms of things like confidentiality.
- It is hard for case study researchers to achieve their aim of investigating situations as they naturally occur without any effect arising from their presence. Because case study research tends to involve protracted involvement over a period of time, there is the possibility that the presence of the research can lead to *the observer effect*. Those being researched might behave differently from normal owing to the knowledge that they are 'under the microscope' and being observed in some way.

Link up with **The Observer effect, p. 53**

Checklist for the case study approach

When undertaking research which involves the case study approach you should feel confident about answering 'yes' to the following questions: ☑

1 Is the research based on a 'naturally occurring' situation? ☐

2 Have the criteria for selection of the case (or cases) been described and justified? ☐

3 Has the case (or cases) been identified as a particular instance of a type of social phenomenon? (e.g. kind of event, type of organization) ☐

4 Have the significant features of the case been described and have they been compared with those to be found elsewhere among the type of thing being studied? ☐

5 Is the case a fairly self-contained entity? ☐

6 Have the boundaries to the case been described and their implications considered? ☐

7 Has careful consideration been given to the issue of generalizations stemming from research? ☐

8 Does the research make suitable use of multiple methods and multiple sources of data? ☐

9 Does the research give due attention to relationships and processes, and provide a 'holistic' perspective? ☐

© M. Denscombe, *The Good Research Guide*. Open University Press.

3

Experiments

What is an experiment?

An experiment is an empirical investigation under controlled conditions designed to examine the properties of, and relationship between, specific factors. It is the bedrock of research in the physical sciences and is regarded by many social researchers as a model of good practice. The idea of an experiment tends to be linked with white-coated scientists working in a laboratory, possibly using highly sophisticated equipment to measure things with extreme precision. The point of conducting an experiment is to isolate individual factors and observe their effect in detail. The purpose is to discover new relationships or properties associated with the materials being investigated, or to test existing theories.

Now, although this draws on a rather idealized image of the way experiments are conducted in the physical sciences, it is not entirely irrelevant for the *social* sciences. It largely succeeds in capturing the essence of the notion and incorporates the three things that lie at the heart of conducting an experiment:

- *The identification of causal factors*. The introduction or exclusion of factors to or from the situation enables the researcher to pinpoint which factor actually causes the observed outcome to occur.
- *Controls*. Experiments involve the manipulation of key variables. The

researcher needs to identify factors that are significant and then introduce them to or exclude them from the situation so that their effect can be observed.

- *Empirical observation and measurement.* Experiments rely on detailed empirical observation of changes that occur following the introduction of potentially relevant factors. They also involve the precise measurement of the changes that are observed.

These essential features of 'the experiment', it is worth noting, are concerned with the aims of the investigation and its design. They do not say anything about *how* exactly the data are to be collected. This is why experiments are better seen as a strategy for research rather than a method. The decision to use an experimental approach is a strategic one in which the researcher decides to investigate the topic under controlled conditions, paying careful attention to the meticulous measurement of what goes on.

Cause and effect

Experiments are generally concerned with determining the *cause* of any changes that occur to the thing being studied. It is not normally enough to show that two things that occur are linked; that they always occur at the same time or they always happen in sequence. Useful though it is to know about such a relationship, experiments usually aim to discover which of the factors is the cause. This requires a distinction to be made between *dependent and independent variables*. It is vital that the researcher has a clear vision of which is which, and sets up the experiment in a way which produces results that show the distinction between the two.

- The independent variable is the one that has the impact on the dependent variable. Its size, number, structure, volume or whatever exists autonomously, owing nothing to the other variable. A change in the independent variable affects the dependent variable.
- The dependent variable is the factor that alters as a result of changes to the independent variable. It literally 'depends' on the independent variable. Any change in the dependent variable does not affect the independent variable.

Example
Tobacco smoking is related to the incidence of lung cancer. Both are variables and both appear to be linked to each other: more smoking, higher incidence of

lung cancer; less smoking, lower incidence. Smoking increases the likelihood of lung cancer. Lung cancer does not increase the likelihood of smoking. In this example, there is clearly a dependent variable and an independent variable. Smoking tobacco is the independent variable, and lung cancer is the dependent variable.

The use of controls

When conducting an experiment the aim is to show that the dependent factor (for example, the incidence of lung cancer in the population) responds to changes in the independent factor (prevalence of smoking in the society). To do this, the researcher needs to be sure it was definitely the prevalence of smoking that was responsible for the observed levels of lung cancer and not some other factor (e.g. diet or amount of exercise) that actually caused it. This requires the experimenter to control variables like smoking, diet, exercise and other factors that could perhaps affect the incidence of lung cancer to ensure that, out of all of them, it is only the one factor, smoking, that could possibly be linked to the level of lung cancer in the population. There are a number of ways in which experiments can be designed to achieve this each of which involves the use of controls.

Introduce a new factor

The most straightforward way to isolate the impact of a variable is to introduce it while keeping all other relevant factors unchanged. Under these circumstances – 'all things being equal' – it is possible to pinpoint the impact of the new factor and to deduce that any observed changes that occur can be attributed to the new factor. Since the introduction of the new factor is the only thing that has changed, it alone can be held responsible for any subsequent changes that occur. In practice, however, researchers face two particular difficulties in this regard. First, it can be extremely difficult to ensure that none of the other variables change. Second, variables are often linked so that a change in one variable might cause changes across a range of other variables.

Eliminate the factor from the experiment

Rather than introduce a new factor to the situation, the researcher might find it easier to eliminate one factor. So, for instance, a study of the link between hyperactivity and diet in children might see the researcher deliberately excluding all artificial colourings from the subjects' diets and then observing any change in behaviour. If other factors remain unaltered, it would be logical to deduce that any observed change was due to the absence of this factor.

Hold the factor constant

In social science, a large number of the key relevant variables come in the form of attributes that cannot be written out of the equation through eliminating them from the situation altogether. Things like income, weight and age are attributes that cannot be eliminated. However, they can be controlled for by 'holding the factor constant'. To prevent the factor from having an unwanted intrusion on the outcome of the experiment, the researcher can devise a situation in which the subjects are all of the same income or of the same weight. Observed outcomes from the experiment, as a result, can be deduced to stem from some factor other than income or weight.

Random selection of groups

If the research subjects are chosen on a random basis there should be a tendency for those factors which are not crucial to cancel themselves out. The principle here is that by the choice of a large enough group of subjects on a random basis, any interference with the results through factors like income or weight would have a nil effect overall, because the random nature of the selection would ensure that all the individual effects would cancel themselves out in terms of the results for the whole research group.

Use of control groups

This is the most used and established way of exercising control over significant variables. The principle is simple. First, it is necessary to identify two groups of people for the experiment. The two groups should be similar in terms of their composition. The start point for the experiment, then, is *two matched groups or samples*. The experiment involves introducing a factor to the experimental group and leaving the other group with no artificially induced changes. Having added the new factor, the experimenter can then look at the two groups again with the belief that any *difference* between the groups can be attributed to the factor which was artificially induced. Note here that it is not the *change* in the experiment group as such which is important. Certain changes over time are likely to happen irrespective of whether an experiment had taken place. Time moves on for all of us. But, if the two groups were as identical as possible at the outset, any change of this kind in one group will also occur in the other group. So, instead of measuring the change from time 1 to time 2, we measure the difference between the control group and the experimental group at the end of the experiment at time 2.

Any differences we observe can be logically deduced to come from the factor which was artificially induced in the experiment (see Figure 2).

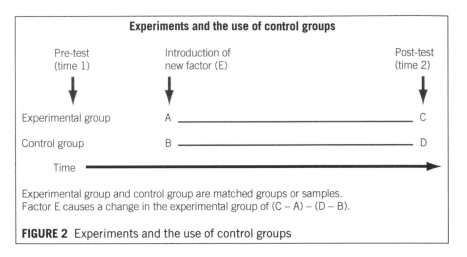

Experiments and the use of control groups

| Pre-test (time 1) | Introduction of new factor (E) | Post-test (time 2) |

Experimental group A ————————————————— C

Control group B ————————————————— D

Time ——————————————————————————————→

Experimental group and control group are matched groups or samples.
Factor E causes a change in the experimental group of (C − A) − (D − B).

FIGURE 2 Experiments and the use of control groups

 Caution

In the case of social research, there are certain limitations to the extent to which circumstances can be manipulated. Basically, a researcher can do things to chemicals and plants that cannot be contemplated with fellow human beings. For the purposes of doing an experiment it may be neither feasible nor, indeed, ethical to manipulate people's lives in order to provide the controlled conditions necessary for a 'social science experiment'. People have feelings, people have rights.

Link up with **Research ethics, pp. 141–51**

Observation and measurement

It might be argued that any form of research involves observation and measurement, but the point about observation and measurement as they are associated with experiments is that they are conducted under conditions that are artificially created (to a greater or lesser extent). They take place under conditions which have been manipulated to allow the greatest rigour and precision. That is why the experiments generally take place in laboratories, because these are purpose-built contexts for the research. They enhance the possibility of precision. There are, though, two points that need to be borne in mind in relation to observations that form part of an experiment.

First, the artificial setting of an experiment can heighten people's sensitivity to being observed. Humans have self-awareness in a sense that makes them very different from the materials studied in other forms of research. When humans become aware that they are the focus of attention for research, there is the very real possibility that they will act differently from normal. They might possibly become self-conscious or alter their behaviour to take account of the purposes of the research. This is known as the 'observer effect' or 'Hawthorne effect'.

Link up with **the Hawthorne studies, pp. 111–12**

Experimenters can take steps to overcome this. They can, for instance, make hidden observations from behind a one-way mirror. Or they can disguise the real purpose of the research to avoid getting altered behaviour in relation to the factor being investigated (see the account of Milgram's research below). But both solutions to the observer effect raise ethical problems and need very careful consideration before being used by the newcomer or project researcher.

The Observer effect

People are likely to alter their behaviour when they become aware that they are being observed.
    Unlike atoms, people can become aware of being studied – conscious of it – and then react in a way that is not usual. They can:

* be embarrassed;
* disguise normal practice/be defensive.

To overcome the effect, researchers are generally advised to:

* spend time on site, so that the researcher becomes 'part of the furniture';
* have minimal interaction with those being observed.

Laboratory experiments

The use of controls, the search for causes and the emphasis on detailed observation and measurement are seen in their most extreme form in *'laboratory experiments'*. Such experiments are characteristically:

- of relatively *short* duration;
- located *'on site'* rather than 'in the field';
- involving *close control* of variables to isolate causal factors;
- with *meticulous observation* and measurements.

Although not necessarily typical of experiments conducted by psychologists, a series of experiments conducted by Stanley Milgram at Yale University between 1960 and 1963 offers an example that illustrates how such laboratory experiments might operate in the case of social research (Milgram, 1974). The aim of the series of experiments was to shed more light on the apparent willingness of ordinary individuals to inflict cruel pain on others when instructed to do so by an authority figure. It formed part of an ongoing debate, prompted by Nazi atrocities during the Second World War, about whether those who inflicted the torture were psychologically different from other people, or whether there is a normal psychological tendency to obey authority, even to the point of following instructions to hurt a fellow human being against whom you bear no personal animosity. Milgram's series of experiments sought to investigate this under strictly controlled conditions.

> The point of the experiment is to see how far a person will proceed in a concrete and measurable situation in which he is ordered to inflict increasing pain on a protesting victim. At what point will the subject refuse to obey the experimenter?
>
> (Milgram, 1974: 3–4)

An advertisement was put in a local newspaper inviting people aged 20 to 50 to participate in 'a scientific study of memory and learning'. The advertisement offered $4 plus 50 cents taxi fare for those willing to give up one hour of their time. Those who took up the offer were met at the university department by a person who said he was in charge of the experiment – a smart looking young man in a laboratory coat. The 'subject' was then introduced to a man who, he was led to believe, was another participant in the experiment. This person was in his late 50s, very mild-mannered and inoffensive, and slightly overweight: not the kind of person you would want to harm. The whole thing, however, was a 'set-up'. The 'experimenter' and the other subject were colleagues of Milgram, and they were actually taking part in a carefully scripted sequence of events. Their words and actions were part of the experiment and in accord with a strict plan which was followed with each new volunteer who came in off the street. This meant that the only real variable was the action of each subject who had volunteered to help. As far as was possible, all other aspects of what happened were controlled to be the same on each occasion.

The subjects were told that they were to take part in a study of the effects of punishment on learning. One of the two participants was to take the role of the 'teacher' administering the punishment, the other was to be the 'learner'. It was rigged so that when drawing a piece of paper out of a hat to determine which subject took which role, Milgram's colleague always got the role of the learner, ensuring that the real subject was left to undertake the teacher role. At this point the 'learner' was taken to a room and sat in a chair. He was strapped down and electrodes were attached to his arm. The whole thing was deliberately set up to resemble the 'electric chair'. In an adjoining room the unsuspecting subject and the 'experimenter' in his lab coat went to an 'impressive shock generator'. The subject was given a 45-volt shock from this generator to make the whole performance that followed convincing. In fact, it was the only real electric shock administered throughout the whole experiment – but the subject was not to know this. The learning experiment consisted of the 'teacher' (the subject) reading out a series of paired words (e.g. fat–neck, blue–girl, nice–day). A stimulus word was then read out, followed by five others, among which was the actual paired word read out in the original series. The learner had to identify which was the correct word out of the five. Each time he made a mistake, the subject had to deliver an electric shock by way of punishment – purportedly to see if this would encourage better learning. Each time a mistake was made, an electric shock 15 volts higher than the one before was apparently administered.

The learner put on a performance. Although he actually received no electric shock at all, he acted as though he did. As the voltage of the shocks was increased he began to moan and protest – all, of course, to a precise script that went with each increase. At 150 volts Milgram's colleague would cry out, 'Experimenter, get me out of here! I won't be in the experiment any more! I refuse to go on!' At 180 volts he would shout, 'I can't stand the pain!' and by 270 volts he would let out an agonized scream. After 330 volts the learner fell silent. The lab-coated experimenter continued to coax the subject to give the electric shocks, and each time the 'learner' protested he gave a carefully scripted reassurance to the real subject: 'No permanent tissue damage is caused; he has to go on because it is part of the experiment.'

The experimental conditions were altered through the series of experiments. The proximity of the subject to the learner was altered, for example, and the nature of the complaints that could be heard by the subject emanating from the pained learner, but the basic design continued. Milgram found that ordinary volunteers were remarkably willing to give dangerously high voltages to a person they believed to be another 'off-the-street' volunteer, a person who was apparently vulnerable to heart attack, an inoffensive person, a person who was quite evidently suffering extreme pain and demanding to be released. Depending on the specifics of the experiment, between one-half and two-thirds of subjects went on to administer up to 450 volts! They did not do so with glee; they often protested and expressed disquiet about the whole thing. But this proportion of ordinary people could be persuaded by the authority of the scientific experimenter in his lab coat to deliver what by any standards is an extremely dangerous and painful 'punishment' to a vulnerable fellow being.

The psychological explanation for this level of obedience to authority is discussed in detail by Milgram, but this is not the point of describing the experiment here. The point of describing it is to illustrate the way in which the use of an experiment relies on controlling as many of the variables as possible to allow an uncontaminated measurement of the factor that is of prime interest and involves precise measurements. It is very unlikely that these could have been achieved had the research not taken place in the laboratory, on home territory where the researchers are able to set things up in a very meticulous fashion and repeat the experiment time and again without interference from outside factors.

Admittedly, most laboratory experiments in the social sciences do not achieve the fame and notoriety of the Milgram experiments, for obvious reasons. They tend to be less provocative in their topic and design. The principles, none the less, remain the same.

Field experiments

The use of experiments by social researchers would appear to be restricted to those situations where they are able to manipulate the situation and impose controls on crucial variables. Laboratories clearly are designed to aid this. There is, though, something of a dilemma here.

> It is often argued that laboratory experiments are of little use because the settings in which they take place are artificial and so the results of the ensuing findings have little validity beyond the confines of the laboratory.
> (Bryman, 1989: 90)

It is not just that the data are generated under artificial conditions: they are actually shaped to some degree by those artificial conditions. Yet, if researchers move outside the laboratories in order to gather data in more natural settings, they are, of course, likely to pay a high price in terms of their ability to control the variables. Beyond the laboratory, the social researcher has far less prospect of managing to manipulate things for the express purpose of a social experiment. Sociologists cannot control levels of incomes in order to conduct experiments on things like poverty. Nor can health educators manipulate levels of smoking among adolescent girls in order to study it. Economists cannot generate a recession in order to investigate its consequences. It is simply not possible to manipulate circumstances like these. It is not feasible, nor would it be ethical.

There are, however, approaches within social research which recognize that it is neither feasible nor ethical to attempt to impose controls on all the relevant factors, yet which strive to retain the logic of the experimental approach, albeit in a watered down version, beyond the bounds of the laboratory. Because they cannot always control all the variables, some social scientists have resorted to a *'quasi-experimental'* approach as a realistic possibility. The quasi (*'as if'*) experimental approach is conducted in the spirit of the classic laboratory experiment, but recognizes that the researcher cannot dictate circumstances and needs to take the role of observing events 'as they naturally occur'. Much like weather forecasters, these social scientists tend to rely on observing events which occur in circumstances over which they have little or no control. Researchers in this case are on the lookout for 'naturally occurring' experiments – situations in which they can see the possibility of observing and measuring the impact of isolated variables through circumstances as they happen, without imposing artificial controls.

Naturally occurring experiments are part of the logic of anthropological studies of simple, 'primitive' societies. As Margaret Mead made the point:

> The study of human development in a primitive society has ... two advantages: contrast with our own social environment which brings out different aspects of human nature and often demonstrates that behaviour which occurs almost invariably in individuals within our own society is nevertheless due not to original nature but to social environment; and a homogeneous and simple social background, easily mastered, against which the development of the individual may be studied. (...) The anthropologist submits the findings of the psychologist who works within our society to the test of observation within other societies.
>
> (Mead, [1930] 1963: 212)

Another example of quasi-experimental research comes in the form of *ex post facto experiments*. In this instance, the starting point for the investigation is the 'effect', and the researcher sets out to deduce what factors could be held to account for this outcome. The idea is to work backwards from the effect to find the cause. For example, the researcher might ask, 'Does imprisonment affect earnings after release from detention?' The research design here would be to identify a number of people who had been to prison. This *independent* variable – imprisonment – is not something the research can or should manipulate. It is a *fait accompli*, existing prior to and quite separate from the research. However, by comparing ex-prisoners with people who in most other respects match them it is possible to deduce whether or not that factor has had a direct effect on the *dependent* variable: earnings. Or, to give another illustration, the starting point for the research might be the discovery of lung cancer in particular people. *Ex post facto* research then sets about trying to identify variables that might explain the incidence of lung cancer in these people. It might be discovered that, compared with the population as a whole, a higher proportion of those with lung cancer smoke tobacco. Controlling for other factors to discount them as possible causes, the researcher might eventually deduce that smoking tobacco is the cause of the higher incidence of lung cancer.

Experimental research	
Laboratory experiments	*Field experiments*
Located 'on site'	Located 'in the field'
Close control of variables	Use available possibilities
Meticulous measurements	Structured observations
Shorter duration	Longer duration

Advantages of experiments

- *Repeatable.* In the case of laboratory experiments, there is every chance that the research will be repeatable. The procedures should have been carefully recorded and the variables controlled for. It is in line with the spirit of scientific research, lending itself to being checked by being repeated by other researchers using identical procedures.
- *Precision.* Again, in the case of laboratory experiments, the context for the research permits the highest possible level of precision when it comes to the measurements that form the basis of the data.
- *Convenience.* In the laboratory, the researcher is on 'home territory'. This has advantages in terms of setting up the research, and there are also some positive benefits when it comes to costs. The researcher does not need to go out into the field and incur the travel costs and the loss of time spent going to research sites.
- *Credibility.* The use of experiments is regarded by many people, including some social scientists, as the most scientific and, therefore, the most credible approach to research. It has a status that trades off an association with 'hard' science.

Disadvantages of experiments

- *Deception and ethics.* There are a number of ethical considerations to be borne in mind when one is considering the use of experimental research. For instance, if the research design employs the use of control groups, which it is likely to, will there be any advantage or disadvantage experienced by those in the respective groups? Is it possible that adverse comparisons might result through different treatments of experimental and control groups?

If there is a significant difference, this could pose both ethical and practical/ political problems for the researcher. Equally, the experiment's success might depend on keeping its purpose secret from the research subjects. This raises a question about the ethics of deception when used in social research.

- *Artificial settings*. With laboratory experiments there are question marks about whether the experimental situation creates conditions comparable with the 'real-world' situations in which the behaviour/decisions would be made, or whether it encourages artificial responses in line with the artificial setting.

- *Representativeness of the research subjects*. For most purposes, experimental researchers will want to use a control group. To use a control group in a valid fashion, the researcher needs to be sure that the experimental group and the control group constitute a 'matched pair'. They need to be very closely matched in terms of those features which are relevant to the experiment and to the broader population from which the research subjects are drawn. This can be difficult to achieve. Are the research subjects typical of the 'population' being studied? Do the subjects share the same prior experiences? Has there been an element of self-selection?

- *Control of the relevant variables*. Being able to control the relevant variables lies at the heart of the experimental method. However, this places a burden on the would-be experimenter to be sure that he or she can do so. And, even if it is practically possible, is it ethical?

Checklist for the experimental approach

When undertaking research which involves experiments you should feel confident about answering 'yes' to the following questions: ☑

1 Have the key variables been identified? ☐

2 Has a clear distinction been drawn between dependent and independent variables? ☐

3 Is it practical to manipulate the independent variable? ☐

4 Does the experimental situation create conditions comparable to the 'real-world' situations in which the behaviour/decisions would be made? ☐

5 Have control groups been used? ☐

   If so, are the control group and the experimental group closely matched in all key respects? ☐

6 Am I satisfied that neither the control group nor the experimental group will have been disadvantaged in any significant way as a consequence of the experiment? ☐

7 Does the experiment explain the causal relationship it observes? ☐

8 Did the research subjects know their true involvement? ☐

   If yes, has the effect of this on the subjects' responses been taken into consideration? ☐

9 Is the research ethical in terms of its treatment of those involved in the experiment? ☐

© M. Denscombe, *The Good Research Guide*. Open University Press.

4

Ethnography

What is ethnography? • The focus of ethnography • Ethnography: description and theory • Ethnographers as part of the world they seek to describe: the issue of reflexivity • Putting the researcher's self into ethnographic research • Access to fieldwork settings • Advantages of ethnography • Disadvantages of ethnography • Checklist for enthnographic research

What is ethnography?

The term *ethnography* literally means a description of peoples or cultures. It has its origins as a research strategy in the works of the early social anthropologists, whose aim was to provide a detailed and permanent account of the cultures and lives of small, isolated tribes. Such tribes were seen, with some justification, as 'endangered species', and the social anthropologists saw the need to map out those cultures before they became contaminated by contact with the industrial world or withered away to extinction.

The image of the pith-helmeted outsider dressed in khaki shorts arriving on the shores of some remote and exotic palm tree island to set up camp and study the lives of the 'native' has become legendary – largely through the works of people like Bronislaw Malinowski (1922) and Margaret Mead (1943). The concerns of such social anthropologists and the research strategy they employed set the scene for much of what is undertaken as 'ethnography' today.

Ethnography, based on the early anthropological origins of the term and on subsequent developments by influential classics in the field (e.g. Whyte, [1943] 1981), has the following characteristics.

- It requires the researcher to spend considerable *time in the field* among the people whose lives and culture are being studied. The ethnographer needs to share in the lives rather than observe from a position of detachment. Extended fieldwork allows for a *journey of discovery* in which the explanations for what is being witnessed emerge over a period of time.
- Routine and normal aspects of *everyday life* are regarded as worthy of consideration as research data. The mundane and the ordinary parts of social life are just as valid as the special events and ceremonies which can all too easily capture our attention.
- There is special attention given to the way the people being studied see their world. Quite distinct from the researcher's analysis of the situation, the ethnographer is generally concerned to find out *how the members of the group/culture being studied understand things*, the meanings *they* attach to happenings, the way *they* perceive their reality. 'To grasp the native's point of view, his relation to life, to realize *his* vision of *his* world' (Malinowski, 1922: 25).
- There is an emphasis on the need to look at the interlinkages between the various features of the culture and to avoid isolating facets of the culture from the wider context within which it exists. Ethnography generally prefers a *holistic approach* which stresses processes, relationships, connections and interdependency among the component parts.
- There is some acknowledgement that the ethnographer's final account of the culture or group being studied is more than just a description – it is a *construction*. It is not a direct 'reproduction', a literal photograph of the situation. It is, rather, a crafted construction which employs particular writing skills (rhetoric) and which inevitably owes something to the ethnographer's own experiences.

> **Key point: the holistic perspective of ethnography**
>
> 'One of the first conditions of acceptable Ethnographic work certainly is that it should deal with the totality of all social, cultural and psychological aspects of the community, for they are so interwoven that not one can be understood without taking into consideration all the others.' (Malinowski, 1922: xvi)

The focus of ethnography

Alien lifestyles: the insider's point of view

As a topic, ethnography refers to the study of cultures and groups – their lifestyle, understandings and beliefs. In doing so, ethnography tends to emphasize the importance of *understanding things from the point of view of those involved*. Rather than explaining things from the outsider's point of view, there is a concern to see things as those involved see things – 'to grasp the native's point of view'. Early anthropologists used to study relatively small groups in societies which were *different* from their own. They hoped the comparison would illuminate aspects of their own society as well as explain the 'primitive' society where their fieldwork was based. Ethnography, in this respect, resembles an anthropological approach, but it does not restrict its attention to remote tribes in distant lands. Indeed, the most popular development of ethnography in recent times has been its application to lifestyles, understandings and beliefs within 'our own' society. The element of *comparison and contrast*, though, is retained as an underlying facet of ethnographic research.

Link up with **Field experiments, pp. 56–8**

The exotic and the routine

In its early days, ethnography 'within our own society' tended to focus on groups who were relatively small in number, and tended to be somewhat alien to the mainstream of society. The anthropological stance was applied to deviant subgroups, oddball cultures that stood out as different from the norm. And, just as with the study of 'natives' in far off lands, there was an immediate attraction for studying such groups. They offered something intrinsically interesting in the way their lifestyles seemed quaint, crazy, even exotic compared with the everyday experience of those who studied the groups and those who read the resulting books. The title of one of the classics illustrates the point. Margaret Mead's (1943) study, originally published in 1928, was titled *Coming of Age in Samoa: A Study of Adolescence and Sex in Primitive Societies*. Such a style of research, in a sense, pandered to a certain voyeurism. When applied to 'our own' society, the focus was on 'deviant' groups, such as hobos, alcoholics, drug users, religious sects, street gangs and the like. There remains, it is true, legacies of an interest in the exotic and the special, with ceremonies and the unusual features of social life. However, the routine and the mundane, the normal and the unspectacular facets of social life have become recognized as equally valid topics for ethnographic enquiry. In recent times, attention has been refocused on to more routine, mainstream aspects of social life – for example, life in classrooms (Woods, 1979) or life on a building site (Reimer, 1979).

Life history

A life history approach involves the in-depth study of individuals, social groups or communities. Mainly, it has come to be associated with the study of individuals. The aim of the approach is to portray the lives of specific people, to map how their experiences change over time, and to link these experiences with the cultural, social or historical context in which they occur. The approach came to prominence through the work of sociologists at the University of Chicago during the 1920s to 1940s who paved the way by conducting detailed empirical studies of individuals, groups and communities (Bulmer, 1984; Denzin, 1970). These ethnographies traced the changes and developments that took place over a period of time and paid particular attention to experiences of those whose lives were being studied. More recently the approach has been associated with feminist research (Devault, 1990) and studies of individuals in relation to occupations (Woods, 1993) and health (Haglund, 2004).

Like biographies, life histories can be based on the whole of a person's life-span from beginning to end, but can also be used to cover portions of lives – extended and substantial parts of people's lives but not the whole of the life.

There are two themes running through most life history research, both of which fit closely with ethnography. The first is that the research provides a 'thick' description of the life of the person. It includes the kind of fine detail that allows the reader to see the complex and multi-layered facets the person's life. The second is that the individual's understanding of things is treated as a crucial part of the life history. As Marshall and Rossman (1999: 121) put it, the life history approach 'understands a culture through the history of one person's development of life within it, told in ways that capture the person's own feelings, views, and perspectives'.

It follows from this that life histories can be *phenomenological* in their approach, treating the core of the research as an attempt to provide an insider's view of life in relation to a particular culture or a particular time in history. The researcher's question is 'How does someone living at that time in that culture really understand things?' and his/her task is to use the person's reflections on their life as the basis for producing an account that enables the reader to see things through the eyes of the person.

Contrasting slightly with this, some life histories are used *descriptively*, their main aim being to use the personal biography as a means to reveal new things about the cultural, historical and social circumstances within which the person lives (or lived). The research, in this instance, attempts to provide insights into the lifestyle and beliefs of a particular culture or group. The idea is that we can learn what things were like from someone who had first-hand experience of being there or who had lived during that period.

Other researchers approach life histories in a more *analytic* fashion. They are more inclined to treat the life history as something that should be interpreted in terms of the wider social structure within which it occurs. There is an issue, here, about whether the life history entails recounting the story of a person's life in the way that they see it, or whether there is a need to bring alternative sources to bear by way of corroborating or challenging the person's version of their own life. Denzin (1970: 238) argues that

The life history must contain reports from persons other than the subject. Not only must users of life histories triangulate methodologies, but they must also triangulate perspectives: (. . .) Unless the perspectives of others are brought to bear upon the subject's statements, observers have no way of assessing the idiosyncrasies of those interpretations.

Despite these differences in emphasis, what life histories share is an approach that uses the

- in-depth study of an individual's life
- in order to get a grasp on their experiences and thinking
- in a way that links these to the cultural, social and historical circumstances in which they occur.

Life histories generally make use of in-depth interviews to collect the data. They can also make use of secondary source data such as public archive material, private archive material, diaries, letters and other forms of documentary data to build the life history. As with most ethnographic research, a distinctive feature of the data collection is that it takes place over a relatively long period and a life history is not something that can be completed quickly.

Usually, it will be gathered over a number of years with gentle guidance from the social scientist, the subject either writing down episodes of life or tape recording them. At its best, it will be backed up with intensive observation of the subject's life, interviews with friends and perusals of letters and photographs.

(Plummer, 2001: 14)

Perhaps the most interesting question of methods in relation to the life history approach is not how the data are collected, but how the informants are chosen. As Plummer (2001: 133) puts is so well: 'Who from the teeming millions of the world population is to be selected for such intensive study and social science immortality?' Obviously, it will be people who are 'information rich' – people with relevant experiences, fascinating insights and stories to tell. The way the researcher finds such people, people who are willing to open-up their lives to the inquisitive gaze of the researcher, can follow a process of 'selective sampling'. The researcher will be looking in certain appropriate places and will have in mind some kind of person who might have the kind of life history that will be revealing and informative. However, when it comes to finding the 'right' person – the one who turns out to have the treasure trove of life experiences – famous instances of life history research show that luck has a large part to play.

Life on the Internet

The Internet is more than a physical network and electronic technology. It enables a cyberworld populated by particular kinds of people. And this has attracted the attention of some ethnographers. For them, the Internet gives rise to a social phenomenon that needs to be investigated and explained. In this vein, research has emerged on:

- the cultural, social and technological conditions giving rise to the Internet and its widespread use;
- the personal attributes of those who use the Internet and the particular facilities it provides.

For others, the Internet is of particular interest because it is seen as a whole new aspect of social existence inhabited by communities with their own distinctive cultures, styles of interaction and modes of personal communication. The interest in 'online cultures' and 'online communities' has given rise to what Hine (2000) has called 'virtual ethnography' and Kozinets (1998, 2002) has termed 'netnography'. Ethnography, in such cases, focuses on the culture of cyberspace.

Ethnography: description and theory

At first glance it would seem easy to associate ethnography with the task of providing straightforward descriptions of things witnessed first hand in the field by the researcher. The crucial factor, from this position, is the depth and detail of the description, the accuracy of what it portrays and the insights it offers to readers about the situation being studied. The purpose of the ethnographic research is to produce detailed pictures of events or cultures – descriptions which stand in their own right without the need to worry about how representative the situation is or what the broader implications might be in terms of other events or cultures of the type, or of contributing to wider theories. The ethnography, from this stance, is a stand-alone 'one-off' that is to be judged by the depth of its portrayal and the intricacy of its description. This is an *idiographic* approach to ethnography.

Link up with **Phenomenology, Chapter 5**

A challenge to the idiographic stance within ethnography comes from those who question the value of producing numerous stand-alone descriptions if there is no attempt to derive something from them which goes beyond the specifics of the situation and which can, in some way or other, link to broader issues. If each ethnographic study produces a one-off, isolated piece of information, these pieces cannot contribute to the building up of any generalized knowledge about human societies, it is alleged. They take the position that ethnographic research should be initiated quite deliberately to develop some theory *grounded* in the detailed observation undertaken.

> Ethnography is directed towards producing what are referred to as 'theoretical', 'analytical', or 'thick' descriptions (whether of societies, small communities, organizations, spatial locations, or social worlds). These descriptions must remain close to the concrete reality of particular events but at the same time reveal general features of human social life.
>
> (Hammersley, 1990: 598)

Some researchers would go still further. They would argue that the purpose of ethnographic research should be to shed some light on an area of life whose significance depends on a theory; to elaborate on a theory or even check on whether the theory really does hold true and explain things as they happen in 'real life' (Porter, 1993).

At one end of the spectrum there are those who regard the main purpose of ethnography as providing rich and detailed descriptions of real-life situations as they really are. At the other end of the spectrum there are those who see the role of ethnographic fieldwork as a test-bed for theories – a means of developing theories by checking them out in small-scale scenarios.

Somewhere towards the middle of the spectrum lies the view 'that "idiographic" and "nomothetic" approaches are not mutually exclusive, and that we can have both rich and intensive description *and* generalizability' (Woods, 1979: 268). Advocates of the middle position are keen to hold on to the idiographic aspect of ethnographic research in as much as it provides a valuable and distinct kind of data – the *detailed descriptions of specifics based on first hand observation in naturally occurring situations*. They also recognize the need for theory within ethnography. They recognize the need to *locate the ethnography within a theoretical context*.

To accommodate the need for ethnography to have some theoretical basis the social researcher should give:

- explicit consideration of how the findings tie in with, or contradict, existing relevant theories and generalizations about human social behaviour (extrapolation from the particular);
- explicit consideration of how the choice of setting might reflect social concerns in the researcher's culture and in the situation being studied (explanation of why the event or culture was selected for study);
- explicit consideration of how the findings compare with those of other similar ethnographies (comparison with other descriptions).

Ethnographers as part of the world they seek to describe: the issue of reflexivity

Ethnographers tend to be very sensitive to the matter of reflexivity and the way it affects their perception of the culture or events they wish to describe. What concerns them is that the conceptual tools they use to understand the cultures or events being studied are not, and can never be, neutral and passive instruments of discovery.

As researchers, the meanings we attach to things that happen and the language we use to describe them are the product of our own culture, social background and personal experiences. Making sense of what is observed during fieldwork observation is a process that relies on what the researcher already knows and already believes, and it is not a voyage of discovery which starts with a clean sheet. We can only make sense of the world in a way that we have learnt to do using conceptual tools which are based on our own culture and our own experiences. We have no way of standing outside these to reach some objective and neutral vantage point from which to view things 'as they really are'. To an extent, we can describe them only 'as we see them', and this is shaped by *our* culture, not theirs.

The question that taxes ethnographers is this: 'How far can my description of the culture or event depict things from the point of view of those involved when I can only use my own way of seeing things, my own conceptual tools, to make sense of what is happening?'

Broadly, ethnographers are conscious of the way in which their account of any particular lifestyle or beliefs is a construction based upon the researcher's interpretation of events. Even when it comes to writing up the ethnography there are deep-rooted doubts about claims to objectivity. The outcome of ethnographic research is generally recognized by those who write it as being a creative work in its own right – the outcome of interpretation, editing and skilful writing techniques as well as a reflection of the reality of the situation they set out to study (Woods, 2006). Inescapably, the account is partial – an edited and abridged version – which owes something to the ethnographer as well as the culture or events observed. There is nothing new to this. Malinowski appreciated the point many years ago.

> In ethnography, the distance is often enormous between the brute material of information – as it is presented to the student in his own observations, in native statement, in the kaleidoscope of tribal life – and the final authoritative presentations of the results. The ethnographer has to traverse this distance in the laborious years between the moment when he sets foot upon a native beach, and makes his first attempts to get into touch with the natives, and the time when he writes down the final version of his results.
>
> (Malinowski, 1922: 4)

Putting the researcher's 'self' into ethnographic research

One of the characteristic features of ethnography is the significance it attaches to the role of the researcher's 'self' in the process of research. The researcher's identity, values and beliefs become part of the equation – a built-in component that cannot be eliminated as an influence on the end-product findings of the project (Ball, 1990).

Ethnographic research, therefore, calls for a certain degree of introspection on the part of the researcher. He or she needs to reflect upon the way that background factors associated with personal experiences, personal beliefs and social values may have shaped the way that events and cultures were interpreted.

However, the ethnographic researcher needs to go beyond mere reflection. This is, in a sense, a private activity. Necessary though it is, it needs to be portrayed more publicly if it is to support the research outcomes. Researchers need to supply their readers with some insights into the possible influence of the researcher's self on the interpretation of events or cultures. *There needs to be a public account of the self which explores the role of the researcher's self.*

The need for a 'public account of the role of the self' means it is necessary to include in the methodology section, and possibly in the preface or introduction, some information about the self and its perceived influence. This account of the self will vary in the amount of detail it provides, depending on the nature of the research topic, the kind of methods used and the audience for whom the ethnography is written. There is obviously a matter of judgement here about the extent to which the account should delve to the depths of detail about researchers' personal matters, and the amount of detail that the readership needs to know in order to arrive at a reasonable evaluation of the likely impact of the 'self' on the research.

A researcher's account of the role of the 'self'

As a broad guideline, the following factors might be considered:

- personal beliefs relating to the topic (politics, values, standpoint);
- personal interests in the area of investigation (vested interest, history of events);
- personal experience linked to the research topic (incidents affecting self or others close to researchers);
- personal expertise in relation to the topic (qualification, experience).

To give an account of the way personal beliefs, interests, experience and expertise might have a bearing on findings, the researcher is likely to need to draw upon personal details about his or her:

- social background (class, family, environment);
- age;
- sex;
- ethnicity;
- education and qualifications;
- work experience and skills.

Access to fieldwork settings

Gaining access to people, places and events is a crucial part of successful ethnographic research. For field researchers this access cannot be taken for granted. Researchers need to set about gaining access, and to do this they need to engage in negotiations that have political, ethical and practical implications.

Naturalism

In order to produce a pure and detailed description, ethnographers will wish to avoid disrupting the situation by their very presence as observers in the field. They will wish to preserve the natural state of affairs. And this is why *naturalism* is a key concern of ethnography. The ethnographer's concern with naturalism derives from the wish to study things in their natural state – undisturbed by the intrusion of research tools or the disruption of experimental designs. Going 'into the field' to witness events first hand in their natural habitat lies at the very heart of what it means to do ethnography.

Link up with **Participant observation, pp. 217–225**

Covert research

It is sometimes possible for an ethnographer to conduct fieldwork without people knowing that they have a researcher in their midst. The researcher can blend into the background by adopting a role that fits in with the normal situation. The researcher can go *undercover* and carry out the research in a clandestine manner. This has benefits as far as ethnography is concerned because (a) it preserves the naturalness of the setting and (b) it generally sidesteps any need to get authorization to conduct the research. However, it gives rise to a different type of problem. The decision to undertake covert research means that the researcher cannot also have 'informed consent' on the part of the subjects of his or her research, and this raises substantial ethical problems (see Humphreys, 1970).

Gatekeepers

Ethnographers do not always work in a covert manner. Indeed, it is fair to say that most ethnographies actually involve some degree of openness about the role of the researcher; that is, *overt* research. When this is the case, the ethical problems cease to be the sole concern. Added to this, ethnographers are faced with the possibility that their explicit research role might disrupt the naturalness of the situation. Most of all, though, an overt research role will most probably bring with it a call for the researcher to make contact with 'gatekeepers' who can help the researcher with the vital business of gaining access to the necessary fieldwork settings.

Identifying key people who can grant permission, and successfully negotiating with them for access to people, places and events, is often a prerequisite without which the fieldwork cannot begin. In informal settings, such sponsors act as guarantors who vouch for the *bona fide* status of researcher. They use their informal status and relationship with subjects as a currency facilitating both contact and trust between researcher and subject or group (e.g. Polsky, 1967; Whyte, [1943] 1981).

> **Key point: access and gatekeepers**
>
> Seeking the permission of gatekeepers or the support of sponsors is often an unavoidable first step in gaining access to the data. Furthermore, the relationships established with such people can have important consequences for the subsequent course of the research. (Hammersley and Atkinson, 1983: 72–3)

Sponsors and gatekeepers, however, cannot be disregarded once their initial approval has been obtained. In reality, they exercise *continued* influence over the nature of the research. Their influence persists in terms of both:

- the kind of initial agreement established about access (influencing the nature of eventual research findings); and
- the need for access to people and places that were not foreseen at the start of the research.

The influence of such gatekeepers, then, goes beyond a simple granting or denial of contact with research subjects. As Burgess (1984) argues, access is a continual *process* in fieldwork research. It is a process because research is generally conducted over a period of time and it is a process, perhaps more importantly, because access needs to be sought to new people, places and events as new lines of enquiry become incorporated in the research. Since field research, especially ethnographic work, tends to evolve and develop in terms of its focus of enquiry, it is unlikely that the researcher could state at the outset of research the precise nature and extent of access that will be required.

Access, in the sense of permission from a gatekeeper, is necessarily renewable and renegotiable, and should be viewed as an 'access relationship' rather than a one-off event.

Gatekeepers' authority to grant or withhold access varies, of course, depending on the degree to which the people, places and events being studied are part of a formal environment. Whereas in the educational context headteachers have formal jurisdiction over entry to school premises and can withhold or grant access to teachers and pupils, in less formal settings the role of the gatekeeper is different. As Whyte illustrated so graphically in his research (Whyte, [1943] 1981), the role of gatekeeper can become more akin to a guarantor for the *bona fide* status of the researcher. Whyte's gatekeeper, 'Doc', had no formal authority to grant or deny access; he used his status with the group to open up the possibility of Whyte making contact with the young men in question, and acted as a sponsor/guarantor to enable some trust relationship to develop. This is an important point. As Hammersley and Atkinson (1983) argue, access is not simply a matter of physical presence or absence. It is far more than a matter of granting or withholding of permission for research to be conducted (Hammersley and Atkinson, 1983: 56). Worthwhile access to people, places and events involves, as well, an opening up to allow the researcher into the world of the persons involved. Being present is one hurdle, but 'access' also involves being trusted with insights and insider knowledge.

Advantages of ethnography

- *Direct observation*. As a research strategy it is based on direct observation via fieldwork, rather than relying on second-hand data or statements made by research subjects.
- *Empirical*. It is essentially grounded in empirical research involving direct contact with relevant people and places.
- *Links with theory*. It can be used as a means for developing theory, and it can also be used for testing theories.
- *Detailed data*. It provides data which are relatively rich in depth and detail. Potentially, it can deal with intricate and subtle realities.
- *Holistic*. Ethnography aspires to holistic explanations which focus on processes and relationships that lie behind the surface events. Potentially, it puts things in context rather than abstracting specific aspects in isolation.
- *Contrast and comparison*. There is an element of contrast and comparison built into ethnographic research in the way the distinct culture or events being studied are 'anthropologically strange' – different from other cultures or events which the researcher and his or her audience to some degree share.
- *Actors' perceptions*. Ethnographic research is particularly well suited to

dealing with the way members of a culture see events – as seen through their eyes. It describes and explores the 'actors' perceptions'.

- *Self-awareness*. It has an open and explicit awareness of the role of the researcher's *self* in the choice of topic, process of research and construction of the findings/conclusions. It acknowledges the inherent reflexivity of social knowledge.
- *Ecological validity*. It is strong in terms of ecological validity, to the extent that the act of researching should have relatively little impact on the setting – retaining things in their 'natural' form.

Disadvantages of ethnography

- *Tensions within the approach*. There is a tension within the realms of ethnography stemming from its twin concerns with naturalism and reflexivity. Ethnographies generally attempt to accommodate an internal contradiction between (a) 'realist' aspirations to provide full and detailed *descriptions* of events or cultures as they naturally exist, and (b) a 'relativist' awareness of the reflexive nature of social knowledge and the inevitable influence of the researcher's 'self' on the whole research endeavour. *Depending on how this tension is accommodated* and the degree to which the ethnography adopts a 'realist' or a 'relativist' position, certain other weaknesses can exist.
- *Stand-alone descriptions*. Ethnographic research has the potential to produce an array of 'pictures' which coexist, but which tend to remain as separate, isolated stories. There is arguably an in-built tendency to scatter these building-block pictures at random, rather than erecting a structure where each is a brick which serves as a base for further bricks to be layered upon it moving ever upwards. To avoid this, ethnographics need to be guided by (or to) a coherent theoretical framework.
- *Story-telling*. There is the potential to provide detailed descriptive accounts at the expense of developing an analytic insight or contributing to a theoretical position. The story-telling can become the sole purpose, leaving a research product which is atheoretical, non-analytic and non-critical.
- *Reliability*. There is a potential weakness of poor reliability and little prospect of generalizing from the ethnographic account of the culture or event.
- *Ethics*. There is also a greater potential than with most other approaches to face ethical problems associated with intrusions upon privacy and with gaining informed consent from research subjects.
- *Access*. Ethnographic research can pose particularly acute difficulties of gaining access to settings, access which avoids disrupting the naturalness of the setting.
- *Insider knowledge*, rather than being a straight advantage, can also cause a 'blind spot', obscuring a vision of 'the obvious'.

Checklist for ethnographic research

When undertaking ethnographic research you should feel confident about answering 'yes' to the following questions: ☑

1 Have lifestyles and meanings been treated as the main interest of the research? ☐

2 Has a holistic approach been adopted, linking all significant contributing factors? ☐

3 Has the research involved sufficient time doing fieldwork, and collected enough empirical data? ☐

4 Has access to the fieldwork settings been negotiated through relevant 'gatekeepers'? ☐

5 Has the research been conducted ethically with due respect to the rights of those being studied? ☐

6 Has the research managed to avoid disrupting the naturalness of the settings? ☐

7 Does the research involve an account of the role of the researcher's 'self'? ☐

8 Is there a description of how the ethnography builds on (or contradicts) existing explanations of the phenomenon? ☐

9 Are the findings compared and contrasted with other ethnographies on similar topics? ☐

10 Has due acknowledgement been given to the fact that the ethnography is a researcher's construction rather than a literal description of the situation? ☐

© M. Denscombe, *The Good Research Guide*. Open University Press.

5

Phenomenology

What is the phenomenological approach?

As an approach to social research, phenomenology is sometimes presented as an alternative to positivism. When a simple dichotomy is called for, phenomenology has been useful for some writers as an umbrella term covering styles of research that do not rely on measurement, statistics or other things generally associated with the scientific method. In direct contrast to positivism it is seen as an approach that emphasizes:

- subjectivity (rather than objectivity);
- description (more than analysis);
- interpretation (rather than measurement);
- agency (rather than structure).

Its credentials as an alternative to positivism are further reinforced by the fact that phenomenological research generally deals with people's:

- perceptions or meanings;
- attitudes and beliefs;
- feelings and emotions.

Link up with **Frequently asked questions, 'What is positivism?', p. 332**

Such a thumbnail portrait of phenomenology serves to set the scene and provide an initial view of its direction as a research strategy. It helps to explain why a phenomenological approach has proved useful for researchers in areas such as health, education and business who want to understand the thinking of patients, pupils and employees (Crotty, 1996; van Manen, 1990). And it gives a clue to why phenomenology is associated with humanistic research using qualitative methodologies – approaches that place special emphasis on the individual's views and personal experiences. Necessarily, though, it also disguises some of the differences and debates that exist in relation to the term. There are always dangers of oversimplification when trying to reduce the variety of approaches to a matter of two opposing camps, and there is also controversy surrounding the use of the term 'phenomenology' to encompass all those approaches that reject positivism. Added to this, different types of phenomenology have emerged as the approach has developed over time, and proponents of phenomenology often differ in the emphasis they place on certain aspects of the underlying principles. Some insight to the alternative types of phenomenology is given later in the chapter. There are, though, certain themes and areas of interest that are shared by the various strands, and it is these that are emphasized in this chapter as an introduction to the phenomenological approach to social research.

Phenomenology is an approach that focuses on how life is experienced

It is not primarily concerned with explaining the causes of things but tries, instead, to provide a description of how things are experienced first hand by those involved. The phenomenological investigation of something like 'homelessness', for instance, would focus on the experience of being homeless. It might be interested in trying to get at the essence of what it means to be homeless. It might try to understand homelessness from the point of view of those who are themselves homeless and try to describe how they see things, how they understand the situation, how they interpret events. What it would not try to do is measure the extent of homelessness, or explain the causes of homelessness. Though both might be worthwhile endeavours, neither would be at the heart of phenomenological research.

Experience

Phenomenology is concerned, first and foremost, with human experience – something denoted by the term 'phenomenology' itself. A phenomenon is a thing that is known to us through our senses. It is seen, heard, touched, smelled, tasted. It is experienced directly, rather than being conceived in the mind as some abstract concept or theory. As such, a phenomenon is something that, though we experience it, is not yet understood through analysis, conceptualization or theorizing. A phenomenon is something that stands in need of explanation; something of which we are aware but something that, as yet, remains known to us only in terms of how it appears to us directly through our senses. A phenomenological approach to research, following from this, concentrates its efforts on the kind of human experiences that are pure, basic and raw in the sense that they have not (yet) been subjected to processes of analysis and theorizing. In contrast to other approaches to research that rely on processes of categorizing things, abstracting them, quantifying them and theorizing about them, phenomenology prefers to concentrate its efforts on getting a clear picture of the 'things in themselves' – the things as directly experienced by people.

Everyday world

Phenomenology is also characterized by a particular interest in the basics of social existence. This stems from a philosophical concern with the nature of 'Being-in-the-world' (Heidegger, 1962) and the lived experience of human beings within the 'life-world' (Husserl, 1970). In practice, this translates into special importance being attached to the routine and ordinary features of social life, and to questions about how people manage to 'do' the everyday things on which social life depends. Sometimes this can involve quite fundamental things associated with the way people experience their lives; for example, coming to terms with the death of a loved one (Seymour, 1999) or the awareness of what it means to be 'different' from others (Moustakas, 1992). On other occasions phenomenological studies have looked at more mundane things such as daydreaming (Morley, 1998) and complaining about chronic pain (Kugelmann, 1999). Such topics might draw on normal, routine facets of the everyday world around us but, from the phenomenological perspective, this does not make them trivial or inconsequential.

Seeing things through the eyes of others

When dealing with the way people experience facets of their lives, phenomenology stresses the need to present matters as closely as possible to the way that those concerned understand them. The phenomenologist's task, in the first instance, is not to interpret the experiences of those concerned, not to analyse them or repackage them in some form. The task is to present the experiences in a way that is *faithful to the original*. This entails the ability to see things through the eyes of others, to understand things in the way that they understand things and to provide a description of matters that adequately portrays how the group in question experiences the situation.

This has some significant implications for social research. First, it places the ideas and reasoning of the group being studied at the core of the investigation. The research necessarily revolves around people and their lives, rather than systems, aggregates and trends operating at a high level of abstraction. Second, it elevates the importance of people's thinking in terms of the research. Rather than being treated as something that is the crude foundation from which to build more sophisticated explanations and theories about the experiences, that thinking becomes the topic of investigation in its own right. Third, people's everyday thinking is given credibility and respected in its own right as valid. It is not necessarily treated as a less rational than or inferior to the 'scientific' thinking of the social researcher, but is considered as rational in its own terms of reference. For these reasons, *phenomenology has an affinity with humanistic perspectives on research that are keen to accord normal people and their own everyday reasoning higher status in research.*

The social construction of reality

Phenomenology is particularly interested in how social life is constructed by those who participate in it, and it makes two points about this. First, it regards people as creative interpreters of events who, through their actions and interpretations, literally make sense of their worlds. From the perspective of the phenomenologist, people do not passively obey a set of social rules; nor do they slot into an external social structure; nor do they simply respond to their internal physiological drives or psychological dispositions. They are viewed instead as 'agents' who interpret their experiences and who actively create an order to their existence. As an approach to understanding the social world this sets phenomenology apart from any belief that things are preordained, that there is a reality to social life that exists independently from the way people experience it or that the way we experience and understand things is structured by the way human minds are programmed to perceive things. Second, it acknowledges that the processes of interpreting sights and sounds into meaningful events are not unique to each individual. Necessarily, they must be shared with others who live in the group or community (Berger and Luckmann, 1967). If they were not, people would find it virtually impossible to interact with one another, since they could be operating on quite different understandings about what is going on. They could be living in different worlds, unable to communicate and unable to grasp the implications of other people's actions. Without some shared basis for interpreting their experiences there would be no way of knowing what others were doing or what their intentions were. There would, effectively, be no basis for social life.

> **Key point**
> Phenomenology deals with the ways people interpret events and, literally, make sense of their personal experiences.

Multiple realities

When the social world is seen as 'socially constructed' it opens up the possibility that different groups of people might 'see things differently'. There is the prospect of alternative realities – realities that vary from situation to situation, culture to culture. In this respect phenomenology stands in stark contrast with positivistic approaches to social research that are premised on the assumption of *one* reality. Whereas positivistic approaches look for explanations that fit one universal reality, phenomenological approaches tend to live with, even celebrate, the possibility of *multiple realities*. Reflecting the fact that the world as experienced by living humans is something that is created through the way they interpret and give meaning to their experiences, phenomenology rejects the notion that there is one universal reality and accepts, instead, that things can be seen in different ways by different people at different times in different circumstances, and that each alternative version needs to be recognized as being valid in its own right.

 Caution

This phenomenological position certainly allows for competing versions of what things are, how they work and what they mean. It implies that there might not be one 'right' explanation and that different theories might be equally valid. It moves researchers away from a mind set where one theory is correct and others are inadequate or wrong. It does *not* imply, however, that there are as many social realities as there are individuals – each interpreting his or her world in their own unique way. As has been stressed, phenomenology does not treat interpretations of the social world as totally individual things. Necessarily, they are shared between groups, cultures and societies, and it is only at these levels that phenomenology recognizes the possibility of there being multiple realities.

Description

When it comes to the matter of how phenomenologists actually do their research, a key characteristic of the approach is its emphasis on describing authentic experiences. Rather than directing their attention to explanations and analyses of experiences in an attempt to discover why they occurred, phenomenologists focus instead on trying to depict the relevant experiences in a way that is as faithful to the original as possible.

To provide a description of the *authentic* experience, phenomenological research first and foremost needs to provide a description that adequately covers the complexity of the situation. One of the crucial benefits of a phenomenological approach is that it deals with things in depth and does not try to gloss over the subtleties and complications that are essential parts of many – possibly most – aspects of human experience. The description, therefore, must be fairly detailed.

> **Key point**
> Good phenomenological research involves a detailed description of the experience that is being investigated.

The phenomenological description should also be prepared to recognize and include aspects of the experience that appear to be self-contradictory, irrational or even bizarre. The researcher's role is not to act as editor for the way people explain their experiences. Nor is it to impose some artificial order on the thoughts of those being studied by trying to remedy any apparent logical inconsistencies. The social world is rarely neat and phenomenology does not involve the attempt to present life experiences as though they are entirely coherent.

A third feature of phenomenological descriptions is that they concentrate on *how* experiences are constructed. It is important to appreciate that phenomenology's emphasis on description is not just a matter of providing a detailed account of any particular set of beliefs, circumstances or events in terms of what they entail. Inevitably this will form part of the research but more fundamentally a phenomenological description focuses on how people come to see things as they are.

The suspension of common-sense beliefs

A phenomenological approach not only encourages the researcher to provide a detailed description of experiences, it also advocates the need to do so with a minimum reliance on the researcher's own beliefs, expectations and predispositions about the phenomenon under investigation.

From a phenomenological perspective researchers are part and parcel of the social world they seek to investigate. Phenomenologists see the social world as existing only through the way it is experienced and interpreted by people – and this includes researchers as much as anyone else. Researchers, like other people, use common-sense assumptions when interpreting events, and this is where phenomenology has an important point to make for researchers. Researchers need to be *aware* of the fact that they rely on such everyday common sense, and make an effort to minimize the impact of these assumptions. They need to stand back from their ordinary, everyday beliefs and question them to see if they are blinkering the researcher's vision of what is happening. As best they can, researchers need temporarily to suspend common-sense beliefs. For the purposes of being able to provide a 'pure' description, researchers need to approach things without predispositions based on events in the past, without suppositions drawn from existing theories about the phenomenon being studied and without using their everyday common-sense assumptions. Such things need to be put to one side for the moment, 'bracketed off' so that researchers are able to describe things not through their own eyes but through the eyes of those whose experiences are being described.

One way of 'bracketing off' presuppositions is to adopt the stance of 'the stranger' (Schutz, 1962). The value of this is that it allows the researcher to see things that would otherwise be hidden from view – things that are so normal and obvious that they would not come to the attention of the researcher as something significant. A stranger is naive about how things work, and needs to figure them out from first principles before he or she can begin to operate as a competent member of the society. A 'stranger' is faced with the prospect of understanding *how* members of the society make sense of events. By adopting the stance of the stranger, then, the researcher is best able to see things for what they are, uncluttered by assumptions that form part of everyday thinking about those things.

> **Key point: suspending common-sense beliefs**
> Researchers who use a phenomenological approach need to be explicit about their own ways of making sense of the world and, in order to get a clear view of how others see the world, they need to suspend (or bracket off) their own beliefs temporarily for the purposes of research.

Members' accounts

Data collection by phenomenology tends to rely on tape-recorded interviews. The interviews are conducted with members of the particular group whose experiences are being investigated. These members can provide insights into the thinking of the group and, through in-depth interviews, their experiences and their reasoning can be described and explained to the researcher in a way that allows the researcher to see things from the member's point of view (Denscombe, 1983).

The process of interviewing is valuable for phenomenologists for a number of reasons. First, it provides the possibility of exploring matters *in depth*. In phenomenological research, interviews tend to be relatively long (in the region of one hour, often more) so that there is plenty of time to delve deeply into issues as they arise. Second, interviews allow the interviewee to raise issues that he or she feels are important. This helps the phenomenologist's investigation by highlighting things that matter to the person being interviewed. It helps to 'see things from the member's point of view'. To encourage this, phenomenological researchers tend to use relatively 'unstructured' interviews. Rather than the interview being conducted using a series of questions devised by the researcher, unstructured interviews allow plenty of scope for interviewees to move the discussion to areas that *they* regard as significant. Third, the interview process gives an opportunity for interviewees to provide an 'account' of their experiences. It is *their* version, spoken in their own words. It allows them both to describe the situation as they see it and to provide some justification or rationale, again from their point of view. Fourth, interviews allow the researcher the opportunity to *check* that he or she is understanding the interviewee correctly. As a normal part of the interview process the researcher can take special care to make sure that what he or she is 'hearing' is really what the interviewee is trying to put across, not a partial or mistaken interpretation resulting from the researcher's common-sense assumptions or presuppositions.

Link up with **Interviews, Chapter 10**

Types of phenomenology: underlying essences or actual experiences

In practice, there are numerous versions of phenomenology and there are sometimes disagreements among those who would call themselves 'phenomenologists' about which is the 'true' version. The social researcher who is thinking about adopting a phenomenological approach should be aware that such differences of opinion exist. Although many versions exist, it is probably most straightforward to characterize phenomenology as consisting of two main types. One version derives from the European tradition of thought and the other, the 'new phenomenology', has a North American origin (Crotty, 1996).

The European version is more steeped in the discipline of philosophy, and can lay claims to being the original version, since it owes much to the founding father of phenomenology, Edmund Husserl. His 'transcendental phenomenology' (Husserl, 1931) approaches the study of human experience with the aim of discovering underlying, fundamental aspects of experience – features that are universal and that lie at the very heart of human experience. Though differing somewhat, the 'existential phenomenology' of Jean-Paul Sartre (1956) and the 'hermeneutic phenomenology' of Martin Heidegger (1962) draw on similar European philosophical roots and have a crucial thing in common. They share a concern with investigating *the essence of human experience*.

The kinds of experience dealt with by these writers tend to revolve around fundamental philosophical questions about 'being-in-the-world' and similar issues relating to 'the meaning of (everyday) life'. However, this form of phenomenology can operate at a more mundane level. For example, it could address something as topical and down-to-earth as bullying in schools. Based on this tradition of phenomenology, the research would be interested in the experience of being bullied and, in particular, it would focus on the essential features of that experience. It would try to identify the core components of the notion of bullying by investigating the experiences of those who have found themselves the victim of bullying. It would not focus on the *extent* of bullying in schools, nor would it try to explain the *causes* of bullying. Its focus would be on the *essence of the experience of being bullied*.

Importantly, though, the European tradition of phenomenology stresses that such essences exist beyond the realms of individual, personal experiences of specific events. While such individual instances might be the starting point for investigation, the purpose is always to use them as a means for getting a clearer picture of the essential qualities of the experience that exist at a general level. In relation to the example of bullying, individual instances of bullying would be of interest only to the extent that they could be used to help the identification of the broader, essential qualities of that experience: they would be valuable as means towards an end, but would not constitute an end in themselves as far as research is concerned.

Contrasting with this tradition, there is the North American version of phenomenology which is more commonly linked to the disciplines of sociology, psychology, education, business studies and health studies. It emanates from the 'social phenomenology' of Alfred Schutz (1962, 1967). Schutz was primarily interested in the mental processes through which humans make sense of the many things they experience. His early work focused on the way that, in order to make sense of the social world, people interpret things through seeing them as specific instances of more general categories – a process that involves what he referred to as 'typifications'. Within the realms of phenomenology this shift in focus had important repercussions. Indeed, through his focus on interpretation of the social world, Schutz's work actually spawned a rather different kind of phenomenology. This kind of phenomenology is less concerned with revealing the essence of experience, and more concerned with describing the ways in which humans give meaning to their experiences. Here lies the defining characteristic of the North American approach: its *concern with the ways people interpret social phenomena.*

This form of phenomenology retains a concern with things like experience, an interest in everyday life and suspending common-sense assumptions in order to provide a description that is true to the way those involved experience things. However, it also incorporates elements of pragmatism and social interactionism into the approach – things that make it controversial in two ways as far as the European phenomenological tradition is concerned. First, the North American phenomenology is comfortable in describing *what* is being experienced (for example, in relation to something such as homelessness), rather than attempting to uncover the essence of what is meant by the term. Second, and linked with this, it also places some value on describing individuals' experiences for their own sake. The new phenomenology might well investigate homelessness by asking what being homeless means to those who are homeless, what events and emotions they have experienced as a consequence of being homeless and what it means to them. The experiences of the individual are taken as significant data in their own right, not something to be put to one side in order to identify the universal essence of the phenomenon.

In practice, it is not always easy to separate the two traditions. Ideas from one area are imported to another, not always reflecting the original very faithfully. It has been argued, for example, that although Heidegger is frequently cited within the North American tradition as a key source, this is not really appropriate. As Crotty (1996: 77) contends, 'Heidegger is after the meaning of Being itself. He is not intent on divining the meanings of real-life experiences.' Such blurring of the boundaries complicates life for the would-be user of a phenomenological approach. This should not, though, deter a researcher from choosing this approach, since many aspects of social research operate in such contested domains. It does, however, alert the would-be user to the need for particular clarity about the purpose of the research the specific way in which the phenomena of human experience will be described, and the ultimate goal of the investigation.

Advantages of phenomenology

- *Offers the prospect of authentic accounts of complex phenomena.* The social world is complex and rarely straightforward. A phenomenological approach allows the researcher to deal with that complexity. It scratches beneath the superficial aspects of social reality. It calls for the researcher to delve into phenomena in depth and to provide descriptions that are detailed enough to reflect the complexity of the social world.
- *A humanistic style of research.* There is a respect for people built into the phenomenological approach. It carries an aura of humanism and, in its efforts to base its enquiry on the lived experiences of people in the everyday world, it represents a style of research that is far removed from any high-minded, abstract theorizing. In effect, the researcher needs to be close to the objects of study.
- *Suited to small-scale research.* Phenomenological research generally relies on in-depth interviews and does not call for technologically sophisticated or expensive equipment for the purposes of data collection and analysis. Coupled with this, it is often undertaken in specific localities such as hospitals, schools or industrial plants. In both respects, it lends itself to small-scale research where the budget is low and the main resource is the researcher him/herself.
- *The description of experiences can tell an interesting story.* There is an inherent potential within (new) phenomenology to describe experiences in a way that is immediately accessible and interesting to a wide range of readers. By unfolding the events and laying bare the feelings experienced by people the research is likely to attract a relatively wide readership. It deals with everyday life and people can generally relate to this.

Disadvantages of phenomenology

- *Lacks scientific rigour.* The emphasis of phenomenology on subjectivity, description and interpretation contrasts with the scientific emphasis on objectivity, analysis and measurement. Although phenomenology is self-consciously non-positivist – and proud to be so – there is the danger that this can be turned against it and be treated as a weakness rather than a strength by those who do not share its stance.

- *Associated with description and no analysis.* The importance attached to providing a detailed and accurate description of the events and experiences being studied can lead to accusations that phenomenology does nothing but provide descriptions. This might not be warranted, in particular where the phenomenologist goes on to develop explanations based on the descriptive material. There is, none the less, the danger that those who are not sympathetic to phenomenology might seize the opportunity to criticize it for its primary focus on description.
- *Generalizations from phenomenological studies.* Phenomenological research does not normally involve large numbers or instances of the phenomenon being studied. This will always raise questions about the representativeness of the data and how far it is justifiable to generalize from the findings. Phenomenologists, for their part, might not regard such a concern as relevant to their work, but many other kinds of researchers will be concerned with this issue.
- *Attention to the mundane features of life.* For phenomenologists the study of routine aspects of everyday life occurs because it is fundamental for understanding the nature of the social world. For others it might be (mis)interpreted as dealing with things that are mundane, trivial and relatively unimportant compared with the big issues of the day in the spheres of social policy, international relations, economic progress and the like.
- *Feasibility of suspending common sense.* In principle, suspending presuppositions about the way things work might seem a reasonable way of trying to get a clearer view of them. However, it is doubtful indeed if it is ever possible to rid ourselves entirely of such presuppositions. Socialization and the use of language make it impossible. What can be done, though, is to be reflective and self-conscious about the way perceptions are shaped by things like common sense and then to try to moderate their impact.

Checklist for phenomenology

When undertaking phenomenological research you should feel confident about answering 'yes' to the following questions: ☑

1 Is the research concerned with on one or more of the following:
   - Looking for the essential features of a phenomenon? ☐
   - Describing the everyday rules by which experience is structured? ☐
   - Describing the content and nature of lived experiences? ☐

2 Does the research provide a description that adequately deals with the complexity and subtlety of the phenomenon? ☐

3 Have efforts been made to bracket off common-sense assumptions and take account of researchers' presuppositions in order to provide a 'pure' description? ☐

4 Does the description authentically represent the way things are seen by those whose experiences are being studied? ☐

5 Does the research look for:
   - Shared ways of interpreting experiences? ☐
   - Underlying essential features of a phenomenon? ☐

   (Rather than just relying on describing an individual's personal experiences.)

6 Does the research take into consideration:
   - The social construction of reality? ☐
   - Multiple realities? ☐

7 Does the research involve the suitable use of interviews and transcripts for checking members' meanings and intentions? ☐

© M. Denscombe, *The Good Research Guide*. Open University Press.

6

Grounded theory

What is the Grounded Theory approach? • When is the Grounded Theory approach useful? • Initial ideas and concepts: the starting point • Methods of data collection • Initial sites for fieldwork • Subsequent sites for fieldwork: theoretical sampling • Analysing the data • Completing the research (theoretical saturation) • Theories and grounded research • Developments in grounded theory • Advantages of Grounded Theory approach • Disadvantages of Grounded Theory approach • Checklist for the Grounded Theory approach

The Grounded Theory approach has become a popular choice of methodology among social researchers in recent times. In particular, it has been adopted by those engaged in small-scale projects using qualitative data for the study of human interaction, and by those whose research is exploratory and focused on particular settings. 'Grounded theory' is cited frequently in such research – not least because it has come to provide a well recognized, authoritative rationale for the adoption of an approach that does not necessarily involve statistical analysis, quantitative data or the quest for representative samples.

What is the Grounded Theory approach?

The approach originated with the work of Barney Glaser and Anselm Strauss and, in particular, their book *The Discovery of Grounded Theory*, which was published in 1967. Since that time, the notion of grounded theory has come to mean slightly different things to different people. There has been a tendency for researchers to 'adopt and adapt' grounded theory and to use it selectively for their own purposes. There are, though, certain basic ideas associated with the Grounded Theory approach that remain fairly constant, and these are outlined in this chapter. They draw principally on the writings of Glaser and Strauss themselves and the main focus is on those components of the Grounded Theory approach that mark it out as distinctive and constitute its core components as an approach to social research.

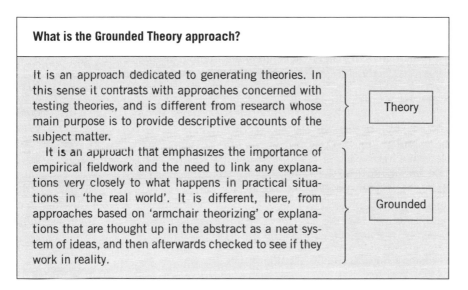

What is the Grounded Theory approach?

It is an approach dedicated to generating theories. In this sense it contrasts with approaches concerned with testing theories, and is different from research whose main purpose is to provide descriptive accounts of the subject matter. } Theory

It is an approach that emphasizes the importance of empirical fieldwork and the need to link any explanations very closely to what happens in practical situations in 'the real world'. It is different, here, from approaches based on 'armchair theorizing' or explanations that are thought up in the abstract as a neat system of ideas, and then afterwards checked to see if they work in reality. } Grounded

Theories should be 'grounded' in empirical research

In the eyes of Glaser and Strauss, it is not good enough to do empirical work and then 'tag on theory'. Their approach directly challenges the value of theorizing at a high level of abstraction and then, subsequently, doing some empirical work to see if the theory actually works. It is much better to develop the theories on the basis of empirical research and gradually build up general theories that emerge from the data.

The insistence that theories should be 'grounded' brings with it the idea that researchers should be engaged with fieldwork as the fundamental part of the work they do. When adopting the Grounded Theory approach the researcher should undertake data collection in the field, not only as the starting point of the research but throughout the course of the research as well.

Theories should be generated by a systematic analysis of the data

Glaser and Strauss were keen to stress that an emphasis on collecting data in the field does not equate their approach with those whose purpose is to amass as much detail as possible about particular situations and then 'let the data speak for themselves'. It differs in this respect from certain kinds of ethnographic research. Always high on the agenda for grounded theory research is a concerted effort to *analyse* the data and to generate theories from the data. And grounded theory is characterized by the specific way in which it approaches the business of analysing the data. Concepts and theories are developed out of the data through a persistent process of comparing the ideas with existing data, and improving the emerging concepts and theories by checking them against new data collected specifically for the purpose.

The selection of instances to be included in the research reflects the developing nature of the theory and cannot be predicted at the start

The instances to be included follow a trail of discovery – like a detective follows a 'lead'. Each new phase of the investigation reflects what has been discovered so far, with new angles of investigation and new avenues of enquiry to be explored. So, in the spirit of 'grounded theory' it is neither feasible nor desirable for the researcher to identify prior to the start exactly who or what will be included in the sample. This, of course, runs right against the grain as far as conventional social research practice is concerned. Normally, the social researcher would be expected to have a very clear vision of the intended sample, chosen on the basis of criteria linked to the ideas and theories being tested by the research.

> **Key point**
> Particularly in the world of business and health, people are very disaffected with preconceived evidentiary proof research because it is not producing findings that make business or health problems any better . . . Grounded theory tells us what is going on, tells us how to account for the participants' main concerns, and reveals access variables that allow for incremental change. Grounded theory is *what is*, not what should, could, or ought to be. (Glaser, 1999: 840, original emphasis)

Researchers should start out with an 'open mind'

In marked contrast to the researcher who sets out to *test* a theory, the researcher who follows the principles of grounded theory needs to approach the topic without a rigid set of ideas that shape what they focus upon during the investigation. Rather than basing an investigation upon whether certain theories do or do not work, *the researcher embarks on a voyage of discovery*.

This should not be seen to imply that a good social researcher starts out with a 'blank' mind.

To be sure, one goes out and studies an area with a particular . . . perspective, and with a focus, a general question or a problem in mind. But the researcher can (and we believe should) also study an area without any preconceived theory that dictates, prior to the research, 'relevancies' in concepts and hypotheses.

(Glaser and Strauss, 1967: 33)

So an open mind is not a blank mind on a subject. It is informed about an area, even quite aware of previous theories that might apply, but does not approach the analysis of data using preordained ways of seeing things. It avoids using previous theories and concepts to make sense of the data and thus is open to discovering new factors of relevance to an explanation of that area.

Theories should be useful at a practical level and meaningful to those 'on the ground'

The Grounded Theory approach has its roots in *pragmatism*, whose guiding philosophy is clearly acknowledged by Glaser and Strauss. Pragmatism places great emphasis on the 'practical' rather than the 'abstract' when it comes to issues of knowledge and truth and it operates on the premise that the value of any theory can only be gauged by how well it addresses real practical needs and how well it works in practice.

> **Key point**
>
> Grounded theory acknowledges its pragmatist philosophical heritage in insisting that a good theory is one that will be practically useful in the course of daily events, not only to the social scientists, but also to laymen. In a sense, a test of a good theory is whether or not it works 'on the ground'. (Locke, 2001: 59)

What this implies is that explanations of events and situations need to be meaningful and relevant to those whose actions and behaviour are involved. If the research involves interaction between teachers and pupils in the school classroom it is vital not only that a grounded theory is based on fieldwork in the classroom setting but also that its explanation makes sense to the teachers and pupils involved and 'rings true' for them.

When is the Grounded Theory approach useful?

The Grounded Theory approach does not purport to be the only proper way of conducting social research. It is one approach among many. What it does claim, however, is that it offers an approach that is well suited to the needs of four kinds of research.

Qualitative research

Although in their original exposition of grounded theory Glaser and Strauss claimed that the approach could be applied to quantitative data as well as qualitative data, and despite subsequent claims that 'It transcends specific data collection methods' (Glaser, 1978: 6), the Grounded Theory approach has become firmly associated over time with qualitative research. The nature of Glaser and Strauss's own research effectively set the tenor for the kind of research that has come to be associated with the Grounded Theory approach and by far the most common use of the Grounded Theory approach by other researchers has been with studies using qualitative data.

Exploratory research

Because there is an emphasis on discovery and because there is a stress on the need to approach investigations without being blinkered by the concepts and theories of previous research, the Grounded Theory approach fits neatly with the needs of researchers who are setting out to explore new territory in terms of either the subject matter of their investigation or the extent to which relevant theories have already been developed. As Goulding (2002: 55) notes, 'usually researchers adopt grounded theory when the topic of interest has been relatively ignored in the literature or has been given only superficial attention'.

Studies of human interaction

The Grounded Theory approach is appropriate for social research that focuses on human interaction, particularly where the researcher wishes to investigate

- practical activity and routine situations;
- the participants' points of view.

This reflects the roots of grounded theory within an approach called *symbolic interactionism*. This is a form of social research that focuses on the way that participants in social settings make sense of situations and events through the use of symbolic actions.

Small-scale research

Grounded theory's affinity with qualitative research, its desire to generate explanations from the study of particular instances, its need for detailed data about activities and practice and its value for exploratory research, combine to make it an approach that is well suited to small-scale research conducted by individual researchers operating within the constraints of a tight budget.

Methods of data collection

There is not a particular method of data collection that is claimed to be unique to grounded theory. Indeed, as Strauss (1987: 1) has indicated, 'Very diverse materials (interviews, transcripts of meetings, court proceedings; field observations; other documents, like diaries and letters; questionnaire answers; census statistics; etc.) provide indispensable data for social research.'

Key point

The novelty of grounded theory lies not in the mode of investigation associated with it, but in the manner in which the information collected is analysed. (Turner, 1983: 335)

Having made this point, there are certain methods that lend themselves better than others to use within a Grounded Theory approach. These are methods that allow the collection of data in a 'raw' state – not unduly shaped by prior concepts or theories. The point is to generate theories, not to test them, and so there is a preference for unstructured interviews rather than structured interviews, for the use of open-ended questions in a questionnaire rather than fixed-choice answers, and the use of fieldnotes rather than observations based on a tick-box schedule. The preference, quite logically, is for the use of methods that produce qualitative data that are relatively unstructured.

Initial ideas and concepts: the starting point

The normal starting point for research is to use findings from previous research as a platform for deciding what is worth investigating and how it needs to be investigated. The Grounded Theory approach, by contrast, expects the researcher to start research without any fixed ideas about the nature of the thing that is about to be investigated or how it operates.

Taken to extremes, this calls for the researcher to approach the topic without being influenced by previous theories or other research relating to the area. A literature review of the subject, by this vision, is prohibited. Taken even further, grounded research could require the researcher to ditch any previous expectations he or she might have about the topic. The researcher might need to forget common sense and everyday knowledge based on personal experience, and approach the topic almost like a new-born person whose vision of the world has not yet been influenced by the process of socialization.

Certainly, it is possible to find evidence for these extremes in the principal writings on grounded theory (Glaser and Strauss, 1967; Strauss and Corbin, 1990), and critics of grounded theory have seized on these points to argue that the Grounded Theory approach is 'bad science' (ignoring the accumulated knowledge of the past) and/or ludicrous in expecting that researchers can forget everything they already know about a topic.

In practice, however, the adoption of a Grounded Theory approach has not actually involved such extremes and, indeed, it is quite clear in some of the writings of the originators of grounded theory that the extreme interpretation was not what they intended to mean. A more moderate and feasible version of the point quite clearly accepts that previous theories and personal experience will have an influence.

> The initial questions or area for observation are based on concepts derived from literature or experience. Since these concepts . . . do not yet have proven theoretical relevance to the evolving theory, they must be considered provisional. Nevertheless, they provide a *beginning focus*, a place for the researcher to start.
>
> (Strauss and Corbin, 1990: 180, original emphasis)

The crucial point is that, whatever the source of the influence on 'what we already know about the topic', the concepts are to be treated as 'provisional' and open to question. They are not fixed, they are not necessarily right. They are simply a tentative starting point from which to launch the investigation.

Initial sites for fieldwork

Researchers who adopt the Grounded Theory approach need to start their investigation by concentrating on a particular situation, event or group. At the beginning, all that is required is that this site is 'relevant'. The criterion for its selection need only be that it might reasonably be expected to provide relevant information on the situation, event or group the researcher is interested in investigating. To illustrate the point, if a researcher wishes to investigate 'classroom control', he or she could initiate research by observing a small number of lessons in one school. In the first instance, the selection of the particular lessons and the specific school does not matter too much. When some lessons have been observed and various participants interviewed, however, the subsequent sites for research will be selected to follow up ideas prompted by the data. From this time forward, the selection of sites becomes far more critical for the research and far more constrained by the need to fit the lines of enquiry suggested by the codes, concepts and categories developing from the research. Following the example above, sites (schools) might be selected as instances where control problems are acknowledged to be rife, and lessons might be selected for observation that offer a relevant contrast in terms of the way they are routinely organized (history and English lessons in a normal classroom being compared with art lessons, sports classes and chemistry laboratory sessions). But, at the very beginning, the relevance of such different contexts might not have been realized.

The criterion of 'relevance' means that the Grounded Theory approach takes a distinct position in its choice of the initial site for fieldwork. It differs from the case study approach in the sense that there is no need for researchers using the Grounded Theory approach to get overly concerned about locating their initial fieldwork in a setting that can be demonstrated as being 'representative', 'typical' or 'extreme' types.

Link up with **Case studies, Chapter 2**

Subsequent sites for fieldwork: theoretical sampling

After having selected the initial site for research (based on its likely relevance for the topic), subsequent sites are selected according to a process of *theoretical sampling*. This form of sampling is a distinctive feature of the Grounded Theory approach and it involves two key features:

• Sites to be included in the research are deliberately selected by the researcher for what they can contribute to the research. Specifically, sites are selected because of their relevance to emerging categories and concepts. They are chosen to allow comparisons and contrast with previous sites and, according to Strauss's version of the approach, they allow the researcher to test out emerging concepts and verify the developing theory as the research goes along. This means that, unlike random sampling, theoretical sampling is a form of non-probability sampling in which the new sites are consciously selected by the researcher because of their particular characteristics. It is a form of 'purposive' sampling.

Link up with **Surveys and sampling, pp. 13–19**

- The researcher following the principles of grounded theory will not want to, or be able to, specify at the outset exactly what the sample will include. They will not be able to state exactly how large the sample will be nor exactly what sites (events or whatever) will be included because the sample *emerges*, reflecting the pursuit of generating theory. The process of research will involve the continued selection of units until the research arrives at the point of *'theoretical saturation'* (see below). It is only when the new data seems to confirm the analysis rather than add anything new that the sampling ceases and the sample size is 'enough'. Here, again, theoretical sampling stands in stark contrast with the conventions that expect researchers to be clear at the outset about the size and nature of their intended sample, and how it constitutes a representative sub-section of the overall group of things that are to be studied.

> *Key point: theoretical sampling*
>
> [The] process of data collection for . . . generating theory whereby the analyst jointly collects, codes, and analyses his data and decides what data to collect next and where to find them, in order to develop his theory as it emerges. (Glaser and Strauss, 1967: 45)

Strauss and Corbin (1990) draw our attention to four other features of theoretical sampling that are important to recognize. First, theoretical sampling is *cumulative*. There is a sense of building on the previous instances that have been sampled to date, and on building up a strong foundation for the concepts and categories that are being refined through the grounded research approach. Events, instances or people sampled early in the research should be considered as an integral part of the overall sample – a vital component in the path of discovery – and not jettisoned as being obsolete, irrelevant or wrong.

Second, theoretical sampling involves an increased *depth of focus*. Initially, the researcher's aim is to generate a large number of categories related to the phenomenon being studied – to keep things as 'open' as possible early on. For this purpose it is necessary to spread the net wide and gather data on a wide range of relevant things. As the work progresses, though, certain initial codes and categories will become relegated in importance and not pursued. As things move on, the researcher will find himself or herself able to concentrate on a smaller number of codes and categories – the ones that emerge as being more crucial to the analysis. And, because these ones are more central to the analysis and are fewer in number, he or she will be in a position to probe them more fully and investigate them in more depth.

Third, theoretical sampling calls for *consistency*. Theoretical sampling is not random or haphazard. It is not based on arbitrary choices, whim or convenience. It follows a rationale. This rationale is based on the contribution that any new additions to the sample might make towards developing and refining codes and concepts. The selection, in this sense, is based on *theoretical relevance*. And, at each stage of the sampling, the selection criteria should be clear, systematic and consistent with the emerging theory.

Fourth, theoretical sampling needs to retain some element of *flexibility*. Although the previous three features of theoretical sampling emphasize focus, relevance and system – a funnelling of the focus of attention that concentrates research on to key components – there also needs to be a degree of flexibility built into the selection process. Partly, this is necessary to allow the researcher to respond to opportunities that arise during the course of fieldwork. Equally, it is vital to permit the exploration of new avenues of investigation that the researcher could not have anticipated as being relevant. Without flexibility, the path of exploration is likely to become set too firmly in its direction too early in the programme of research, curtailing potentially useful lines of enquiry and closing off areas of investigation that might have proved to be illuminating – possibly crucial – to the eventual explanation of the situation being studied.

> **Key point**
>
> A certain degree of flexibility is . . . needed because the investigator must respond to and make the most out of data relevant situations that may arise while in the field. By flexibility, we mean the ability to move around and pursue areas of investigation that might not have been foreseen or planned, yet that appear to shed light upon or add a new perspective to one's area of investigation. (Strauss and Corbin, 1990: 178)

Analysing the data

Analysis involves the separation of things into their component parts. More specifically, it involves the study of complex things in order to identify their basic elements. It calls on the researcher to discover the key components or general principles underlying a particular phenomenon so that these can be used to provide a clearer understanding of that thing. The analysis of data in the Grounded Theory approach sticks closely to this task.

Link up with **Analysis of qualitative data, Chapter 14**

Codes, categories and concepts

The search for core elements starts by taking the raw data (interviews, field notes, documents, etc.) and looking for themes that recur in the data that appear to be crucial for understanding that phenomenon. The first stage of analysis here involves the coding and categorizing of the data. This means that the researcher begins to assign bits of the 'raw data' to particular categories. Careful scrutiny of the data (for example, an interview transcript) will allow the researcher to see that certain bits of the data have something in common. Possibly they will refer to the same issue. Possibly they will involve statements about the same emotion. Possibly they will share the use of a similar word or phrase in relation to a specific topic. Whatever it is, the chunks of raw data have something in common that the researcher can identify and that allows those chunks of data to be coded (tagged) as belonging to a broader category. It is worth noting that there are a number of commercially available software programs that can help researchers with this process.

Link up with **Computer Assisted Qualitative Data Analysis, pp. 304–5**

Unlike codes used with quantitative data, in grounded theory the codes are open to change and refinement as research progresses. Indeed, it is to be expected that initial codes and categories will be refined as the research progresses. Strauss (1987) suggests that initially the researcher starts to establish codes and concepts from the data by approaching things with an open mind.

The codes will be fairly descriptive and are likely to involve labelling chunks of data in terms of their content. This is referred to as *open coding*. As the codes take shape, the researcher will look for relationships between the codes – links and associations that allow certain codes to be subsumed under broader headings and certain codes to be seen as more crucial than others. This is referred to as *axial coding*, since it shifts the analysis towards the identification of key (axial) components. Eventually, the researcher should be in a position to focus attention on just the key components, the most significant categories, and concentrate his or her efforts on these. This *selective coding* focuses attention on just the core codes, the ones that have emerged from open and axial coding as being vital to any explanation of the complex social phenomenon.

The aim of this process is to arrive at *concepts* that help to explain the phenomenon – basic ideas that encapsulate the way that the categories relate to each other in a single notion. These concepts then form the cornerstone for the generation of theories that provide an account of things and, in some sense or other, explain why things happen as they do. In the words of Strauss and Corbin (1990), 'Concepts are the basis of analysis in grounded theory research. All grounded theory procedures are aimed at identifying, developing, and relating concepts.'

The constant comparative method

The Grounded Theory approach uses the constant comparative method as a means for analysing the data. This entails a commitment to comparing and contrasting new codes, categories and concepts as they emerge – constantly seeking to check them out against existing versions. By comparing each coded instance with others that have been similarly coded, by contrasting instances with those in different categories, even using hypothetical possibilities, the researcher is able to refine and improve the explanatory power of the concepts and theories generated from the data. Such comparison helps the researcher to refine the codes, categories and concepts by

- highlighting the similarities and differences that exist (promoting better categories and descriptions);
- allowing researchers to integrate categories and codes under common headings (facilitating the reduction of complex phenomena to simpler elements);
- allowing researchers to check out their developing theories as they emerge (incorporating a way to verify them or refute them at the stage of production rather than after the event).

By using the constant comparative method the researcher can never lose sight of the data, or move the analysis too far away from what is happening on the ground. It ensures that any theory developed by the research remains closely in touch with its origins in the data – that it remains 'grounded' in empirical reality. This, of course, is of vital importance to the whole approach.

Note that an important distinction occurs here between the analysis of qualitative data and that of quantitative data. Following the Grounded Theory approach, the concepts that form the foundation of the theory/analysis emerge from the process of the research activity itself and are not, as is the case with quantitative data, established *prior* to the investigation itself.

Analysis of data using the Grounded Theory approach

This involves:

- coding and categorizing the raw data (e.g. interview tapes),
- constantly comparing the emerging codes and categories with the data and
- checking them out against new data specifically collected for the purpose, with a view to
- generating concepts and theories that are thoroughly grounded in the data and that
- have relevance to the practical world from which they were derived.

Completing the research (theoretical saturation)

How much research is enough? This is, necessarily, rather difficult to specify when using the Grounded Theory approach. Whereas survey researchers using quantitative data will know at the start how many items are to be collected, and will be able to plan the duration of the research project around this, those who opt for a Grounded Theory approach face the uncomfortable prospect of not knowing in advance how long the research will take or how much data they will need to collect. In principle, they will be expected to continue theoretical sampling to test and validate the developing codes, categories and concepts until reaching the point of *theoretical saturation.*

> **Key point: theoretical saturation**
>
> 'when additional analysis no longer contributes to discovering anything new about a category.' (Strauss, 1987: 21)

This point cannot be predicted accurately at the start of the research but the researcher will recognize when he or she has arrived there because, at this point, the collection of further bits of data ceases to contribute anything new to the properties of the codes, categories and concepts being developed. Additional field research will tend to confirm the concepts, codes and categories that have been developed to date – serving only to confirm and verify the theory, not to refine it. Further research, in effect, adds nothing new to the researcher's understanding.

Theories and grounded research

The Grounded Theory approach, when it was originally conceived by Glaser and Strauss, was a reaction against the kind of 'grand' theories produced through the *logico-deductive method* of science that Glaser and Strauss encountered during the late 1950s and early 1960s. As Layder (1993: 42) points out, 'Such theories are generally "speculative" in nature because they have not grown directly out of research, and thus remain ungrounded. As a consequence, these theories very often lack validity because they do not "fit" the real world and thereby remain irrelevant to the people concerned.' Glaser and Strauss were dissatisfied with this approach and argued that a theory developed through the Grounded Theory approach would have distinct advantages over those derived from the more traditional 'scientific' methods.

First, it is unlikely that new data will be found that serve to refute the theory. Since the theory has been built upon substantive data extracted from field-work, the theory should already take account of all the crucial aspects of the situation it explains so that there should be no 'nasty surprises' waiting to be uncovered that will point to a major weakness in the theory. This contrasts, of course, with theories that have been logically deduced and that are then subjected to test by seeing if they work in practice. The 'scientific' approach certainly is susceptible to such nasty surprises and radical rethinks about the theory when findings do not support the theory. In grounded theory, the testing is conducted as an integral part of the development of the theory – as an ongoing process – not as a separate process conducted after the theory has been put together in an abstract form.

Key point

Theory based on data can usually not be refuted by more data or replaced by another theory. (Glaser and Strauss, 1967: 4)

Second, the theory has more credibility. Because the theory emerges from the data there ought to be a comfortable fit between the facts of the situation and the theory used to explain them. Put rather simply, the theory is shaped by the facts, and therefore there should be a good fit. There should be a close correspondence between the realities of the situation and the theories used to explain them. On this basis, there can be no allegations that researchers are in any sense *forcing* a fit between the data and the theory. By contrast, the process of testing theories can involve a search, more or less consciously, for facts that fit the theory. Without necessarily intending to do so, researchers can have their vision of facts shaped by the theory they are setting out to test. They can end up being selective about what they 'see' and what they find, managing to corroborate their theory by a process of selective perception in which facts that do not fit the theory get subtly edited out of the picture as irrelevant or non-existent.

Substantive theory and formal theory

There are two kinds of theory that can be generated using the Grounded Theory approach. The first is linked closely to the empirical situation that has been the subject of study. It is a fairly localized kind of theory and is known as *substantive theory*. This is by far the most common kind of theory associated with the approach. The other kind of theory is more conceptual, with more general coverage and application to circumstances beyond particular settings. This is known as *formal theory*. Substantive theory is closely linked to practice, interaction and specific kinds of settings, whereas 'when we speak of formal theory . . . we usually refer to those areas of inquiry that operate at a high level of generality, such as systems theory, agency theory, population ecology, and contingency theory' (Locke, 2001: 35). Ultimately, the aim is to move from a growing body of good, grounded substantive theories towards the integration of these in higher-level formal theories.

Developments in grounded theory

Since the notion of a Grounded Theory approach was first coined, subsequent works by the originators have moved in slightly different directions. This divergence reflects two potential stances that coexist within the Grounded Theory approach. On the one hand there is Glaser's version (Glaser, 1978, 1995, 1999), which rests on the belief that: (a) the researcher should maintain a distance and independence from the data; and (b) the meaning of the data will emerge inductively from the data if studied using a suitably neutral methodology. This is really quite positivistic in outlook.

Contrasting with this, there is Strauss's version (Strauss, 1987; Strauss and Corbin, 1990, 1998), which is more in line with interpretivism, in that the role of the researcher is to go looking for the meaning that the data hold, possibly probing beyond their superficial meaning. Things like 'coding paradigms' provide a fairly extensive and detailed framework that is intended to help researchers to *make* sense of the data; that is, to interpret the data in a systematic way.

To complicate matters further, as noted at the beginning of this chapter, researchers have selectively adapted the approach to suit their specific needs, with the consequence that 'grounded theory' appears in a number of guises. And, on top of this, there are approaches that have branched off from grounded theory (see Goulding, 2002) or incorporated elements of the approach within distinct new approaches (Layder, 1998).

The researcher who wants to use the Grounded Theory approach needs to be aware that such debates and developments exist under the umbrella term 'grounded theory'. They might even need to delve into the schisms and controversies in order to defend their research as being in line with a particular version of grounded theory. Professional researchers and those using grounded theory as a core feature of a PhD would fall into this category. Project researchers, however, are less likely to need to pursue the methodology to this depth. Provided they adhere to the key points listed below, they should be justified in saying that they have adopted a Grounded Theory approach because these items incorporate the core tenets of the approach.

Key points of the Grounded Theory approach

- Uses empirical field research as its starting point (the researcher starts the fieldwork research early in the investigation).
- Develops its analysis with constant reference to fieldwork data (an iterative process).
- Produces explanations that are recognizable to the subjects of research.
- Is geared to modest localized explanations based on the immediate evidence.
- Adopts an emergent design (based on theoretical sampling).
- Generally is linked with qualitative research, exploratory investigations, small-scale studies and research focusing on human interaction in specific settings.

 Caution

The term 'grounded theory' is often used in a rather loose way to refer to approaches that accept some of the basic premises but do not adopt the methodological rigour espoused by the originators of the term. All too frequently, Glaser and Strauss are cited by way of justification for methodologies that actually bear few of the hallmarks of the strict conception of 'grounded theory'.

Worse than this, there is a very real danger that the term 'grounded theory' can be hijacked and cited as justification for what is, in reality, *sloppy research*. Taken out of context, 'grounded theory' can be misused as a rationale for approaching research

- without too clear an idea of the topic of research;
- without a clear basis in mind for selecting the sample;
- with a general 'jump in at the deep end', 'try it and see', 'find out as we go' approach.

This is certainly not in tune with the spirit of grounded theory and its clear concern with rigour in the analysis of qualitative data.

Advantages of Grounded Theory approach

- The notion of grounded theory has currency in the research community and it has become a *recognized rationale for qualitative research*. Grounded theory provides a standard justification that can fend off potential criticism from those who might otherwise question the rigour of small-scale qualitative research.
- The approach is *fairly adaptable*, lending itself to use with a variety of qualitative data collection methods (e.g. interviews, observation, documents) and forms of data (interview transcripts, fieldwork, texts).
- There is a *focus on practice* (human interaction) and what is practical (pragmatic philosophy), which makes the approach well suited to studies in areas, such as health, business and education, that are concerned with understanding and improving matters in terms of interpersonal relations.
- The *systematic way of analysing qualitative data*, especially as developed by Strauss, can be helpful to the newcomer who might wonder how on earth he or she can make sense of the data and how he or she can move towards developing concepts and ultimately theories.
- The *analysis can draw on computer software* for help with the coding and sorting of the qualitative data.
- The approach includes *the means for developing theoretical propositions from data*, and should boost project researchers' confidence in the realms of theorizing. All researchers – not just the venerable experts – are encouraged to arrive at modest theories on the basis of the data that they have collected.
- *Explanations are grounded in reality*. Concepts and theories are developed with constant reference to the empirical data and this means that, unlike with speculative, abstract theory, they are built on a sound foundation of evidence. This ensures that grounded theories are kept in touch with reality.
- The approach permits a degree of flexibility in both the selection of instances for inclusion in the sample and the analysis of the data – both of which are *well suited to the exploration of new topics and new ideas*.

Disadvantages of Grounded Theory approach

- *The approach does not lend itself to precise planning.* The use of 'theoretical sampling' means that it is not possible to predict in advance the nature of the sample that will be used. And the need to achieve 'theoretical saturation' makes it impossible to state at the outset the eventual size of the sample. The voyage of discovery comes with a price and that price is the ability to plan all aspects of the research in advance and anticipate when the research will be completed.

- By focusing research on specific instances of behaviour in particular settings, there is a *tendency to divorce the explanation of the situation being studied from broader contextual factors*. In particular, there is the danger that the theory generated from the data might ignore the influence of social, economic and political factors (e.g. globalization, migration, social class, gender and race inequalities) and the historical background to events, which might be vital to any full and valid theory explaining the phenomenon.

- *An 'open-minded' approach to the data is something that can operate at a variety of levels.* The need to approach things with an 'open mind' is a fundamental principle of the Grounded Theory approach but, in practice, it raises some awkward questions. Researchers are inevitably influenced by prior conceptions based on their own culture and personal experience. The question is: how far can these be put to one side for the purposes of analysing the data? There is also the controversial point about how far previous concepts and theories should be allowed to influence matters. Should grounded theory researchers avoid undertaking a literature review in order to avoid having their minds 'contaminated' by existing concepts and theories? And, if so, does this invite the possibility of 'reinventing the wheel' or failing to learn from what has been researched in the past? Within the Grounded Theory approach different researchers adopt different positions on such issues.

- The systematic way of analysing data developed by Strauss and Corbin (1990, 1998) can be daunting in terms of the *complexity of the process*. Indeed, Strauss's development of 'guidance' for the analysis of qualitative data actually incensed his former collaborator, Barney Glaser, who saw the template and framework for analysis as unnecessary and going against the spirit of grounded theory by 'forcing' categories and codes on to the data, rather than letting them naturally 'emerge'.

- *Interpretivists will be unhappy with any suggestion that substantive theories provide the one correct explanation of things.* Yet within the writings of Glaser and Strauss there are occasions when this position is taken. There is a positivistic strand of thought in which the 'grounding' of theory means that it is not liable to be refuted by the later discovery of facts that do not fit the theory. If the theory emerges from the data and is meaningful to the participants, then it is a good theory that stands in its own right – *not open to alternative interpretation*.

- *The approach can be criticized as being 'empiricist'.* By looking to fieldwork data as the source of its theories, and by setting itself against the use of general theories, it opens itself to the criticism that it relies too heavily on the empirical data – expecting an explanation to exist within the accumulated data, waiting to be 'discovered' by the researcher. This inductive approach is rather naive about the complex relationship between theory and data collection and the way it calls for researchers to approach the data without the use of prior theories and concepts (Layder, 1998).

Checklist for the Grounded Theory approach

When undertaking grounded theory research you should feel confident about answering 'yes' to the following questions: ☑

1 Is the aim of the research to generate concepts and theory geared to 'localized' explanations (substantive theory)? ☐

2 Have empirical data been used as the foundation for generating the concepts and theories? ☐

3 Has the research focused on issues of practical significance to participants in the setting? ☐

4 Have the data been analysed through a systematic process of coding and categorization (open coding, etc.)? ☐

5 Were the codes, categories and concepts developed with constant reference to the fieldwork data (constant comparative method)? ☐

6 Is there an explicit justification for the choice of the initial site for fieldwork in terms of its relevance to the area of research? ☐

7 Have subsequent sites been selected on the basis of theoretical sampling? ☐

   If so, have the criteria been clearly stated? ☐

8 Has the research produced explanations that are recognizable to the subjects of research? ☐

   If so, how was this confirmed? ☐

9 Did the research continue until it reached a point of theoretical saturation? ☐

   If so, how was this checked? ☐

10 Have measures been taken to aid an open-minded approach to the investigation? ☐

    If so, have these been explained? ☐

11 Has the Grounded Theory approach been adapted to meet the needs of the research? (For example, have the concepts and theories been linked to wider social, political, economic and historical factors?) ☐

© M. Denscombe, *The Good Research Guide*. Open University Press.

7

Mixed methods

What is the Mixed Methods approach? • When is it appropriate to use a Mixed Methods approach? • Types of mixed methods design • Mixed model research designs • Pragmatism and the Mixed Methods approach • Advantages of the Mixed Methods approach • Disadvantages of the Mixed Methods approach • Checklist for mixed methods research

The term 'mixed methods' applies to research that combines alternative approaches within a single research project. It refers to a research strategy that crosses the boundaries of conventional paradigms of research by deliberately combining methods drawn from different traditions with different underlying assumptions. At its simplest, a mixed methods strategy is one that uses both qualitative and quantitative methods.

There is nothing startlingly new about the strategy. It is easy to find examples throughout the history of social research in which researchers successfully mixed their methods. However, the identification of something called the 'Mixed Methods approach' is relatively new. As an approach, with a recognized name and research credibility, it has only come to the fore in recent years championed by writers such as Creswell (2003), Creswell and Plano Clark (2007), Gorard and Taylor (2004), Greene *et al.* (1989), Johnson and Onwueg-buzie (2004) and Tashakkori and Teddlie (1998, 2003). This chapter focuses mainly on this new 'movement'. Partly this reflects its new rise to prominence; partly it reflects the valuable way this movement has explored the underlying rationale for mixing methods. It would be wrong, however, to infer that others have not explored the prospects of combining qualitative and quantitative research and made valuable contributions in their own right to a broader notion of a mixed methods strategy in social research (see, for example, Bryman, 1988, 2006; Layder, 1993, 1998; Silverman, 1985, 2000). While such writers might not accept all the tenets of the 'new Mixed Methods approach' (in particular the use of pragmatism as its philosophical foundation) there is consensus on one fundamental point – the belief that *treating qualitative and quantitative approaches to research as incompatible opposites is neither helpful nor realistic when it comes to research activity*.

A number of different names have been given to mixed methods strategies. 'Mixed methodology', 'multi-strategy research', 'integrated methods', 'multi-method research' and 'combined methods' research are just some of the alternatives. The names bear testimony to the variety of ways in which research can be mixed and the many aspects of the research process that can be involved. The most common form of mix, however, involves a mix of methods and, in practice, the term *mixed methods* has come to be used in a general sense to cover the spectrum of ways in which mixing can occur in the research process. In effect, it has given its name to a broad approach to research.

What is the Mixed Methods approach?

The Mixed Methods approach has three characteristic features that set it apart from other strategies for social research. These can be summarized as follows:

- *Use of qualitative and quantitative approaches within a single research project.* At the heart of the approach is the idea that researchers can bring together within a single research project certain elements that have conventionally been treated as an 'either/or' option. In most cases the distinction is drawn between 'qualitative' and 'quantitative' with researchers variously writing about using both qualitative and quantitative *methods*, qualitative and quantitative *data* or qualitative and quantitative *research*.
- *Explicit focus on the link between approaches* (Triangulation). The Mixed Methods approach emphasizes the need to explain why the alternative approaches are beneficial and how the alternatives are to be brought together. Particular attention is given to the design of mixed methods research and especially the role of triangulation in justifying the use of the alternative approaches.

Link up with **Triangulation, pp. 134–9**

- *Emphasis on practical approaches to research problems* (Pragmatist). The Mixed Methods approach is 'problem-driven' in the sense that it treats the research problem – more specifically *answers* to the research problem – as the overriding concern. Other approaches, of course, share a concern for practical solutions to real-world problems. But, advocates of the Mixed Methods approach regard it as the crucial driving force behind decisions about which methods to use. This means they are prepared to use methods that come from different philosophical traditions, provided their use produces findings that are of practical value for addressing the research problem. The Mixed Methods approach, in this sense, challenges the premise that social research should strive for consistency between the various components of the research process – the questions, the design, the data collection, the data analysis – in terms of their underlying assumptions about the nature of the social world and the possibilities this opens for research. It adopts instead a *pragmatist* position that allows it to bring together methods drawn from 'paradigms' of research conventionally regarded as incompatible.

When is it appropriate to use a Mixed Methods approach?

Drawing on reviews of published mixed methods studies (Bryman, 2006; Collins *et al.*, 2006; Greene *et al.*, 1989; Rocco *et al.*, 2003) it is evident that social researchers use mixed methods strategies for one or more of the following purposes.

Improved accuracy

Researchers can improve their confidence in the accuracy of findings through the use of different methods to investigate the same subject. In line with the principles of triangulation, the Mixed Methods approach provides the researcher with the opportunity to check the findings from one method against the findings from a different method. In the words of Greene *et al.* (1989: 259) this use of the Mixed Methods approach 'seeks convergence, corroboration, correspondence of results from the different methods'. Where different methods produce data that are more or less the same the researcher can feel more confident in assuming that the findings are accurate.

Using the same principle of triangulation, researchers can also check on the impact of a particular research method. For example, if a researcher wants to know whether online questionnaires 'distort' the kind of answers that are given by respondents he/she could compare the findings from this method of data collection with findings from a similar set of respondents completing a conventional paper questionnaire. If there is no marked difference between the methods in terms of the data collected the researcher can be more con-fident that the use of the online questionnaires does not have a distorting impact on the data (at least, no impact that is different from the conventional paper questionnaire).

The Mixed Methods approach is valuable, too, as a means for developing research instruments. For example, researchers who are designing a questionnaire for use in a survey can employ qualitative data through focus groups and interviews to improve the validity of a subsequent survey questionnaire that produces quantitative data. The qualitative data collected through interviews and focus groups can be valuable initially as a way of shaping the kind of questions that are relevant and then subsequently to ensure that the questions have been worded suitably.

In sum, then, the mixing of methods can be a valuable research strategy for:

- the validation of findings in terms of their accuracy;
- checking for bias in research methods;
- the development of research instruments.

A more complete picture

The use of more than one method can enhance the findings of research by providing a fuller and more complete picture of the thing that is being studied. The benefit of the Mixed Methods approach in this instance is that the data produced by the different methods can be complementary. They can provide alternative perspectives that, when combined, go further towards an all-embracing vision of the subject than could be produced using a mono-method approach. In terms of the Mixed Methods approach this tends to involve the use of both qualitative and quantitative methods as a means for seeing things from alternative perspectives and, thereby, getting a more complete overview of the subject.

Consider, for example, research that focuses on smoking and the health-related behaviour of young people. A quantitative survey approach would certainly produce evidence of the extent of smoking by under-16s and could provide good demographic details that will help us to understand the social backgrounds of those involved. A series of focus groups involving young smokers could be used to provide qualitative data that would help to explain why the underage smokers started smoking and what motivates them to continue. In their own rights, both the quantitative and the qualitative methods are valuable and can make a worthwhile contribution to what is known on the matter. Combining the methods, however, allows the researcher to produce a fuller account of the situation that covers not only the scale of the issue (e.g. numbers involved, age, sex, ethnic group) but also gives some insight into the motivational factors that give rise to the behaviour (e.g. self-image, stress, peer groups).

Compensating strengths and weaknesses

Recognizing that different methods have their respective strengths and weaknesses, one of the valuable uses of mixing methods is to offset any inherent weakness or bias in a particular method by combining it with a different one that can compensate for this weakness or bias. In Denzin's words:

> By combining multiple observers, theories, methods and data sources, (researchers) can hope to overcome the intrinsic bias that comes from single-methods, single observer, and single theory studies.
>
> (Denzin, 1989: 307)

A shrewd combination of methods allows the researcher to exploit the strengths of a particular method without leaving him/herself vulnerable to criticism in connection with that method's weakness. To illustrate the point, a researcher who chooses to use semi-structured interviews as the main data collection method might also choose to supplement this method with the use of a closed-answer questionnaire. The choice of semi-structured interviews could reflect the researcher's need to gain an in-depth understanding of the motivations of a particular group of people – say, airline pilots. The choice of semi-structured interviews might seem appropriate because this method is particularly good at allowing the researcher to explore in depth the thoughts, feelings and reasoning of the pilots. But because interviews generally take time to organize, conduct and analyse, the numbers involved are generally quite small – which makes the researcher vulnerable to the criticism that the data are not representative. To compensate for this weakness, a mixed methods strategy can be adopted that involves a questionnaire survey of airline pilots, possibly including pilots from other countries and employed by other airlines. The initial findings from the interviews can be checked with the broader population of airline pilots using questionnaires which, as a research method, lend themselves far better to use with large numbers across wide geographical areas. Questionnaires, of course, would not have provided the kind of depth of information that the semi-structured interviews did but, by combining the methods, the researcher is in a position to avoid potential criticism linked to either the relatively small sample size associated with the interview method or the relative superficiality of data collected via questionnaires.

Developing the analysis

Within a mixed methods strategy contrasting methods can be used as a means for moving the analysis forward, with one method being used to inform another. In this sense, an alternative method is introduced as a way of building on what has been learned already through the use of the initial method. It is used to produce *further data* that might shed light on things. This is different from using another method to produce a fuller picture of things; the new method is introduced specifically to address a research issue arising through findings produced by another method.

A classic study illustrates this use of a mixed methods strategy: the Hawthorne studies. These were a series of studies conducted at the Western Electric company's Hawthorne plant in Chicago between 1924 and 1933. The purpose of the studies was to discover what factors affected worker productivity. Initially, management at the plant conducted a sequence of quasi-experiments in which they altered the level of lighting to see if this was linked with productivity. Subsequently, researchers from Harvard Business School joined the investigation and conducted a further series of studies designed to investigate the link between fatigue, monotony and worker productivity (Mayo, [1933] 2003; Roethlisberger and Dickson, [1939] 2003). All these controlled, quasi-experimental studies produced rather puzzling and inconclusive results and this caused the researchers to introduce a new method of enquiry in 1932. Instead of trying to *observe* the factors that affected productivity they decided to *ask* the workers what motivated them. The researchers embarked on a huge programme of interviews with the workforce. What they found out about workers' motivation through the interviews helped the researchers to make sense of the findings from the experimental/observational phases of the research and it laid the foundations for a further observational phase of the research designed to check their conclusions. The interviews revealed that the workers were motivated by factors other than just money; there were personal and social rewards from work that affected their productivity as well. Once the researchers understood this, they could see that the results of the earlier observation studies had been influenced by the eponymous 'Hawthorne effect' in which the process of observing people can have an impact on the nature of those people's behaviour. In the case of the Hawthorne studies, members of the experimental groups reacted to being observed in as much as they felt more valued and appreciated by management. This increased the group's morale which had the knock-on effect of increasing their productivity. This impact on their productivity had nothing directly to do with the factor of fatigue that was being investigated and it helped to explain why changes introduced to affect the level of worker fatigue did not have a predicted impact on productivity. A confounding variable – worker morale – was interfering with the process. But the crucial point in relation to mixing methods is that by interviewing the workforce the researchers were able to understand why their quantitative methods had not supplied 'the answer'. The qualitative research, in this sense, informed the quantitative research. It explained that worker productivity owed as much to worker motivation as it did to physical fatigue, and that worker motivation stemmed from social and psychological factors such as morale, recognition and group cohesion.

Link up with **Experiments, Chapter 3**

An aid to sampling

Using a mixed methods strategy, information from one method can be used as the basis for selecting a sample of people who will participate in the research through a different and contrasting method. Sometimes this involves the use of a quantitative pilot study to provide background information that researchers use to guide their selection of the individuals who will participate in subsequent qualitative research involving things like focus groups and interviews. Other times, as Collins *et al.* (2006) found, qualitative research can precede quantitative research as a means for identifying the appropriate kind of people to take part in a piece of research and as a means of filtering out those who might not be suitable. Indeed, interviews and focus groups can be used in a variety of ways to help recruit participants for a survey or panel study. The qualitative methods can aid the quantitative methods by identifying the kind of people who are required for the study, by finding out what things might influence their willingness to take part in the study, and even by finding out at a later stage what caused some recruits to drop out from the research.

 Caution

The Mixed Methods approach does not mean 'anything goes'. As with cooking, there are certain ingredients that go together well and others that do not. Ingredients need to be mixed in the right order and in the right amount if they are to be successful, and there is no sense in which the Mixed Methods approach promotes a careless throwing-together of ingredients in a haphazard fashion: that would be a recipe for disaster. To qualify as a mixed methods strategy *the research needs to have a clear and explicit rationale for using the contrasting methods.* Equally, the use of mixed methods is not automatically applicable to *all* research questions or issues. In practice, there might be no need for – no benefit from – using alternative methods. The Mixed Methods approach should not be adopted without considering whether there will be particular benefits to be gained.

Types of mixed methods design

Researchers who advocate the use of the Mixed Methods approach generally make a distinction between QUAL and QUAN where:

- QUAL stands for qualitative data in the form of text or pictures that provide the basis for interpretations of the meaning they convey;
- QUAN stands for quantitative data in the form of numbers that provide objective measurements of observed events.

The mix of QUAL and QUAN can take a number of forms and it is possible to construct a complex range of possibilities for combining them within a single research project. Basically, though, the key decisions facing the social researcher in this context boil down to two things:

- *In what order should the alternative methods be used?*
- *Should greater importance be attached to one or other of the alternative methods?*

When a research design involves the use of methods or strategies drawn from different paradigms, the order in which the methods/strategies are used is significant. Given that they are used as part of the same investigation of the same research question, the sequencing reflects the researcher's beliefs about how the combination of methods and strategies works best. For some purposes it might be better to have QUAN followed by QUAL; for other purposes the opposite might be true. Possibly, more phases within a research project might be most useful, in this case calling for a sequence of three or more QUAL/QUAN components.

There might be occasions when the research is best served by conducting the contrasting alternatives alongside each other at the same time. This would involve the 'simultaneous' use of QUAL and QUAN. A further variation might involve the use of QUAL and QUAN with different 'levels' of research. Such a 'multilevel research' design, for example, might use a QUAL approach to the study of individual pupils in classroom (e.g. their feelings and experiences in relation to homework), use a QUAN approach to investigate features of whole classes (e.g. test scores and attendance rates), use a QUAN approach for looking at the school (e.g. truancy rates and exam pass rates), and complement these with a QUAL approach looking at the history and environment of the school (e.g. reports by school inspectors, local newspaper articles). Of course, a multilevel design such as this could operate either simultaneously or sequentially.

Taking the factors of sequencing and level into account, a large number of possibilities exist in relation to mixed methods research design. The basic principles of such designs, however, can be depicted in the following way:

Sequential studies   e.g.   **QUAL ⟶ QUAN**
                                        QUAN ⟶ QUAL
                                        QUAN ⟶ QUAL ⟶ QUAN

Simultaneous studies   e.g.   **QUAN ⟍**
                                        QUAL ⟋ ⟶

Multilevel designs   e.g.   **QUAN** at macro level ↑
(simultaneous or sequential)   **QUAL** at micro level ↓

Research designs that incorporate aspects of both QUAL and QUAN need not necessarily attach equal weight to the two. Indeed, there is a strong likelihood that researchers will tend to regard one as the 'main' and the other as the 'subsidiary' counterbalance or check. For example, the researchers might start by collecting and analysing a relatively small amount of qualitative data as an exploratory phase of the investigation. They might use interviews or focus groups to get a feel for the relevant issues and to explore the way things are perceived. Armed with this knowledge, the researchers can then produce a questionnaire (or other quantitative research instrument) that can build on information obtained in advance. Some psychology and marketing research adopts this approach, using the QUAL as a preliminary checking device to ensure the validity of a QUAN research instrument. In this approach, it is the QUAN data that is treated as the most important material for the investigation.

In contrast to this, the design might treat QUAL as the dominant, perhaps preceding the quan subsidiary. An example of this would be the use of a detailed case study that is followed up with small-scale questionnaire survey to check the case study findings. The research design, in this instance, centres on the collection and analysis of qualitative data. It might, for example, consist of interview data collected from employees within a particular business. From these interviews the researchers might reach certain conclusions. At this point, they might choose to conduct a survey of other businesses to check if these conclusions tend to be borne out in other situations. The key points might be included in a questionnaire distributed to a representative sample of businesses nationwide, with the hope that the responses they receive will corroborate the conclusions based on the detailed case study. The main thrust of the investigation, in this example, is the QUAL (interviews) with the quan (questionnaire survey) being used in a supporting role.

In a simplified depiction of the range of possibilities, the sequencing and dominance of methods from different research paradigms might take one of the following forms:

Equivalent status e.g. **QUAL ⟶ QUAN**
                              QUAN ⟶ QUAL ⟶ QUAN

Dominant/ less dominant status e.g. **qual ⟶ QUAN**
                                          QUAL ⟶ quan

Caution

The mixed methods research designs that make use of QUAL and QUAN phases of research have not normally included any provision for *emergent* designs. Although there is nothing inherent in the notion of the Mixed Methods approach that would prevent the use of, for example, a Grounded Theory approach, writers promoting the Mixed Methods approach have tended to focus heavily on research designs that are established prior to the start of data collection and which do not change to reflect emerging themes or directions in the data.

Mixed model research designs

The mix of alternative approaches within a single research project can involve more than just the data collection methods or the kind of analysis. It is possible to mix methods at a more fundamental level, building the mix into the fabric of the research strategy and design so that it is not just the methods and analysis that are mixed, but the nature of the research questions and whole style of research. This is termed 'mixed model' research (see Tashakkori and Teddlie, 1998: 57). Conventionally, social research has followed one of two broad paths when it comes the style and nature of the investigation. Either the research has set out to test hypotheses and check predictions based on theories by conducting '*confirmatory investigations*'. Or, it has aimed to discover things by engaging in '*exploratory investigations*' which are not based on any firm hypothesis at the beginning. Mixed model research designs break the mould by incorporating both kinds of approach within the same project.

Pragmatism and the Mixed Methods approach

Pragmatism is generally regarded as the philosophical partner for the Mixed Methods approach. It provides a set of assumptions about knowledge and enquiry that (a) underpins the Mixed Methods approach; and (b) distinguishes the approach from purely quantitative approaches that are based on a philosophy of positivism and purely qualitative approaches that are based on a philosophy of interpretivism. In the context of research, pragmatism tends to revolve around the following core ideas:

- Knowledge is based on practical outcomes and 'what works'. The key criterion for judging knowledge is how useful it is perceived to be and how well it works when applied to some practical problem.
- Research should test what works through empirical enquiry.
- There is no single, best 'scientific' method that can lead the way to indisputable knowledge.
- Knowledge is provisional. What we understand as truth today may not be seen as such in the future. Knowledge is seen as a product of our times. It can never be absolute or perfect because it is inevitably a product of the historical era and the cultural context within which it is produced. The quest for absolute 'Truth' is consequently seen as hopeless cause.
- Traditional dualisms in the field of philosophy and science are regarded as not helpful. In particular, there is scepticism about the distinction between quantitative and qualitative research, but there is also a rejection of distinctions like facts/values, objectivism/subjectivism and rationalism/empiricism.

For some mixed methods researchers, these tenets of pragmatism leave the door open for the use of purely quantitative research or purely qualitative research – providing the use of either in isolation can produce the kind of findings that work sufficiently well to answer a research problem. It leads them to regard the use of mixed methods as a third alternative – another option open to social researchers if they decide that neither quantitative nor qualitative research alone will provide adequate findings for the particular piece of research they have in mind. Rather than see positivism and interpretivism as having become obsolete, these researchers regard the Mixed Methods approach as simply an alternative research strategy that can be used if, and when, necessary. 'What answers my question' is their guiding principle.

Others, seeking to challenge what are regarded as sterile and unproductive dualisms, favour a search for common ground between the 'old' philosophies of research. They focus on areas of compatibility between quantitative and qualitative research, and between positivism and interpretivism. Theirs is an eclectic approach in which the traditional paradigms of research are brought together and emphasis is placed on how elements of the paradigms can be combined to good effect. 'What meets my needs' is their guiding principle.

There are some mixed methods researchers, as we have seen, who operate on the assumption that good social research will almost inevitably require the use of both quantitative *and* qualitative research in order to provide an adequate answer. For them, the Mixed Methods approach is built on the belief that not only is it allowable to mix methods from alternative and incompatible paradigms of research but it is also *desirable* to do so in order to provide answers that work – or, at least, that work better than those based on the use of just quantitative or just qualitative research. For some of the main advocates of the Mixed Methods approach (e.g. Johnson and Onwuegbuzie, 2004; Tashakkori and Teddlie, 1998, 2003) pragmatism represents an advance in thinking about social research – a new paradigm that is replacing the earlier paradigms based on positivism and interpretivism. 'What works best' is their guiding principle.

Despite this difference of emphasis within the mixed methods camp, there is still some broad agreement that social research should not be judged by how well it fits in with the quantitative paradigm (positivism) or with the premises of the competing camp – the qualitative paradigm (interpretivism). The decision to use a mixed methods strategy should be based on how *useful* the methods are for addressing a particular question, issue or problem that is being investigated. For those who adopt the Mixed Methods approach the crucial consideration is how well the research tools *work* rather than how well they fit within a specific research philosophy.

Key issues in the Mixed Methods approach

- **Order**: in what order do the methods get used?
- **Timing**: at what points are methods changed or combined?
- **Proportion and priority**: which methods are seen as dominant?
- **Comparison and contrast**: linked with triangulation, are the methods similar or markedly different?
- **Use and benefit**: for what purposes are the alternative approaches combined?

Advantages of the Mixed Methods approach

- *A more comprehensive account of the thing being researched.* A Mixed Method approach can provide a fuller description and/or more complete explanation of the phenomenon being studied by providing more than one perspective on it. By encouraging the use of qualitative and quantitative methods and by facilitating a blend of exploratory and explanatory research, the findings are likely to address a wider range of the questions relating to 'how', 'why', 'what', 'who', 'when' and 'how many'.
- *Clearer links between different methods and the different kinds of data.* The Mixed Methods approach places emphasis on the integration of alternative approaches and encourages the researcher to provide an explicit account of how and why the different methods and data complement each other. The approach is particularly sensitive to the nature of the mix and how the qualitative methods relate to the quantitative methods in the research. To this extent, the Mixed Methods approach avoids any arbitrary 'mix-and-match' approach where methods get thrown together in a random or *ad hoc* way.

- *Good use of triangulation.* Following on from its emphasis on the rationale for combining different approaches, the Mixed Methods approach involves a heightened sensitivity to the nature of triangulation. In effect, the use of a Mixed Methods approach calls for a clear appreciation of 'triangulation' and makes good use of its potential.
- *A practical, problem-driven approach to research.* As a movement, the Mixed Methods approach is problem-driven rather than theory driven. Its underlying philosophy is that of pragmatism. As such, it gives voice to the general practice of a large proportion of social researchers who have, for years, used methods from different research paradigms because it has been practical to do so.

Disadvantages of the Mixed Methods approach

- *The time and costs of the research project can increase.* The combination of phases can extend the time-frame for research design and data collection.
- *The researcher needs to develop skills with more than one method.* The researcher needs to develop and exercise skills covering both qualitative and quantitative approaches. This adds demands on the researcher and opens up the possibility of 'missing the mark' for experts in either camp.
- *The QUAL/QUAN distinction tends to oversimplify matters.* Although the labels QUAL and QUAN are convenient to use and easy to understand, a clear dividing line between qualitative and quantitative approaches is hard to sustain at either a practical or philosophical level (Coxon, 2005; Halfpenny, 1997; Hammersley, 1996; Reichardt and Rallis, 1994). In reality, it is hard to find examples of research that are entirely QUAL or entirely QUAN. As Gorard and Taylor (2004: 6) make the point, 'all methods of social science research deal with qualities, even when the observed qualities are counted. Similarly, all methods of analysis use some form of number, such as "tend, most, some, all, none, few" and so on.' So, qualitative social research involves some quantification and measurement; quantitative social research involves some element of interpretation. When using the QUAL/QUAN distinction, therefore, mixed methods researchers need to be aware that the clarity and simplicity of the terms mask a more complicated reality.
- *The mixed methods designs that are generally recommended do not allow for emergent research designs.* Mixed methods research designs that are based on the sequencing of the QUAL and QUAN components of research do not sit comfortably with the kind of emergent research designs associated with grounded theory approaches or some other forms of qualitative enquiry. Within the Mixed Methods approach discussions of the research design tend to presume that the sequencing of the QUAL/QUAN components is something that can and should be determined at the outset of the research.

For many purposes this is good practice. However, it does not really provide for the kind of flexibility required by emergent research designs. Nor does it really allow for 'developing the analysis' in which unexpected results can prompt the researcher to bring on board a different research method in direct response to unforeseen outcomes. There is, though, no reason in principle why a Mixed Methods approach cannot adopt an emergent design.

• *The underlying philosophy of the Mixed Methods approach – pragmatism – is open to misinterpretation.* There is a common-sense use of the word pragmatic which implies expediency and a certain lack of principles underlying a course of action. There is the danger, then, that the Mixed Methods approach gets associated with this understanding of the word and thus becomes regarded as an approach in which 'anything goes'. It should be stressed that this is not the philosophical meaning of pragmatism and it is not a meaning that should be associated with the Mixed Methods approach.

• *Findings from different methods might not corroborate one another.* If findings from the different methods do not corroborate one another, the researcher can be faced with an awkward situation. In particular, when the Mixed Methods approach is being used to check the validity of findings (rather than to complement findings) any disparity between the findings can pose a challenging and possibly unwelcome occurrence. The Mixed Methods approach, to a large degree, operates on the assumption that findings will coincide and that this will be a positive contribution to the research project. If the findings do not coincide, however, the researcher can be faced with a problem. *In principle*, the non-alignment of results need not be a set-back. It should spur further research to investigate the difference in findings. The contradictions could be very interesting – revealing limitations to the methods of data collection or teasing out fascinating complications within the phenomenon being studied. In practice, though, non-corroboration can have negative consequences. Project researchers and contract researchers can be under pressure to arrive at conclusions within a given time-frame. They can be expected to produce reports that have to be delivered by a given deadline. But, at the end of the project they could be left with contradictory findings from the alternative methods (or data sources) and no firm conclusion. Where people look to research to provide concrete findings or practical solutions to a pressing problem, they might not be very receptive to conclusions that are based on conflicting data from different methods. The audience for the research (e.g. funders, examiners) might feel dissatisfied that the completion of the project does not provide a clear-cut finding. They might even interpret things to mean that one or other of the methods (or data sources) employed was 'wrong' and should not have been used within the project.

Checklist for mixed methods research

When undertaking mixed methods research you should feel confident about answering 'yes' to the following questions: ☑

1 Does the research
  - make use of more than one research method? ☐
  - combine more than one kind of research data? ☐
  - ask questions based on different models? (exploratory/explanatory) ☐

2 Does the research have a clear design showing the sequence and dominance of the QUAN and QUAL parts? ☐

3 Are the QUAN and QUAL components integrated in an explicit way? ☐

  Does this occur in relation to the:

  - methods of data collection? ☐
  - quantitative and qualitative data? ☐
  - kinds of data analysis? ☐

4 Has a clear statement been made about the benefits of using a mixed methods strategy compared with using just one method? ☐

  Are the benefits linked explicitly to the research problem? ☐

5 Is the rationale for using a mixed methods strategy based on one or more of the following criteria?
  - the needs of the particular research question; ☐
  - improving the accuracy of data; ☐
  - providing a more complete picture; ☐
  - developing the analysis; ☐
  - an aid to the sampling of participants; ☐
  - a means for compensating the strengths and weaknesses of particular methods; ☐
  - the principle that mixed methods research is fundamentally good practice. ☐

© M. Denscombe, *The Good Research Guide*. Open University Press.

8

Action research

What is the Action Research approach? • The practical nature of action research • Change and professional self-development • Action research as a cyclical process • Participation in the research process • Issues connected with the use of action research • Advantages of action research • Disadvantages of action research • Checklist for action research

What is the Action Research approach?

Action research is normally associated with 'hands-on', small-scale research projects. Its origins can be traced back to the work of social scientists in the late 1940s on both sides of the Atlantic, who advocated closer ties between social theory and the solving of immediate social problems. More recently, action research has been used in a variety of settings within the social sciences, but its growing popularity as a research approach perhaps owes most to its use in areas such as organizational development, education, health and social care. In these areas it has a particular niche among professionals who want to use research to improve their practices.

Action research, from the start, was involved with practical issues – the kind of issues and problems, concerns and needs, that arose as a routine part of activity 'in the real world'. This specifically practical orientation has remained a defining characteristic of action research. Early on, action research was also seen as research specifically geared to changing matters, and this too has remained a core feature of the notion of action research. The thinking here is that research should not only be used to gain a better understanding of the problems which arise in everyday practice, but actually set out to alter things – to do so as part and parcel of the research process rather than tag it on as an afterthought which follows the conclusion of the research. This, in fact, points towards a third defining characteristic of action research: its commitment to a process of research in which the application of findings and an evaluation of their impact on practice become part of a cycle of research. This process, further, has become associated with a trend towards involving those affected by the research in the design and implementation of the research – to encourage them to participate as collaborators in the research rather than being subjects of it.

Together, these provide the four defining characteristics of action research.

- *Practical*. It is aimed at dealing with real-world problems and issues, typically at work and in organizational settings.
- *Change*. Both as a way of dealing with practical problems and as a means of discovering more about phenomena, change is regarded as an integral part of research.
- *Cyclical process*. Research involves a feedback loop in which initial findings generate possibilities for change which are then implemented and evaluated as a prelude to further investigation.
- *Participation*. Practitioners are the crucial people in the research process. Their participation is active, not passive.

Action research quite clearly is a *strategy* for social research rather than a specific method. It is concerned with the aims of research and the design of the research, but does not specify any constraints when it comes to the means for data collection that might be adopted by the action researcher. This point is captured by Susman and Evered:

Action research can use different techniques for data collection . . . Action researchers with a background in psychology tend to prefer questionnaires for such purposes . . . while action researchers with a background in applied anthropology, psychoanalysis or socio-technical systems tend to prefer direct observation and/or in-depth interviewing . . . Action researchers with any of these backgrounds may also retrieve data from the records, memos and reports that the client system routinely produces.

(Susman and Evered, 1978: 589)

The practical nature of action research

Action research is essentially practical and applied. It is driven by the need to solve practical, real-world problems. It operates on the premise, as Kurt Lewin put it, that 'Research that produces nothing but books will not suffice' (Lewin, 1946: 35).

But being practical would not be enough to set it apart from other approaches to research. After all, many approaches can lay claim to this territory. Many can claim with justification to offer applied research. While it certainly does embrace this aim, being 'practical' has a second sense as far as action research is concerned, and it is this which helps to give it a unique identity as a research strategy. The research needs to be undertaken *as part of practice* rather than a bolt-on addition to it.

> **Key point**
> Action research [rejects] the concept of a two-stage process in which research is carried out first by researchers and then in a separate second stage the knowledge generated from the research is applied by practitioners. Instead, the two processes of research and action are integrated. (Somekh, 1995: 34)

Clearly, if the processes of research and action are integrated, then action research must involve 'the practitioner' very closely. And this provides a further meaning which can be added to the practical nature of action research: *practitioner research*. However, although it may be linked with the notion of practitioner research, it is important to appreciate that action research is not exactly the same thing as practitioner research. Edwards and Talbot stress this point:

> Practitioner research can only be designated action research if it is carried out by professionals who are engaged in researching (. . .) aspects of their own practice as they engage in that practice.
>
> (Edwards and Talbot, 1994: 52)

It is not enough for the research to be undertaken as part of the job, because this could include all kinds of data gathering and analysis to do with remote people and systems, the findings from which might have no bearing on the practitioner's own activity. To accord with the spirit of action research, the researcher needs to investigate his or her *own* practices with a view to altering these in a beneficial way.

Change and professional self-development

Action research is wedded to the idea that change is good. Initially, this is because studying change is seen as a useful *way of learning more about the way a thing works* (Bryman, 1989). Change, in this sense, is regarded as a valuable enhancer of knowledge in its own right, rather than something that is undertaken after the results of the research have been obtained. But, of course, the scale and the scope of changes introduced through action research will not be grand. The scale of the research is constrained by the need for the action researchers to focus on *aspects of their own practice as they engage in that practice.* So change as envisaged by action research is not likely to be a wide-scale major alteration to an organization. The element of change will not be in the order of a large-scale experiment such as changes in the bonus schemes of production workers at Ford's car assembly plants. No. Because, action research tends to be localized and small-scale, it usually focuses on change at the micro level.

One of the most common kinds of change involved in action research is at the level of *professional self-development.* It is in keeping with the notion of professional self-development that a person should want to improve practices and that this should involve a continual quest for ways in which to change practice for the better. Action research provides a way forward for the professional which, while it entails a certain degree of reflection, adds the systematic and rigorous collection of data to the resources the professional can use to achieve the improvement in practice.

It is important to recognize that reflection may be of itself insufficient to make the professional's endeavour 'action research'. The reflection needs to be systematic if it is to qualify as action *research.* Merely *thinking* about your own practice – though possibly a valuable basis for improving practice – is not the same as researching that action. And here a distinction needs to be made between the 'reflective practitioner' (Schön, 1983) as one who strives for professional self-development through a critical consideration of his or her practices, and the action researcher who, while also being a reflective practitioner, adds to this by using research techniques to enhance and systematize that reflection.

Action research as a cyclical process

The vision of action research as a cyclical process fits in nicely with the quest for perpetual development built into the idea of professionalism (see Figure 3). The purpose of research, though it might be prompted by a specific problem, is seen as part of a broader enterprise in which the aim is to improve practice through a rolling programme of research.

The crucial points about the cycle of enquiry in action research are (a) that *research feeds back directly into practice,* and (b) that *the process is ongoing.* The critical reflection of the practitioner is not only directed to the identification of 'problems' worthy of investigation with a view to improving practice, but can also involve an evaluation of changes just instigated, which can, in their own right, prompt further research. It is fair to point out, however, that this is something of an ideal and that, in reality, action research often limits itself to discrete, one-off pieces of research.

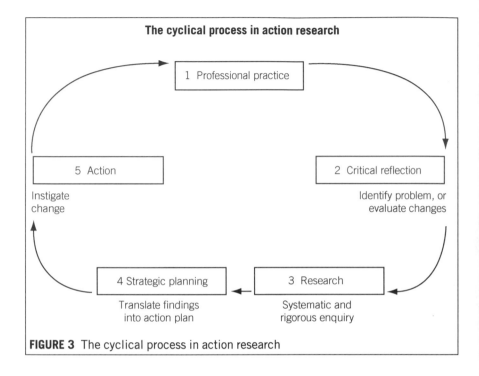

FIGURE 3 The cyclical process in action research

Participation in the research process

The participatory nature of action research is probably its most distinctive feature, since, in some ways, it hits at the heart of conventions associated with formal social research. Conventionally, research is the province of the expert; the outside authority who is a professional. This researcher more often than not initiates the process of research, sets the agenda and designs the collection and analysis of data. After the research is concluded, those involved might receive some feedback in the form of results from the research. They may, or may not, instigate changes on the basis of such findings. Broadly speaking, the act of doing research is separated from the act of making changes (Boutilier *et al.*, 1997). Action research, by contrast, insists that practitioners must be partici-pants, not just in the sense of taking part in the research but in the sense of being *a partner in the research.*

Partnerships, of course, take many forms. Grundy and Kemmis (1988: 7) argue that 'in action research, all actors involved in the research process are equal participants, and must be involved in every stage of the research'. With action research it can be the practitioner, not some outside professional researcher, who wants to instigate a change and who consequently initiates the research (Elliott, 1991). The research, in this sense, is practitioner-driven, with the practitioner not just an equal partner but a sponsor and director of the research process. And if this sounds radical, there are others who would push the matter further, insisting that the practitioner should be the dominant partner – calling the shots at all stages and in all aspects of the research.

Even in less radical revisions to the conventional relationship between researcher and practitioners, the inclusion of participation as a fundamental feature of action research brings with it a shift in the direction of *democratizing the research process*. Control is transferred away from the professional researcher and towards the practitioner. Power shifts towards the insider who is the practitioner. There is, of course, still a role for the outside expert, but that role shifts in the direction of mutual collaboration in the research process, or even to the position where the outside expert has the role of *facilitator* of the practitioner's own project, a resource to be drawn upon as and when the practitioner sees fit.

Behind this shift in the relationship there rests a *respect for the practitioner's knowledge*. Again, this respect may not be unique to action research, but it is an aspect of action research which is distinctive and built into an approach which is broadly sympathetic to democratizing the research process by challenging the separation of expert from lay person in research.

There can be an explicitly political angle to the participatory aspect of action research, with its 'democratization' of the research process and 'respect for practitioner knowledge'. Zuber-Skerritt (1996) refers to this as *'emancipatory'* action research. This type of action research is quite clear about the nature of the change which is brought about through action research; it is change which challenges the existing system. It is change which goes beyond *technical*

Three approaches to action research

1 Technical action research aims to improve effectiveness of educational or managerial practice. The practitioners are co-opted and depend greatly on the researcher as a facilitator.

2 Practical action research, in addition to effectiveness, aims at the practitioners' understanding and professional development. The researcher's role is . . . to encourage practical deliberation and self-reflection on the part of the practitioners.

3 Action research is emancipating when it aims not only at technical and practical improvement and the participant's better understanding, along with transformation and change within the existing boundaries and conditions, but also at changing the system itself of those conditions which impede desired improvement in the system/organisation.

(Zuber-Skerritt, 1996: 4–5)

matters that can have a bearing on the effectiveness or efficiency of the professional's current practice. It is change which goes beyond *practical* matters that can have a bearing on the way practitioners interpret the task at hand. For sure, emancipatory action research incorporates these, but it also challenges the fundamental framework within which the practice occurs.

Issues connected with the use of action research

'Ownership' of the research

The participatory nature of action research brings with it a question mark concerning who owns the research and its outcomes. With conventional approaches to research this tends to be less complicated. To offer something of a caricature, the outsider research initiates the process and approaches practitioners to gain their permission for the research to be conducted (by the outsider). Having obtained authorization from relevant people, research proceeds, with the outsider 'owning' the data collected and having full rights over the analysis and publication of findings. Of course, complications arise with various forms of sponsored research and consultancy, where authorization might include certain restrictions on the rights of the two parties over the research and its findings. However, these are likely to be *explicitly* recognized as a result of negotiating access.

In the case of action research, the *partnership* nature of work can make matters rather less clear cut. Who is in charge? Who calls the shots? Who decides on appropriate action? Who owns the data? These and similar issues need to be worked out sensitively and carefully by the partners to *ensure that there are shared expectations about the nature of participation* in action research.

Ethical issues associated with action research

The distinct ethical problem for action research is that, although the research centres on the activity of the practitioner, it is almost inevitable that the activity of colleagues will also come under the microscope at some stage or other, as their activity interlinks with that of the practitioner who instigates the research. Practitioners are not 'islands' – isolated from routine contact with colleagues and clients. Their practice and the changes they seek to make can hardly be put in place without some knock-on effect for others who operate close by in organizational terms.

The idea that the action researcher is exempt from the need to gain authorization, as a consequence, evaporates. Because the activity of action research almost inevitably affects others, it is important to have a clear idea of when and where the action research necessarily steps outside the bounds of collecting information which is purely personal and relating to the practitioners alone. Where it does so, the usual standards of research ethics must be observed: permissions obtained, confidentiality maintained, identities protected.

Two things follow. First, there is a case for arguing that those who engage in action research should be open about the research aspect of their practice. It should not be hidden or disguised. Second, the need for informed consent from those involved in the research should be recognized.

Ethics in action research

- The development of the work must remain visible and open to suggestions from others.
- Permission must be obtained before making observations or examining documents produced for other purposes.
- Description of others' work and points of view must be negotiated with those concerned before being published.
- The researcher must accept responsibility for maintaining confidentiality.

(Winter, 1996: 17)

Reflexivity and action research

Practitioners who engage in action research have a privileged insight into the way things operate in their particular 'work-sites'. They have '*insider knowledge*'. This can be a genuine bonus for research. However, it can also pose problems. The outsider – 'the stranger' – might be better placed to see the kind of thing which, to the insider, is too mundane, too obvious, to register as an important factor. Because the practitioner cannot escape the web of meanings that the 'insider' knows, he or she is constrained by the web of meanings. The outsider 'expert' may not have the 'right' answer, but can possibly offer an alternative perspective which can help the practitioner to gain new insights into the nature of the practical problem.

Link up with **Ethnography and reflexivity, p. 68**

So, although action research respects the knowledge of the practitioners, it would be rather naive to assume that practitioners' knowledge – of itself – provides all the answers. Particularly in relation to *practical* action research, and *emancipatory* action research, their aim is to enhance practitioner understanding and this is likely to call upon some modicum of outsider advice.

Resources and action research

The action researcher's investigation is necessarily fairly localized and relatively small-scale. None the less, the action researcher faces the difficulty of trying to combine a probably demanding workload with systematic and rigorous research. *Time constraints*, alone, make this hard to accomplish. Even if, as should be the case, action research is integrated with practice rather than tagged on top of practice, the routine demands of the job are unlikely to be reduced by way of compensation. In the short run, prior to positive benefits emerging, the action researcher is likely to face extra work.

Generalizability and action research

Given the constraints on the scope of action research projects, it might be argued that their findings will rarely contribute to broader insights. Located as they are in the practitioner's work-site, there are not very good prospects for the *representativeness* of the data in action research. The setting and constituent features are 'givens' rather than factors which can be controlled or varied, and the research is generally focused on the one site rather than spread across a range of examples. Action research, therefore, is vulnerable to the criticism that the findings relate to one instance and should not be generalized beyond this specific 'case'.

Link up with **Case studies, Chapter 2**

In one sense this reservation needs to be acknowledged. Surely, practice-driven research in local settings hardly lends itself to conclusions with universal application. New truths and new theories will be unlikely to find foundation in such studies alone. And this caution is worth taking to heart for the action researcher: beware of making grandiose claims on the basis of action research projects. However, it can rightly be argued that action research, while practice-driven and small-scale, should not lose anything by way of rigour. Like any other small-scale research, it can draw on existing theories, apply and test research propositions, use suitable methods and, importantly, offer some evaluation of existing knowledge (without making unwarranted claims). It is the rigour, rather than the size of the project or its purpose, by which the research should be judged.

Advantages of action research

- It addresses practical problems in a positive way, feeding the results of research directly back into practice. In the words of Somekh (1995: 340), 'It directly addresses the knotty problem of the persistent failure of research in the social sciences to make a difference in terms of bringing about actual improvements in practice.'

• It has personal benefits for the practitioner, as it contributes to professional self-development.

• It should entail a continuous cycle of development and change via on-site research in the workplace, which has benefits for the organization to the extent that it is geared to improving practice and resolving problems.

• It involves participation in the research for practitioners. This can democratize the research process, depending on the nature of the partnership, and generally involves a greater appreciation of, and respect for, practitioner knowledge.

Disadvantages of action research

• The necessary involvement of the practitioner limits the scope and scale of research. The 'work-site' approach affects the representativeness of the findings and the extent to which generalizations can be made on the basis of the results.

• The integration of research with practice limits the feasibility of exercising controls over factors of relevance to the research. The setting for the research generally does not allow for the variables to be manipulated or for controls to be put in place, because the research is conducted not alongside routine activity but actually as part of that activity.

• The nature of the research is constrained by what is permissible and ethical within the workplace setting.

• Ownership of the research process becomes contestable within the framework of the partnership relationship between practitioner and researcher.

• Action research tends to involve an extra burden of work for the practitioners, particularly at the early stages before any benefits feed back into improved effectiveness.

• The action researcher is unlikely to be detached and impartial in his or her approach to the research. In this respect, action research stands in marked contrast to positivistic approaches, as Susman and Evered (1978) point out. It is clearly geared to resolving problems which confront people in their routine, everyday (work) activity, and these people therefore have a vested interest in the findings. They cannot be entirely detached or impartial in accord with the classic image of science.

Checklist for action research

When undertaking action research you should feel confident about answering 'yes' to the following questions: ☑

1 Does the research project address a concrete issue or practical problem? ☐

2 Is there participation by the practitioner in all stages of the research project? ☐

3 Have the grounds for the partnership between practitioner and any outside expert been explicitly negotiated and agreed? ☐

4 Is the research part of a continuous cycle of development (rather than a one-off project)? ☐

5 Is there a clear view of how the research findings will feed back directly into practice? ☐

6 Is it clear which kind of action research is being used – 'technical', 'practical' or 'emancipatory'? ☐

7 Has insider knowledge been acknowledged as having disadvantages as well as advantages for the research? ☐

8 Is the research sufficiently small-scale to be combined with a routine workload? ☐

9 Have ethical matters been taken into consideration? ☐

© M. Denscombe, *The Good Research Guide*. Open University Press.

Part II

Methods of social research

There are four main methods that social researchers can use: questionnaires, interviews, observation and documents. Each of these methods provides an alternative tool available to the researcher for the collection of empirical data. In many ways they are the social scientist's equivalent of the microscope, the scales and the micrometer that natural scientists might use in relation to material objects in the physical world. They are tools that help the researcher to get:

- a clearer picture of things;
- an accurate measurement of things;
- facts and evidence about the subject matter.

Selecting methods – a matter of 'horses for courses'

In the following chapters there is guidance about the key features of each method. However, before choosing and using any of the tools, it is important to consider five points.

First, although certain research strategies have come to be associated with the use of certain research methods this does not rule out the possibility of choice. Surveys tend to be linked with questionnaires, for example, while ethnography tends to be associated with participant observation. And there are some sound theoretical reasons which explain the tendency of strategies to be linked with particular methods. The linkage, however, is not watertight and it is important for the project researcher to recognize that there is likely to be some scope to choose among different methods for use within any specific strategy.

Second, each of the methods has its particular strengths and weaknesses. Each method approaches the collection of data with a certain set of assumptions and produces a type of data whose usefulness depends on what the researcher is trying to achieve. This means that none of the possible methods for data collection can be regarded as perfect and none can be regarded as utterly useless.

Third, when it comes to choosing a method researchers should base their decision on the criterion of 'usefulness'. Rather than trying to look for a method that is superior to all others in any absolute sense, they should look for the most appropriate method in practice. Researchers should ask themselves which method is best suited to the task at hand and operate on the premise that, when *choosing a method for the collection of data, it is a matter of 'horses for courses'*.

Fourth, research methods do not need to be seen as mutually exclusive. If no method is intrinsically better than others, and if methods are to be chosen pragmatically, then this opens up the possibility of combining methods and using a mixed method approach. More than one method can be used for the research with the clear intention that weaknesses in one method can be compensated for by strengths in another method.

Fifth, the use of more than one method allows the researcher to use *triangulation*. The combination of different methods can be used by the researcher to look at the research topic from a variety of perspectives, as a means of comparison and contrast, with each method approaching the topic from a different angle.

Link up with **Mixed methods, Chapter 7**

Triangulation

Triangulation involves the practice of viewing things from more than one perspective. This can mean the use of different methods, different sources of data or even different researchers within the study. The principle behind this is that the researcher can get a better understanding of the thing that is being investigated if he/she views it from different positions.

The notion of triangulation draws on trigonometry and the geometric laws associated with triangles. There are many applications of these laws but one extremely valuable application concerns the ability to find the exact location of a point if it is viewed from two other known positions. The combination of information about angles and distances from these two other positions has been used extensively, for example, to help with navigation and surveying.

Caution

When used by social scientists, triangulation does not equate literally with the use of triangulation by geologists, surveyors, navigators and others concerned with measuring exact locations of things in the physical world. It is used in a *metaphorical* sense. The reason for this is that social researchers are not able to make use of fixed/objective positions, universally agreed, from which to make their observations – not in the same way that surveyors, engineers and others rely on absolute, objective positions in the physical world. What social research has adopted, however, is the principle that viewing something from more than one viewpoint allows you to get a better 'fix' on it – to get a better knowledge of it.

Social researchers have applied the principle of triangulation in a variety of ways. Building on the work of Denzin (1970) the possibilities include the following.

Methodological triangulation (between-methods)

This is the most common form of triangulation adopted by social researchers. The use of alternative methods allows the findings from one method to be contrasted with the findings from another. More often than not the difference between methods takes the form of 'qualitative' data compared with 'quantitative' data. There are two main benefits accruing to this form of triangulation:

- Findings can be corroborated or questioned by comparing the data produced by different methods.
- Findings can be complemented by adding something new and different from one method to what is known about the topic using another method.

The key to this form of triangulation is to use approaches that are markedly different and which allow the researcher to see things from as widely different perspectives as possible.

Methodological triangulation (within-methods)

Comparisons using similar methods can provide a check on the accuracy of findings. This is particularly useful for:

- the analysis and evaluation of quantitative data; and
- the development of research instruments or questionnaire items.

If similar methods produce the same results, it would seem reasonable to conclude that the findings are accurate and that they are authentic (rather than being some artificial by-product of the methods used). This is the form of triangulation used by Campbell and Fiske (1959) and Webb *et al.* (1966) in their pioneering work on triangulation. The use of widely contrasting methods would not be the best option in this instance because it would increase the possibility that any difference in the findings might reflect the difference in methods rather than the actual factor that is being checked (McFee, 1992).

Data triangulation (use of contrasting sources of information)

The validity of findings can be checked by using different sources of information. This can mean comparing data from different informants (informant triangulation) or using data collected at different times (time triangulation). The notion also incorporates the idea of space triangulation (the use of more than one cultural, social or geographical context).

Investigator triangulation (use of different researchers)

As a check against bias arising from the influence of any specific researcher, the findings from different investigators can be compared for consistency. Do the researchers 'see' things in the same way? Do they interpret events similarly? Do they attach the same codes to the same source of data (e.g. interview transcript, observed event)? To the extent that they do, the findings can be accepted with more confidence. Where they do not,

- quantitative researchers will want to refine the coding schedule or conduct further training with the data collectors;
- qualitative researchers will be interested in the identity of the researchers and how this might have influenced the researchers' interpretation of the situation or the process of data collection itself (e.g. interaction with participants).

Theory triangulation

This involves the use of more than one theoretical position in relation to the data. Different theories can shape the kind of data that are collected and the way the data are interpreted. These different perspectives can be based on the approaches of different disciplines. So, for example, researchers might choose to contrast a sociological with a psychological approach to the particular topic being investigated.

Example of triangulation in social research

Imagine a case study in which the focus of attention is on disruptive behaviour by students in a secondary school. The researcher could elect to use observation as the method for collecting data, and would, of course, want to justify this choice in relation to the kind of data desired and practical factors affecting the research. To enhance confidence in the validity of the findings, however, it might be decided to make use of more than one method. After all, interviews with the staff and pupils involved could shed light on the topic. Questionnaires administered to all staff and pupils might gather other relevant information, and documents such as school records could supply a further avenue for exploring the topic. As Figure 4 illustrates, in this instance triangulation between the methods could be used to (a) check the accuracy of the findings (e.g. about the frequency of disruptive behaviour) and (b) provide a fuller picture (e.g. of the significance of disruptive behaviour in terms of its meaning for staff and students).

Methodological triangulation

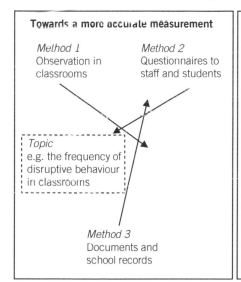
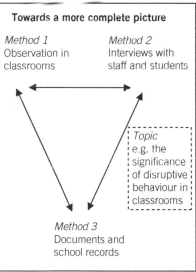

FIGURE 4 Methodological triangulation

Advantages of triangulation

The rationale for using triangulation in social research is that by viewing something from more than one viewpoint the researcher can get a better knowledge of it. And this better knowledge can take two forms:

- *Improved accuracy* (a means of validation). This use of triangulation focuses on the validation of the findings in terms of their accuracy and authenticity. The alternative methods are used as confirmation – a check on one another in terms of the corroboration of findings.
- *Fuller picture* (a source of complementary data). This approach focuses on producing complementary data that enhances the *completeness* of the findings. Researchers can use triangulation to get a fuller version or a version that incorporates different facets of the thing being studied. Or triangulation can be used to develop a line of enquiry, building on findings produced by a different viewpoint. In this sense, the triangulation is used to *complement* information from other sources.

Whether the aim is to get improved accuracy or to get a fuller picture, the use of triangulation can give the researcher added confidence in his/her research data and findings. The opportunity to corroborate findings and the chance to see things from a different perspective can enhance the *validity* of the data. It can bolster confidence that the meaning of the data has some consistency across methods and that the findings are not too closely tied up with a particular method used to collect the data.

 Caution

Triangulation cannot *prove* that the researcher has 'got it right'. In view of the nature of social reality and the nature of social measurement devices, triangulation's potential needs to be seen more cautiously as 'providing more support', 'increasing confidence' and 'reducing the possibility of error'.

Disadvantages of triangulation

Weighed against the benefits of using triangulation there are three factors that ought to be borne in mind. The first of these concerns the sacrifices that need to be made in order to accommodate the use of different methods. Since most research is restricted by the amount of time and money available to conduct the investigation, it is very likely that the use of more than one method will require sacrifices elsewhere. The researcher will need to cut out aspects of the investigation that would have been included had the research used just one method. The most obvious extra demand on the research comes in the form of the multi-skilling that is required. If the researcher is to use more than one method in order to triangulate, he/she must become proficient in the use of the alternative methods – and this takes time. The consequence is that the time-scale for data collection and analysis will get squeezed, requiring the researcher to limit the scope of the research, narrow the range of research questions addressed or reduce the volume of data collected. Inevitably, there is a cost to the use of triangulation.

Second, data analysis becomes more complex when using triangulation. Not only does the researcher need to use more than one kind of analysis, there is also the need to compare, contrast and integrate the findings in a way that is more demanding. In many cases this will involve the combination of quantitative and qualitative findings – a task that is more challenging than sticking with just one method.

Third, the use of triangulation can be risky. There tends to be an implicit assumption underlying the use of triangulation that the alternative perspectives will indeed support one another and that data from one perspective will be corroborated by data from others. But what happens if this does not turn out to be the case? What are the implications for the research when triangulation produces contradictory results? In the spirit of good research, of course, any non-corroboration should lead the researcher to explore the situation further and conduct enquiries that might help to explain the reasons for the contrasting findings. In the short-run, though, the situation can be awkward for the researcher. Where the research has deadlines to meet or examiners/funders to satisfy it can mean the findings appear 'inconclusive' or it might be seen to imply that there was some fundamental 'fault' with the research.

> **Key point: guidelines for the use of triangulation**
>
> - Be very clear and explicit about the purpose of using triangulation: is it intended to *improve accuracy* or to provide a *fuller picture?*
> - Avoid any naive use of triangulation. Appreciate that different methods might point in a similar direction but are unlikely to meet at some precise, unequivocal point of true reality.
> - When writing up the research, give special attention to comparing, contrasting and integrating the data rather than leaving the different sources as separate, stand alone sections.

Data protection

In the collection and use of data, social researchers need to be conscious of the legislation relating to 'personal data'. Most societies have some form of such legislation. In the UK, it is covered by the Data Protection Act 1998. This defines personal data as data relating to living, identifiable individuals. The legislation covers paper documents as well as computer files covering all forms of personal data, no matter how they are collected and stored. Under the legislation, data users are required to:

- supply details of their data to a public register;
- abide by a set of data protection principles.

In practice, researchers in the UK do not always need to go through the process of notifying their research to the public register. One reason for this is that where their research is conducted under the auspices of some organization the organization itself might have a 'notification' that already covers the activity of the researcher. Students and staff at universities are likely to be covered in this way, particularly with respect to research conducted for academic dissertations and coursework.

There are also a number of exemptions contained in the Act that serve to help small-scale academic research by allowing personal data to be held *without* necessarily going through the process of 'notifying' the details of the data to the Data Commissioner or being required to abide by the data protection principles. For example, research is exempted from the requirements of the legislation where the data are not used to influence any decisions concerned with the treatment of the individual concerned. So, for example, examination results collected as part of a dataset relating to personal data on students would be exempt if used by someone as part of an academic research project tracing an association between examination performance and other factors, but would be covered by the legislation if kept by a university and used as part of the decision-making process about the award of a degree qualification. The holding of personal data by academic researchers doing dissertations might also be exempted under section 36 of the Data Protection Act 1998, which specifically exempts from the need to comply with the data protection principles any 'personal data processed by an individual only for the affairs of that individual's personal, family or household affairs (including recreational purposes)'.

Even when they are formally exempted from the provisions of the Act, it is good practice for researchers to recognize the data protection principles and operate within the spirit of the law. It is good research practice to:

- *Collect and process data in a fair and lawful manner.* There is an obligation on researchers to stick within the law in the way they collect their data and, equally, to avoid deception or subterfuge in order to get their information.
- *Use data only for the purposes originally specified.* It is not legitimate under the legislation to collect data for one purpose and then use them for some other purpose that was not stated at the time the data were collected.
- *Collect only the data that are actually needed.* Researchers should not collect vast amounts of data anticipating that some of it might come in useful now or at some time in the future. The data collection should be targeted at the current and actual needs of the project.
- *Take care to ensure the data are accurate.* Researchers, like other data collectors, have a duty of care to make sure the data they hold are accurate and, where appropriate, kept up to date.

- *Keep data no longer than is necessary.* Although researchers do not need to erase data after any given time, the legislation establishes the principle that data should be kept for use rather than simply accumulated. Obviously, in research terms there is some real value in retaining data for future comparison and checking.
- *Keep the data secure.* Very importantly, data should be kept safe. Depending upon the sensitivity of the data, appropriate measures need to be taken to avoid the possibility of them falling into the wrong hands by being lost or stolen. With data held on computers, this entails a suitable use of passwords or encryption to prevent unauthorized access to the data. With paper documents, the data need to be kept under lock and key.
- *Not distribute the data.* Legislation here relates mainly to the commercial use of data and conditions under which personal data can be passed on to other organizations. Under specific exemptions in the UK legislation, it is legitimate for researchers to hand their data to other researchers for specifically research purposes.
- *Restrict access to data.* Although the legislation gives people the right to demand access to the data held about them, this does not generally apply in the case of research where the results and statistics are not made available in any way that allows the individual to be identified.
- *Keep data anonymous.* If the data are anonymous and cannot therefore be traced to any particular individual, the legislation does not apply. If this is the case, contributors should be informed at the time the data are collected that the information will be used in an anonymized form and that it will not be possible for individuals to be identified in any report or other publication arising from the research. Clearly, the researcher should consider whether it is really necessary to collect data that are linked to identifiable individuals since anonymized data are exempted from legislation.

Research ethics

Social researchers should be ethical. In the collection of their data, in the process of analysing the data and in the dissemination of findings, they are expected to:

- respect the rights and dignity of those who are participating in the research project;
- avoid any harm to the participants arising from their involvement in the research;
- operate with honesty and integrity.

On moral grounds, these principles stem from the belief that people should be protected from researchers who might be tempted to use any means available to advance the state of knowledge on a given topic. The principles rest on the assumption that researchers have no privileged position in society that justifies them pursuing their interests at the expense of those they are studying – no matter how valuable they hope the findings might be.

There are practical reasons, too, why social researchers need to adopt an ethical approach to their investigations. Protection of the public from the unscrupulous collection and use of data has become enshrined in legislation. Prompted by the potential of computers to store and process vast quantities of personal data, and given further impetus by the growth of the Internet, most societies have some *data protection laws* that lay down conditions governing the legitimate collection and storage of personal data, and *human rights legislation* that has implications for the way in which researchers go about their business. Both kinds of legislation provide a framework within which researchers must operate if they are to stay within the law. Although it might be a good thing for those conducting small-scale research projects to make themselves familiar with the relevant legislation in their own society, some of the burden of this is relieved by the fact that professional research associations almost always publish an explicit code of conduct that they expect their members to abide by, and these codes embody the key points of legislation (as well as trying to establish a standard of conduct that is both moral and professional).

Key point: professional associations and codes of research ethics

The disciplines that make up the social sciences have their own professional associations and their codes of conduct are usually available through their websites.

There is a large degree of overlap between the various disciplines' codes. This is hardly surprising since in many cases they are responding to the same sets of laws. The similarity, however, stems from more than just the laws: it owes much to a shared sense of values in relation to research. Certainly, there is scope for some difference. Market research associations approach things in a slightly different way from medical associations, reflecting the different nature of the procedures the researchers are likely to use and the potential harm that might be done to participants. Market researchers collecting data on consumer preferences are not likely to be exposing participants to the same kind of risk, psychological or physical, as health researchers investigating the effectiveness of a new drug or surgical procedure. So there are some differences in emphasis. More striking, though, is the level of agreement about the underlying ethical principles that should guide the activities of researchers. These fall under three headings.

Principle 1: the interest of participants should be protected

There is general agreement that people should not suffer as a consequence of their involvement with a piece of research. Those who contribute to research as informants or as research subjects should be no worse off at the end of their participation than they were when they started. Nor should there be longer-term repercussions stemming from their involvement that in any sense harm the participants.

In accord with this principle, researchers have a duty to consider in advance the likely consequences of participation and to take measures that safeguard the interests of those who help with the investigation. First of all, they need to ensure that participants do not come to any physical harm as a result of the research. This might sound like an issue more appropriate to health research, but it is something that is also coming to the foreground in social research. Increasingly, *safety considerations* are built into research design. Safety is something that can no longer be taken for granted and it is something to which researchers should give serious consideration in the design of their investigation. To illustrate the point, a good researcher will consider the issue of personal safety when arranging the time and location to meet someone for an interview. The researcher will bear in mind any potential dangers, such as the prospect of being attacked on the way to the interview, recognizing that, while the possibility might be quite remote, they have a responsibility to foresee and avoid the risk as far as possible.

Second, care needs to be taken to *avoid psychological harm* resulting from research. Again, this consideration should be built into the design of the research because any investigation that is potentially going to lead to trauma, stress or other psychological harm will not be considered ethical. On this point, researchers need to bear in mind the extent to which the investigation will be intrusive, touch on sensitive issues or threaten the beliefs of the participants.

Third, participants should suffer no personal harm arising from the disclosure of information collected during the research. Disclosure of personal information could be embarrassing for the participants and, depending on the type of information, it could also involve economic loss or even the prospect of legal action being taken against participants on the basis of the disclosed information if it was to come to the attention of relevant authorities (e.g. employers, Inland Revenue, social security inspectors, the police, customs officials). There is broad agreement, therefore, that researchers need to protect the interests of the participants by ensuring the *confidentiality of information* that is given to them. Research data should be kept secure and, when publishing results, care needs to be taken not to disclose the personal identities of individuals who have contributed to the findings.

Principle 2: researchers should avoid deception or misrepresentation

There is a general expectation that researchers should operate in an honest and open manner with respect to their investigation. Codes of conduct include reference to providing fair and unbiased analysis of findings and, crucially in the current context, researchers are expected to avoid deception or misrepresentation in their dealings with informants or research subjects. They are expected to be open and explicit about what they are doing – to let people know that they are researchers and that they intend to collect data for the purposes of an investigation into a particular topic. Furthermore, they are expected to tell the truth about the nature of their investigation and the role of the participants in that research.

There are, though, occasions when it is not feasible for the researcher to be completely open and honest with participants. To be so would automatically jeopardize any prospect of the investigation actually taking place or would cause participants to react to the research in a way that would contaminate the results. Research on illegal activity and research on sensitive issues are obvious examples of instances where the researcher might feel the need to be economical with the truth. Even with more mundane areas of investigation, there are many occasions where total openness about the research and its aims at the start of the investigation could hinder the collection of data or skew the findings. Many psychology experiments, for example, would be ruined if the subjects knew in advance what the researcher was investigating, and it has been estimated that about three-quarters of psychology experiments involve giving participants information that, in one respect or another, actually misleads them about the purpose of the experiment.

When some form of deception is seen as necessary, researchers face an ethical dilemma: from the point of view of good research design deception is regarded as essential, yet from the point of view of ethical research such deception is bad practice. Fortunately, there is a way round the problem. It is recognized in the vast majority of the codes of conduct published by professional associations that, on certain occasions, some deception by researchers might be warranted as absolutely necessary for the purposes of the research. The conditions under which it might be acceptable generally require the researcher to:

- acknowledge that the deception entails a transgression of a core ethical principle;
- provide an explicit justification for why it was deemed necessary on this particular occasion;
- use a 'debriefing' session in which, after the event, participants are put in the picture about the true nature of the enquiry and why they could not be informed about this at the beginning.

Exceptionally, there are occasions when researchers use deception in order to collect their data and do not at any time tell those people being studied about the fact that they have been involved in a research project. Some types of ethnographic study, for example, involve fieldwork where it might be dangerous to disclose the researcher's identity even after the event. Such occasions, though, need to be treated as exceptions to the rule – ones that can be justified only on the basis of the very special circumstances surrounding the particular investigation.

Principle 3: participants should give informed consent

People should never be forced or coerced into helping with research. Their participation must always be voluntary, and they must have sufficient information about the research to arrive at a reasoned judgement about whether or not they want to participate. These are the premises of 'informed consent'. Of course, as with the other ethical principles, there are exceptions because it is not always feasible to gain consent from people. Observation of crowd behaviour at football matches and observation of the movements of visitors to art galleries are clearly situations where it would prove impossible to get the consent of all involved. As with the other exceptions, the codes of conduct of the professional associations generally include clauses that acknowledge such situations. And, as before, the conditions under which researchers can collect data ethically without getting informed consent involve the recognition that it is an exception to the general principle coupled with an explicit justification for not seeking it on this particular occasion. The grounds for not seeking informed consent tend to centre on the claims that: (a) it is not feasible to get such consent; or (b) the form of data collection is unlikely to involve much by way of personal risks to the informant (e.g. clipboard questionnaire research conducted on the streets on a topic that is not particularly controversial or sensitive).

For those kinds of research that call for greater personal involvement on the part of the participant, where the research is more lengthy or ongoing and particularly where the kind of information collected is of a sensitive nature, there is normally a need to get informed consent. But, more than this, there is a need to get that consent *in writing*. When the consent is in writing it acts as a way of formally recording the agreement to participate and confirming that the participant has been informed about the nature of the research. This protects the researcher from any possible accusation that he or she acted improperly when recruiting people to take part in the research.

The following items should be included in any form that is used for obtaining written consent from participants.

The consent form

Identity of the researcher

Participants are entitled to know who is conducting the research and where they can be contacted. The consent form, therefore, should include

- the name(s) of the researcher;
- an address and other contact details at which he or she can be contacted;
- where appropriate, the name of the organization under whose auspices the research is being conducted.

Information about the research

There needs to be a statement providing enough detail for the participant to understand, in broad terms, the aims, methods and anticipated outcomes of the research. This must be brief since participants will not normally wish to spend a lot of time reading page after page of details. Some researchers present the information on a separate sheet that can be left with the participant for future reference. At other times, the statement is limited to a few sentences on the consent form itself. Either way, participants need to be provided with a brief description of:

- what the research is investigating;
- how it is to be conducted;
- what benefits are likely to emerge from the investigation.

Expectations about the participant's contribution

Informed consent presumes that participants know in advance what tasks the researcher expects them to undertake and what, if any, reward they might expect for their efforts. They will need to be told whether they are expected to take part in an interview, take part in a laboratory experiment or complete a questionnaire. And they should be given some indication of how much time this is likely to take. They might also need to know whether any expenses they incur will be paid for by the researcher, and whether they will receive some kind of payment or other incentive (such as a free copy of the final report of the research). The consent form, then, should specify:

- what tasks the participant will undertake;
- how much of their time this is likely to take;
- what rewards or incentives there might be for taking part in the research.

The right to withdraw consent

Signing a consent form does not oblige participants to continue in the role if, at some subsequent stage, they no longer wish to do so. The consent form is not a contract that binds a person to the task of helping with the research – and this should be made clear on the consent form itself. Participants should be made aware that, should they wish to do so, it is their right to withdraw their consent at any time.

Confidentiality and security of data

The consent form needs to incorporate some commitment by the researcher with regard to the conduct of the research and the treatment of the data. Any agreement to take part in research ought to be made with an understanding of what code of ethics the researcher will use and what measures will be taken to safeguard the data and protect participants from any disclosure of their individual identity. Such assurances could include:

- specifying which professional association's code of ethics will be adhered to during the course of the research;
- what security measures will be taken to ensure the confidentiality of the data;
- how anonymity of the data will be guaranteed (if appropriate).

Signature of the participant, with date

This signature can incorporate an acknowledgement that the participant has been advised about the requirements of the research and understood what is involved (e.g. 'I have read and understood the written details provided for me about the research, and agree to participate in the project. Signed . . .').

Counter signature of the researcher, with date

It is good practice for the researcher to sign the consent form as well as the participant, effectively committing the researcher to uphold his or her side of the agreement.

The need for Ethics Committee approval

The importance attached to research ethics is evident in the fact that most social researchers will need to get prior approval for their investigation from an *Ethics Committee*. In particular, this is the case where the proposed research involves collecting data directly from people, or collecting personal data about living people. Even with small-scale research, it is increasingly the case that before the research can be conducted it will need to have been scrutinized by a committee of suitably qualified experts to ensure that the design of the research includes appropriate measures to protect the interests of the people and groups covered by the research. Researchers in the field of health will find that medical ethics committees are powerful in this respect, and those conducting investigations as part of an educational qualification will normally be required to have their plans vetted by an ethics committee within their university before they are allowed to start the investigation. Submissions to ethics committees will be judged according to the broad principles for ethical research outlined above, and might include further specific stipulations depending on the field of the research. And the need to get approval from such ethics committees reinforces the point that a concern with ethics is not an option – it is a fundamental feature of all good research.

Ethics and Internet research

Internet-based research involves the same principles of research ethics as all other research but it brings with it some issues that warrant particular attention. A considerable amount of attention has been paid to the new kinds of challenge faced by Internet research in terms of things like informed consent, privacy and deception, confidentiality and legislation (see for example Bruckman, 2002; Buchanan, 2004).

Informed consent

With Internet research the process of gaining informed consent is not necessarily straightforward. Giving the information to would-be participants is relatively easy. An outline of the research can be emailed to them. Alternatively, they can be asked to visit a website where the information is held. Or, again, with bulletin boards and chat rooms the information and consent details can be posted ahead of the time when it is proposed to begin the research.

Confirming that the would-be participant has read the information, and understands it, is rather more difficult. One possibility here that has been used by Internet researchers is to ask for the email, the attachment, the posting or the web page containing the information to be sent back to the researcher as a way of confirming that it has been read and understood, and that there is agreement to participation. If sent back from email or a web page, the form could contain a tick box (yes/no) that allows the would-be participants to confirm their willingness to take part – a kind of proxy signature that, though it is not as good as a formal signature, at least signals agreement to take part in a project whose details have been made available. Alternatively, those who have been contacted could be asked to print off a copy of the downloaded form, sign it and return it to the researcher through the ordinary post. This provides a more robust kind of informed consent, but takes more effort on the part of the would-be participant and might well have the effect of deterring them from agreeing to participate.

Special care needs to be taken in the case of research that, intentionally or otherwise, includes children and young people. Permission from parents or someone with equivalent parental authority is needed according to most codes of conduct for research and this applies just as much to Internet research as it does to conventional data collection methods. Although it is difficult to be certain about the age of contacts on the Internet, researchers are still expected to:

- use their best endeavours to identify any respondents who might be aged under 16;
- where appropriate, seek parental permission (or its equivalent) on behalf of such young people;
- abide by relevant national laws relating to contact with children and young people.

Privacy and deception

Respect for the privacy of participants is becoming an increasingly significant issue. In the context of Internet research this concern arises frequently through the way such research offers the opportunity to conduct covert observations. It allows researchers to observe events secretly by hiding in the background and not declaring their presence. It enables them to enter chat rooms and observe proceedings by 'lurking' rather than joining in. Researchers can read postings to bulletin boards, again observing proceedings without disturbing the natural course of events. The question is, does this involve a form of *deception*? Should the Internet researcher be morally obliged to declare their presence and state openly the purpose for observing events? There is a position on research ethics that would say 'yes'. Others, however, would argue that the information provided through these channels has been made open and public by those who supplied it, arguably removing any need on the part of the researcher to disclose the existence of the research activity or to try to get consent from those who are to become the objects of study. On the understanding that such information is 'public', some Internet researchers (e.g. Denzin, 1999) have chosen to proceed without being open about who they are and what they are doing. Under specific circumstances they argue that it is not necessary to get permission to use the postings as data for research. Any researcher contemplating such Internet research needs to be aware of the alternative views and should explicitly state their considered position on this issue.

As with any research, there can be situations where researchers argue that some degree of deception is unavoidable; when it is *not expedient* to disclose research activity because to do so would be to jeopardize the research aims. A good illustration of this is provided by Glaser *et al.* (2002), who collected data from chat rooms associated with white racist groups. They wanted to find out what kind of events or circumstances triggered such people into advocating physical violence against ethnic groups, and covertly conducted semi-structured interviews with 38 participants through these chat rooms. The sensitivity of the issue meant that they did not seek informed consent. They argued that racists appear to 'express their views rather freely [on the Internet], at least when they are interacting with those they perceive to be like-minded' (p. 181) and that revealing the researchers' identity and purpose would have been likely to deter such openness. In this specific case, under these special circumstances, they were able to gain the approval of the relevant ethics committee (at Yale University) on the grounds that:

- the respondents' statements were made in a public forum under conditions that were entirely normal for the chat room and so were naturally occurring data;
- the deception was absolutely necessary in order for the research to be undertaken;
- respondents' identities were carefully protected.

Confidentiality

It is difficult, arguably impossible, for researchers using the Internet to *guarantee* that respondents' contributions will be private and will not be traced back to them. Despite the efforts of individuals and organizations to protect the anonymity of sources of Internet communications, and despite the potential of encryption, the reality is that governments and security agencies have the power and the ability to trace just about any kind of Internet communication should they wish to do so (O'Dochartaigh, 2002; Stanton and Rogelberg, 2001). Researchers, therefore, should be wary about making promises they are not in a position to keep, and should word statements about the confidentiality of data supplied via the Internet in a way that acknowledges the point, yet also reassures the respondent that all reasonable precautions will be taken to avoid the disclosure of identities.

Coomber's (1997) research highlighted the issue of confidentiality in relation to research with drug dealers. The concern was that anyone responding to the request for information might be traced through the communication and open themselves to criminal investigation. Not only this, the researcher could also become embroiled – possibly being required by law to hand over to the police the email addresses of those who had contributed to the survey. As Coomber points out, there are some ingenious ways in which the origins of responses can be hidden from view, and it is in the interests of both respondents and researcher when investigating illicit activities to ensure that the data collection procedures do what is reasonable to protect the identities of respondents. Ultimately, though, there remains the possibility that communications can be traced to their senders if authorities consider it sufficiently important to do so.

Legislation

There are laws that need to be observed. These vary from country to country and are evolving to meet the repercussions of the spread of the Internet. Mann and Stewart (2000) suggest that, in the face of this uncertainty, researchers are best advised to make a clear statement to participants about which country's legal jurisdiction is being applied as far as the research is concerned – normally the country in which the researcher is based. Complications arise when researchers wish to base their research in more than one country – for example, with collaboration between universities in the UK, Russia and the USA. Such complications are fairly unlikely to trouble the small-scale research project. Broadly, though, there are three aspects of legislation that are likely to affect Internet research and that need to be reflected in the researcher's use of the Internet for data collection.

- *Data protection*: the data should be collected, stored and used in accord with relevant data protection legislation (see above).
- *Copyright*: downloading text and images is simple, but the *use* of text and images needs to be in accord with copyright conventions and legislation concerned with things like trademarks and intellectual property rights.
- *Sensitive Issues*: researchers hold no special position in the eyes of the law and need to exercise particular caution when investigating topics that are politically sensitive or that involve things like pornography or terrorism.

9

Questionnaires

What is a questionnaire? • When is it appropriate to use a questionnaire for research? • What kinds of data are collected by questionnaires? • Planning the use of questionnaires • Checklist for planning the use of a questionnaire • Routine essentials for questionnaire design • Internet questionnaires • The length of the questionnaire • Constructing the questions • Types of questions • Evaluating questionnaires • Advantages of questionnaires • Disadvantages of questionnaires • Checklist for the production of a questionnaire

What is a questionnaire?

There are many types of questionnaires. They can vary enormously in terms of their purpose, their size and their appearance. To qualify as a research questionnaire, however, they should:

- *Be designed to collect information which can be used subsequently as data for analysis.* As a research tool, questionnaires do not set out to change people's attitudes or provide them with information. Though questionnaires are sometimes used for this purpose – for instance, as a way of marketing a product – it is not strictly in keeping with the spirit of a *research* questionnaire, whose purpose is to discover things.
- *Consist of a written list of questions.* The important point here is that each person who answers the particular questionnaire reads an identical set of questions. This allows for consistency and precision in terms of the wording of the questions, and makes the processing of the answers easier. (Occasionally, pictures might be used instead of written questions.)

- *Gather information by asking people directly* about the points concerned with the research. Questionnaires work on the premise that if you want to find out something about people and their attitudes you simply go and ask them what it is you want to know, and get the information 'straight from the horse's mouth'.

There is an assumption in this chapter that the kinds of research questionnaire being considered are the postal type and the Internet type – not the face-to-face clipboard questionnaire that involves more personal, interactional factors. If a clipboard-style questionnaire is being considered, the effect of such interactional factors must be considered in addition to many of the points related here.

When is it appropriate to use a questionnaire for research?

Different methods are better suited to different circumstances, and questionnaires are no exception. Although they can be used, perhaps ingeniously, across a wide spectrum of research situations, questionnaires (both postal and Internet) are at their most productive:

- when used with *large numbers* of respondents in many locations;
- when what is required tends to be fairly *straightforward information* – relatively brief and uncontroversial;
- when the *social climate is open* enough to allow full and honest answers;
- when there is a need for *standardized data* from identical questions – without requiring personal, face-to-face interaction;
- when the respondents can be expected to be *able to read and understand the questions* – the implications of age, intellect and eyesight need to be considered.

In relation to postal questionnaires there are two further points. They are best used:

- when *time allows for delays* caused by production, piloting, posting and procrastination before receipt of a response;
- when *resources allow for the costs* of printing, postage and data preparation.

What kinds of data are collected by questionnaires?

Questionnaires rely on written information supplied directly by people in response to questions asked by the researcher. In this respect, the kind of data is distinct from that which could be obtained from interviews, observation or documents. The information from questionnaires tends to fall into two broad categories – 'facts' and 'opinions' – and it is vital that at all stages of using questionnaires the researcher is clear about whether the information being sought is to do with facts or to do with opinions.

Factual information does not require much in the way of judgement or personal attitudes on the part of respondents. It just requires respondents to reveal straightforward information (such as their address, age, sex, marital status or number of children). An example of a 'fact' question might be 'Which TV programmes did you watch last night?'

Opinions, attitudes, views, beliefs, preferences, etc. can also be investigated using questionnaires. In this case, though, respondents are required to reveal information about feelings, to express values and to weigh up alternatives in a way that calls for a judgement about things rather than the mere reporting of facts. An example of an 'opinion' question might be 'Which is your favourite TV programme?'

It is worth stressing that, in practice, questionnaires are very likely to include questions about both facts and opinions. Political opinion polls, for instance, might include factual questions about how people actually voted at the last election as well as questions about feelings of support for particular political parties' policies, and market researchers might want to know factual information about the age, social class, sex, etc. of the people whose opinions, attitudes and preferences they are investigating.

Planning the use of questionnaires

Questionnaires tend to be 'one-offs'. In general, researchers do not have the time or resources to repeat pieces of research which involve the use of questionnaires; nor do they have the opportunity to make amendments and corrections to the questionnaire once it has been printed and distributed. And the vast majority of respondents are likely to be less than sympathetic to a plea from the researcher to fill in the questionnaire a second time in order to overcome a mistake in the first version. There is, therefore, a lot of pressure to *get it right first time*.

Bearing this in mind, the successful use of questionnaires depends on devoting the right balance of effort to the planning stage, rather than rushing too early into distributing the questionnaire. If the questionnaire is to produce worthwhile results, the researcher needs to have a clear plan of action in mind and some reasonable idea of the costs and timescale involved in the venture.

Link up with **Surveys, Chapter 1**

Planning, right from the start, involves the researcher in consideration of the following points:

Costs

What are the likely costs of producing, distributing, collecting and analysing the results of the questionnaire? Production might entail printing costs. There might be postal charges and the need for envelopes (increased by the need to follow up non-respondents). Will the costs include supplying a stamped addressed envelope? Is there the intention to use a computer to analyse the results and, if so, what costs might emerge in terms of the necessary software, web hosting services and data preparation? The shrewd researcher works out the resource implications before embarking on the use of questionnaires.

Production

The production of a well designed questionnaire can take time. First, there is the lead-in time of developing the suitable questions and piloting the questionnaire. Second, if using a large postal survey, there can be time delays arising from the printing and production stage.

Organization

The process for distribution, collection and analysis of results from question-naires demands an eye on organization. A fundamental skill of good research is tight organization, and nowhere is this needed more than in the use of a questionnaire survey. From the outset the researcher must keep a record of how many questionnaires are sent out, to whom they are sent and when they were sent. Unless the questionnaire is anonymous, responses can then be checked off against the mailing list and an accurate follow-up survey of non-respondents undertaken at an appropriate time. Obviously, a filing system of some sort is vital.

Schedule

Questionnaires, especially when used as part of a broad postal survey, do not supply instant results. The researcher, therefore, needs to consider what *timescale* is likely to be involved before the results from the questionnaire are available for analysis. The timescale for the research, it should be stressed, involves all the time spent in the production, distribution and collection of the questionnaires. It is not just the time between sending out the questionnaires and receiving the completed returns; the planning should involve the whole period between the conception of the research and the receipt of data. The researcher needs to be aware of this and plan accordingly.

Permission

Depending on the nature of the questionnaire and the people to whom it is being sent, there may be the need to gain permission from those in authority to conduct the survey. For example, if a questionnaire is being contemplated for use with young people and it is intended to distribute the questionnaires by hand at schools or youth clubs, staff and the local authorities are likely to want to give approval before allowing the survey to proceed using their facilities. The researcher needs to be cautious on this score. It is dangerous to short-circuit proper channels of authority. However, gaining permission from appropriate authorities can take time and this consideration needs to be built into the schedule.

Checklist for planning the use of a questionnaire

When using a questionnaire you should feel confident about answering 'yes' to the following questions: ☑

1 Has time been scheduled for:
- The planning stage itself? ☐
- The design of an initial draft? ☐
- The production of an initial draft? ☐
- The piloting of this initial draft? ☐
- The design of a subsequent draft? ☐
- The production of the subsequent draft? ☐
- Turnaround time: time for respondents to complete and return the questionnaire? ☐
- Time to pursue non-respondents; the 'follow-up' to boost response rates? ☐
- The analysis of the results? ☐

2 With postal questionnaires, has allowance been made for:
- Packing, posting and distribution the final version? ☐
- The collection and checking of questionnaires? ☐

3 Have resources been allocated for all the costs involved in production and distribution of the questionnaire? ☐

4 Has access been granted from:
- Appropriate authorities? ☐
- Respondents (if appropriate)? ☐

© M. Denscombe, *The Good Research Guide*. Open University Press.

Routine essentials for questionnaire design

Designing a good questionnaire involves attention to certain routine matters, quite separate from the more creative and taxing aspects, such as constructing the questions themselves (see below). However, such routine matters are absolutely vital.

Background information about the questionnaire

From both an ethical and a practical point of view, the researcher needs to provide sufficient background information about the research and the questionnaire. Each questionnaire should have some information about:

- *The sponsor*. Under whose auspices is the research being undertaken? Is it individual research or does the research emanate from an institution? Headed notepaper is an obvious way to indicate the nature of the institution from which the questionnaire comes.
- *The purpose*. What is the questionnaire for, and how will the information be used? It is important here to reveal sufficient information to explain the purpose of the research without going too far and 'leading' the respondent into a line of answering. A brief paragraph should suffice.
- *Return address and date*. It is vital that the questionnaire contains in it somewhere quite visibly the name and contact address (postal or email) of the person(s) to whom the completed questionnaire is to be returned and the date by which it is required.
- *Confidentiality*. Assuming that the research is operating according to the normal code of ethics for social researchers, the information collected will not be made publicly available. Respondents should be reassured on this point.
- *Voluntary responses*. In the vast majority of cases, researchers collect information from respondents who volunteer to co-operate with the research. Rewards are not generally used (though in market research there may be some enticements offered), and people are not usually obliged to respond. Again, this point should be acknowledged on the cover page and respondents reassured that the questionnaire is to be completed voluntarily.
- *Thanks*. It follows from the fact that questionnaires are normally voluntarily completed that the researcher is beholden to those who co-operated. Courtesy suggests that some word of thanks from the researcher should appear either on the front cover or right at the end of the questionnaire.

Instructions to the respondent

It is very important that respondents are instructed on how to go about answering the questions. It is no good assuming that it is self-evident; experience will soon prove that wrong. Mistakes that occur can invalidate a whole questionnaire, so it is worth being meticulously careful in giving instructions on how to complete the answers.

- *Example*. It is useful to present an example at the start of the questionnaire. This can set the respondent's mind at rest and indicate exactly what is expected of him or her.
- *Instructions*. Specific instructions should be given for each question where the style of question varies throughout the questionnaire (e.g. put a tick in the appropriate box, circle the relevant number, delete as appropriate).

The allocation of serial numbers

With web-based questionnaires, the serial numbers are added automatically. Other forms of questionnaire might need serial numbers to be added manually. In this case, each questionnaire should be numbered so that it can be distinguished from others and located if necessary. The serial number can be used to identify the date of distribution, the place and possibly the person. But note: if the questionnaires are anonymous, such serial numbers should only allow general factors such as the date and location to be identified – not the identity of any individual person.

Internet questionnaires

Using the Internet, questionnaires can be delivered in one of three main ways. With each of these the basic principles of planning and good design remain much the same as they do for questionnaires in general.

An email questionnaire includes the questions as part of the email itself. Such questionnaires have the virtue of being simple to construct and easy to answer. The respondent only needs to complete the answers and then use the reply button to send back the questionnaire. The disadvantages are that (a) the questionnaire may not be completed properly and (b) the design of the questionnaire is necessarily rather 'basic'. For technical reasons an email questionnaire cannot be made to look very attractive, since there are limitations on the design features that can be incorporated (e.g. no buttons, restricted layout).

A questionnaire sent as an attachment to an email offers much more by way of design features. Using word processing or spreadsheet software it is simple to produce and can be made quite attractive. The disadvantage, however, is that the reply is not as easily executed as it is with the email questionnaire. The respondent needs to open, complete and save an attachment and then reattach it to the email reply.

A web-based questionnaire is designed as a web page and located on a host site where visitors to the site can access it. This has two advantages. First, the design can take advantage of all the usual web page features that people find attractive (buttons, icons, frames). The questionnaire can be colourful and attractive and can incorporate graphics. Respondents can select from a predefined range of answers and simply 'submit' the completed form at one keystroke. The researcher can get answers via tick boxes and text-entry boxes. Second, the responses can be read automatically into a spreadsheet or database, which has the twin benefits of speed and accuracy in terms of data collection. The disadvantages of this approach are that it requires rather more by way of technical skill and access to web hosting resources than the other types do, and that it relies on people coming to the website. This latter problem can be addressed by emailing people telling them about the survey and including in the email a hypertext link to the website so that all the respondent needs to do is double click on the link in order to go to the website and open the questionnaire.

Link up with **Internet surveys, pp. 9–10**

The length of the questionnaire

There is no hard and fast rule about the number of questions that can be included in a questionnaire. This will depend on factors like the topic under investigation, how complex the questions are, the nature of the respondents who have been targeted and the time it takes to complete the questionnaire. Decisions about the size of a questionnaire are ultimately a matter of judgement on the part of the researcher, who needs to gauge how many questions can be included before the respondent is likely to run out of patience and consign the questionnaire to the waste paper bin.

> **Key point**
> It is worth remembering that there is, perhaps, no more effective deterrent to answering a questionnaire than its sheer size.

In most cases, researchers do not get a second chance to follow up issues they might have missed in the initial questionnaire. Conscious of this 'one-shot' constraint, there may be the temptation to ask about everything that might possibly be of relevance. It is, after all, vital to cover all key matters if the questionnaire is to supply data which permit a reasonable analysis by the researcher. But the shrewd researcher realizes that it is counter-productive to include everything that might *feasibly* have some relevance to the research issues. Every effort should be made to keep the questionnaire as brief as possible by restricting the scope of the questions to crucial issues related to the research, and avoiding any superfluous detail or non-essential topics.

When designing a questionnaire, then, the researcher has to walk a tightrope between ensuring coverage of all the vital issues and ensuring the questionnaire is brief enough to encourage people to bother answering it.

To accomplish this balancing act there are certain rules to bear in mind.

- *Only ask those questions which are absolutely vital for the research.* The better the research is planned, the easier it will be to identify the absolutely crucial questions and discard the 'just in case I need this information later' questions.
- *Be rigorous in weeding out any duplication of questions.* For example, if a questionnaire contains as separate questions, 'What is your date of birth?' and 'How old are you?' we need to ask just how vital it is that both are included. A moment's reflection might lead the researcher to the conclusion that one or other will supply adequate information for the particular purposes of the investigation – or that one can be deduced from the other.
- *Make the task of responding to the questionnaire as straightforward and speedy as possible.*
- *Pilot the questionnaire to see how long it takes to answer* and then consider whether it is reasonable to expect the specific target group to spare this amount of time supplying the answers.

Constructing the questions

Identifying the key issues

A questionnaire needs to be crisp and concise, asking just those questions which are crucial to the research. This means that the researcher must have a clear vision of exactly what issues are at the heart of the research and what kind of information would enlighten those issues. *There is little room for vagueness or imprecision.*

> **Key point**
> The wording of the questions is one of the most difficult features of
> questionnaire design. It is also one of the most important to get right.

Before focusing on the exact wording and structure of the questions, the researcher needs to consider a few broader points that will influence the style and direction of the questions. First of all, the researcher needs to consider whether the information being sought from the respondent is amenable to direct questions, or whether it will need to be measured by indirect means. This has a bearing on the matter of the 'validity' of the questionnaire. Yet again, the importance of the researcher having a clear conception of the issues under examination becomes evident. Where the information being sought is of an overt, factual nature, there is not normally a problem on this point. The questions will take the form of 'How many times . . .? or 'When did you last . . .? However, questionnaires are frequently geared to less straightforward matters, where a direct question would be inappropriate. If, for example, the researcher wishes to know what social class the respondent comes from, it would not be wise to ask the straightforward question, 'What is your social class?' Apart from the fact that some people might find this offensive, the term social class has different meanings for different people, and the question will produce inconsistent answers. In this case, the researcher needs to pinpoint exactly what he or she defines as social class and then devise questions that will supply the type of information which will allow the respondent's social class to be deduced. For this purpose, indirect questions will be used about occupation, income, education, etc.

The wording of the questions

The researcher needs to be confident that:

- *The questions will not be irritating* or annoying for the respondents to answer. The success of the questionnaire depends on the willingness of the respondents to supply the answer voluntarily.
- *The respondents will have some information,* knowledge, experience or opinions on the topic questions. It is no good designing perfect questions where the responses are likely to be a series of 'don't knows' or 'not applicable'.
- *The proposed style of questions is suited to the target group.* Questions geared to 14-year-olds will need to be different in terms of conceptual complexity and wording from ones aimed at, for example, members of a professional association.
- *The questions require respondents to answer only about themselves* or matters of fact they can realistically answer for others. It is not good practice, generally speaking, to ask respondents to answer for other people. For example, it would be inappropriate to ask a parent to say which TV programmes were their children's favourite. The parent's perception might differ from the children's and, in any case, each child is likely to prefer something different. If we really wish to know the children's favourite TV programme we should devise a questionnaire that the children will answer.
- *The questions are on a topic and of a kind which the respondents will be willing to answer.* This point applies, in particular, where questions are on highly personal matters or moral/legal indiscretions.

There are some specific things the researcher needs to bear in mind when devising the questions:

- *Avoid the use of 'leading' questions.* These are questions which suggest an answer or which prompt the respondent to give a particular kind of answer (e.g. Would you agree that there should be controls on the emission of carbon dioxide from cars?).

- *Avoid asking the same question twice in a different fashion.*
- *Make sure the wording is completely unambiguous.*
- *Avoid vague questions.* The more specific and concrete the question, the easier it is to give a precise answer. And, in all probability, the answer will prove to be of more value to the researcher.
- *Be sure to include sufficient options in the answer.* If the list might prove too long, selecting the main possibilities and then tagging on the 'Other (please specify)' option is a good strategy.
- *Use only the minimum amount of technical jargon.* In terms of a questionnaire, the aim is not to see how clever people are.
- *Keep the questions as short and straightforward as possible.* This will avoid unnecessary confusion and wasted time re-reading questions or trying to decipher the meaning of the question.
- *Include only those questions which are absolutely vital for the research.*
- *Pay attention to the way the questions are numbered.* Obviously they should be sequential, but there are clever ways of using sub-questions (e.g. 4a, 4b and so on) which can help the respondent to map his or her way through the series of questions.
- *Don't make unwarranted presumptions in the questions.* It can be annoying to the respondent who does not match the presumption. For example, questions about people's reading habits should not start with something like 'How many novels have you read in the past 12 months?' This presumes that all respondents read novels. It would be better to ask first (1) 'Do you read novels?', and if the answer is yes, follow this up with a supplementary question: (1a) 'How many novels have you read in the past 12 months?'
- *Avoid words or phrases which might cause offence.* If, for example, the questionnaire involves ethnic minority issues, it is important to use the 'politically correct' terms.

The order of the questions

The ordering of the questions in a questionnaire is important for three reasons. First and foremost, questions asked at an earlier point in the questionnaire can affect the answers supplied at a later stage. This is evident in many commercial 'marketing/sales questionnaires', where there is a conscious attempt to make use of this feature of questionnaires.

The second way in which the ordering of questions can be important is that it can entice or deter the respondent from continuing with the exercise of providing answers. If the respondent is immediately faced with the most complex of the questions at the start of the questionnaire, this might deter him or her from going any further. However, if the questionnaire starts with straightforward questions and then gradually moves towards such questions at a later stage, there is a greater likelihood that the respondent will persevere. This same point is true for those questions which might be perceived as more personal and on sensitive issues. There will be a greater chance of success if such questions appear later in the questionnaire than if they appear right at the start.

Key points on the order of the questions

In a nutshell, the researcher should be sure that:

- the most straightforward questions come at the start;
- the least contentious questions and least sensitive issues are dealt with at the beginning of the questionnaire;
- the sequence of questions does not lead the respondents towards 'inevitable' answers, where the answers to later questions are effectively predicated on the answers to earlier ones.

Types of questions

There are a variety of ways in which questions can be put in a questionnaire. These are outlined below. However, from the outset it is worth giving some thought to whether the overall questionnaire will benefit from using a variety of kinds of questions, or whether it is better to aim for a consistent style throughout. Variety has two potential advantages. First, it stops the respondent becoming bored. Second, it stops the respondent falling into a 'pattern' of answers where, for example, on a scale of 1 to 5 he or she begins to put 4 down as the answer to all questions. Aiming for a consistent style of question, for its part, has the advantage of allowing the respondent to get used to the kind of questions so that they can be answered quickly and with less likelihood of confusion or misunderstanding. There is no hard and fast rule on this point: it is down to a judgement call on the part of the researcher.

'Open' and 'closed' questions

Open questions are those that leave the respondent to decide the wording of the answer, the length of the answer and the kind of matters to be raised in the answer. The questions tend to be short and the answers tend to be long. For example, the questionnaire might ask, 'How do you feel about the inclusion of nuclear arms as part of Britain's defence capability?' and then provide a number of empty lines which invite the respondent to enter his or her thoughts on the matter.

The advantage of 'open' questions is that the information gathered by way of the responses is more likely to reflect the full richness and complexity of the views held by the respondent. Respondents are allowed space to express themselves in their own words. Weighed against this, however, there are two disadvantages which are built into the use of open questions. First, they demand more effort on the part of the respondents (which might well reduce their willingness to take part in the research). Second, they leave the researcher with data which are quite 'raw' and require a lot of time-consuming analysis before they can be used.

Closed questions structure the answers by allowing only answers which fit into categories that have been established in advance by the researcher. The researcher, in this case, instructs the respondent to answer by selecting from a range of two or more options supplied on the questionnaire. The options can be restricted to as few as two (e.g. 'Yes' or 'No'; 'Male' or 'Female') or can include quite complex lists of alternatives from which the respondent can choose.

The advantages and disadvantages of the 'closed' question are more or less a mirror image of those connected with the open, unstructured approach. In a nutshell, the main advantage is that the structure imposed on the respondents' answers provides the researcher with information which is of uniform length and in a form that lends itself nicely to being quantified and compared. The answers, in fact, provide pre-coded data that can be easily analysed. Weighed against this, there are two disadvantages. First, there is less scope for respondents to supply answers which reflect the exact facts or true feelings on a topic if the facts or opinions happen to be complicated or do not exactly fit into the range of options supplied in the questionnaire. The closed question allows for less subtlety in the answers. Second, and largely as a result of the first disadvantage, the respondents might get frustrated by not being allowed to express their views fully in a way that accounts for any sophistication, intricacy or even inconsistencies in their views.

 Caution

Closed questions, in general, lend themselves to the production of quantitative data. However, it is very important for the researcher to be clear *at the design stage* about which particular kind(s) of quantitative data will be collected (nominal, ordinal, etc.) and what specific statistical procedures will be used. Unless the researcher thinks ahead on this point there is a very real danger that the data collected will turn out to be inappropriate for the kind of analysis that the researcher eventually wants to undertake.

Link up with **Analysis of quantitative data, Chapter 13**

Nine types of question that can be used in a questionnaire

1 A statement

Example:
What do you think about the UK's membership of the European Union?

_____

_____

_____

2 A list

Example:
Please list the issues you feel are most important in relation to the UK's membership of the European Union:

_____

_____

_____

3 A 'yes/no' answer

Example:
Have you travelled from the UK to another European country in the past 12 months?   Yes/No

4 Agree/disagree with a statement

Example:
Would you agree or disagree with the following statement?
European unity carries economic advantages which outweigh the political disadvantages.   Agree/Disagree

5 Choose from a list of options

Example:
Which ONE of the following list of European countries do you feel has the strongest economy?

Spain	UK	Belgium	Netherlands
Ireland	France	Germany	Italy

6 Rank order

Example:
From the following list of European countries choose the THREE which you feel have the strongest economies and put them in rank order: 1 = strongest, 2 = second strongest, 3 = third strongest.

Spain	UK	Belgium	Netherlands
Ireland	France	Germany	Italy

7 Degree of agreement and disagreement: *the Likert Scale*

Example:

Membership of the European Union is a good thing for the UK.

Strongly agree	Agree	Neutral	Disagree	Strongly disagree

8 Rate items

Example:

How significant would you rate the following factors in affecting further European integration?

	Not significant						Very significant
political sovereignty	1	2	3	4	5	6	7
national identities	1	2	3	4	5	6	7
past history	1	2	3	4	5	6	7
religious differences	1	2	3	4	5	6	7
language barriers	1	2	3	4	5	6	7

9 Feelings about a topic: *the semantic differential*

Example:

European unity is:

Boring	1	2	3	4	5	Interesting
Unlikely	1	2	3	4	5	Likely
Risky	1	2	3	4	5	Safe
Important	1	2	3	4	5	Unimportant
Difficult	1	2	3	4	5	Easy

Evaluating questionnaires

There are four basic criteria for evaluating a research questionnaire. The first of these concerns an assessment of the likelihood that the questionnaire will provide *full information* on the particular topic(s) of research. The value of the questionnaire will depend in no small measure on the extent to which it includes coverage of all *vital* information pertaining to the area of research.

The second criterion concerns the likelihood that the questionnaire will provide *accurate information*. What confidence do we have that the responses on the questionnaires are as full and honest as they can be – free from mischievous attempts to scupper the research, errors arising through ambiguous questions, etc.?

Third, the questionnaire can be evaluated according to its likelihood of achieving a decent *response rate*. In order to get a representative picture, the questionnaire needs to avoid 'turning people off' by being poorly presented, taking too long to complete, asking insensitive questions, etc.

Fourth, the questionnaire needs to adopt an *ethical stance*, in which recognition is given to the respondents' rights to have the information they supply treated according to strict professional standards. Apart from legal requirements associated with data protection when personal information is stored on computer, there is some moral obligation on the researcher to protect the interests of those who supply information and to give them sufficient information about the nature of the research so that they can make an informed judgement about whether they wish to co-operate with the research.

 Caution

When it comes to the use of questionnaires there is no 'golden formula' that can guarantee success and protect the researcher from any possible criticism. Almost inevitably the researcher will need to apply discretion, make trade-offs and exercise judgement when producing and implementing a questionnaire. However, the guidelines in this chapter provide signposts for good practice that, if followed, should minimize the prospect of 'getting it badly wrong'.

Advantages of questionnaires

- *Questionnaires are economical*, in the sense that they can supply a considerable amount of research data for a relatively low cost in terms of materials, money and time.
- *Easier to arrange*. Questionnaires are easier to arrange than, for example, personal interviews. There is no need to 'arrange' it at all, in fact, since the questionnaire may be simply sent unannounced to the respondent. (Some researchers, though, have sought to improve the response rate by contacting respondents before they send a questionnaire to them. This contact can be by phone, email or letter.)
- *Questionnaires supply standardized answers*, to the extent that all respondents are posed with exactly the same questions – with no scope for variation to slip in via face-to-face contact with the researcher. The data collected, then, are very unlikely to be contaminated through variations in the wording of the questions or the manner in which the question is asked. There is little scope for the data to be affected by '*interpersonal factors*'.

- *Pre-coded answers.* A further, and important, advantage of the questionnaire is that it encourages pre-coded answers. As we have seen, this is not an essential facet of questionnaires, because unstructured answers can be sought. However, particularly with questionnaires, the value of the data is likely to be greatest where respondents provide answers that fit into a range of options offered by the researcher. These allow for the speedy collation and analysis of data by the researcher. They also have an advantage for the respondents, who, instead of needing to think of how to express their ideas, are faced with the relatively easy task of needing to pick one or more answers which are spelt out for them.
- *Data accuracy.* Surveys using the Internet can be designed so that the data contained in the completed questionnaires can be fed straight into a data file, thus automating the process of data entry. This effectively eliminates the human error factor that inevitably arises when people need to read the responses to a paper questionnaire and then enter the data manually via the computer keyboard. More advanced design techniques can ensure that all sections of the Internet questionnaire get completed, an advantage even when compared with paper questionnaires that are designed to be read automatically via an optical mark reading (OMR) machine.

Disadvantages of questionnaires

In many respects the potential disadvantages of questionnaires go hand in glove with the potential advantages. You can't have one without the other.

- *Pre-coded questions can be frustrating for respondents and, thus, deter them from answering.* The advantage for the researcher of using pre-coded answers set out in the questionnaire carries with it a possible disadvantage. While the respondents might find it less demanding merely to tick appropriate boxes they might, equally, find this *restricting and frustrating.* So, on the one hand, the 'tick box' routine might encourage people to respond but, on the other hand, this same routine might be experienced as negative and put people off co-operating with the research.

Link up with **Response rates, pp. 22–5**

- *Pre-coded questions can bias the findings towards the researcher's, rather than the respondent's, way of seeing things.* Questionnaires, by their very nature, can start to impose a structure on the answers and shape the nature of the responses in a way that reflects the researcher's thinking rather than the respondent's. Good research practice will minimize the prospect of this, but there is always the danger that the options open to the respondent when answering the questions will channel responses away from the respondent's perception of matters to fit in with a line of thinking established by the researcher.

- *Questionnaires offer little opportunity for the researcher to check the truthfulness of the answers given by the respondents.* Because the researcher does not meet the respondent and because the answers are given 'at a distance', the researcher cannot rely on a number of clues that an interviewer might have about whether the answers are genuine or not. The interviewer might see some incongruity between answers given by the same interviewee and be able to probe the matter. Or the interviewer might note a disparity between a given answer and some other factor (e.g. stated occupation and apparent level of income). In the case of the questionnaire, however, if a respondent states their occupation to be a 'dentist', it would seem at first glance that the researcher has little option but to accept this as true. Likewise, on matters of taste or opinion, if the respondent answers along a particular line, the questionnaire researcher would seem to have no solid grounds for challenging the answer. This is all the more true if the questionnaires are anonymous.

Key point: advantages and disadvantages of questionnaires	
Advantages	**Disadvantages**
• Wide coverage.	• Poor response rate.
• Cheap.	• Incomplete or poorly completed
• Pre-coded data.	answers.
• Eliminate effect of	• Limit and shape nature of
personal interaction with	answers.
researcher.	• Cannot check truth of answers.

Checklist for the production of a questionnaire

When producing a questionnaire for research you should feel confident about answering 'yes' to the following questions: ☑

1 Has the questionnaire been piloted? ☐

2 Is the layout clear? ☐

3 Is there an explanation of the purpose of the questionnaire? ☐

4 Is there a contact address on the questionnaire? ☐

5 Have thanks been expressed to the respondents? ☐

6 Are there assurances about confidentiality of information or anonymity? ☐

7 Have serial numbers been given to the questionnaires? ☐

8 Are there clear and explicit instructions on how the questions are to be completed? ☐

9 Have the questions been checked to avoid any duplication? ☐

10 Are the questions clear and unambiguous? ☐

11 Are the essential questions included? ☐

12 Are the non-essential questions excluded? ☐

13 Are the questions in the right order? ☐

14 Has the questionnaire been checked for spelling and typographical errors? ☐

© M. Denscombe, *The Good Research Guide*. Open University Press.

10

Interviews

What is an interview? • When is it appropriate to use interviews for research? • Types of research interview • Focus groups • The interviewer effect • Internet interviews and online focus groups • Planning and preparation for face-to-face interviews • Interview skills • Conducting the interview • Recording the interview • Transcribing audio recordings of interviews • Representing data: the use of interview extracts in research reports • The validity of interview data: how do you know the informant is telling the truth? • Advantages of interviews • Disadvantages of interviews • Checklist for the use of interviews

What is an interview?

Interviews are an attractive proposition for project researchers. At first glance, they do not seem to involve much technical paraphernalia and they draw on a skill that researchers already have – the ability to conduct a conversation. The reality, though, is not quite so simple. Although there are a lot of superficial similarities between a conversation and an interview, interviews are actually something more than just a conversation. Interviews involve a set of assumptions and understandings about the situation which are not normally associated with a casual conversation (Denscombe, 1983; Silverman, 1985). When someone agrees to take part in a research interview:

- *There is consent to take part.* From the researcher's point of view this is particularly important in relation to research ethics. The interview is not done by secret recording of discussions or the use of casual conversations as research data. It is openly a meeting intended to produce material that will be used for research purposes – and the interviewee understands this and agrees to it.

- *Interviewees' words can be treated as 'on the record' and 'for the record'.* It is, of course, possible for interviewees to stipulate that their words are *not* to be attributed to them, or *not* to be made publicly available. The point is, though, that unless interviewees specify to the contrary, the interview talk is 'on record' and 'for the record'.
- *The agenda for the discussion is set by the researcher.* Although the degree of control exercised by the researcher will vary according to the style of interviewing, there is a tacit agreement built into the notion of being interviewed that the proceedings and the agenda for the discussion will be controlled by the researcher.

 Caution

The superficial similarity between an interview and a conversation can generate an illusion of simplicity. We all have conversations and it is likely that most of us do not have too much difficulty with them. So an interview should be fairly straightforward. As long as we know to whom we are going to talk and what we want to ask, the rest should be plain sailing. Here lies the problem. The researcher can be lulled into a false sense of security. The superficial similarity can encourage a relaxed attitude to the planning, preparation and conduct of the method that would be unlikely were it to involve questionnaires or experiments. In reality, interviewing is no easy option. It is fraught with hidden dangers and can fail miserably unless there is good planning, proper preparation and a sensitivity to the complex nature of interaction during the interview itself.

When is it appropriate to use interviews for research?

Although interviews can be used for the collection of straightforward factual information, their potential as a data collection method is better exploited when they are applied to the exploration of more complex and subtle phenomena. If the researcher wants to collect information on simple and uncontroversial facts, then questionnaires might prove to be a more cost-effective method. But, when the researcher needs to gain insights into things like people's opinions, feelings, emotions and experiences, then interviews will almost certainly provide a more suitable method – a method that is attuned to the intricacy of the subject matter. To be specific, interviews – in particular *in-depth* interviews – lend themselves to the collection of data based on:

- *Opinions, feelings, emotions and experiences*. The nature of these means that they need to be explored in depth and in detail rather than simply reported in a word or two.
- *Sensitive issues*. When the research covers issues that might be considered sensitive or rather personal there is a case to be made for using interviews. Using a careful and considerate approach, participants can be encouraged to discuss personal and sensitive issues in open and honest manner.
- *Privileged information*. Here, the justification for interviews is based on the value of contact with key players in the field who can give privileged information. The depth of information provided by interviews can produce best 'value for money' if the informants are willing and able to give information that others could not – when what they offer is an insight they have as people in a special position 'to know'.

The decision to use interviews for a research project, of course, needs to take account of their feasibility as a data collection method. Before embarking on a programme of interviews the researcher needs to feel assured that:

- *It is possible to gain direct access to the prospective interviewees*. There is obviously no point in pursuing the idea of conducting interviews unless there are good grounds for believing that the necessary people can be accessed, and that some agreement can be obtained from all the parties involved in the research.
- *The interviews are viable in terms of the costs in time and travel involved*. With limited resources, the researcher needs to ensure that the people are not distributed too widely across a large geographical area and that conducting the interviews will not incur prohibitive costs.

Types of research interview

Structured interviews

Structured interviews involve tight control over the format of the questions and answers. In essence, the structured interview is like a questionnaire which is administered face to face with a respondent. The researcher has a predetermined list of questions, to which the respondent is invited to offer limited-option responses. The tight control over the wording of the questions, the order in which the questions occur and the range of answers that are on offer have the advantage of 'standardization'. Each respondent is faced with identical questions. And the range of pre-coded answers on offer to respondents ensures that data analysis is relatively easy. The structured interview, in this respect, lends itself to the collection of quantitative data.

Structured interviews are often associated with social surveys where researchers are trying to collect large volumes of data from a wide range of respondents. Here, we are witnessing the replacement of interviewers armed with clipboards and paper questionnaires with those using laptop computers to input information direct into a suitable software program. Such *computer-assisted personal interviewing* (CAPI) has the advantage of using software with built-in checks to eliminate errors in the collection of data, and it allows quick analysis of the data. However, its relatively large initial costs, caused by the purchase of the laptop computers, the development of suitable software and the training involved, means that CAPI is better suited to large-budget, large-number surveys than to small-scale research.

Link up with **Questionnaires, Chapter 9**

Whether using a laptop computer, telephone or printed schedule of questions, the structured interview, in spirit, bears more resemblance to questionnaire methods than to the other types of interviews. For this reason, *this chapter focuses on semi-structured and unstructured interviews rather than structured interviews.*

Semi-structured interviews

With semi-structured interviews, the interviewer still has a clear list of issues to be addressed and questions to be answered. However, with the semi-structured interview the interviewer is prepared to be flexible in terms of the order in which the topics are considered, and, perhaps more significantly, to let the interviewee develop ideas and speak more widely on the issues raised by the researcher. The answers are open-ended, and there is more emphasis on the interviewee elaborating points of interest.

Unstructured interviews

Unstructured interviews go further in the extent to which emphasis is placed on the interviewee's thoughts. The researcher's role is to be as un-intrusive as possible – to start the ball rolling by introducing a theme or topic and then letting the interviewee develop their ideas and pursue their train of thought.

Semi-structured and unstructured interviews are really on a continuum and, in practice, it is likely that any interview will slide back and forth along the scale. What they have in common, and what separates them from structured interviews, is their willingness to allow interviewees to use their own words and develop their own thoughts. Allowing interviewees to 'speak their minds' is a better way of discovering things about complex issues and, generally, semi-structured and unstructured interviews have as their aim 'discovery' rather then 'checking'.

One-to-one interviews

The most common form of semi-structured or unstructured interview is the one-to-one variety which involves a meeting between one researcher and one informant. One reason for its popularity is that it is relatively easy to arrange. Only two people's diaries need to coincide. Another advantage is that the opinions and views expressed throughout the interview stem from one source: the interviewee. This makes it fairly straightforward for the researcher to locate specific ideas with specific people. A third advantage is that the one-to-one interview is relatively easy to control. The researcher only has one person's ideas to grasp and interrogate, and one person to guide through the interview agenda. And a fourth advantage of conducting one-to-one interviews becomes evident when the researcher embarks on transcribing the interview tape: it is far easier to transcribe a recorded interview when the talk involves just one interviewee. There is only one voice to recognize and only one person talking at a time.

Group interviews

A disadvantage of the one-to-one interview is that it limits the number of views and opinions available to the researcher. Listening to one person at a time effectively restricts the number of voices that can be heard and the range of views that can be included within a research project. Group interviews, however, provide a practical solution to this. By interviewing more than one person at a time the researcher is able to dramatically increase the number and range of participants involved in the research.

A group interview can be undertaken very much like a one-to-one interview in the sense that the interviewer remains the focal point of the interaction that takes place. The questions and answers are channelled through the interviewer. The difference is that instead of each question prompting a response from just one interviewee the researcher can get perhaps four responses from four people during the interview.

Increasing the numbers involved can have benefits in terms of the representativeness of the data. The inclusion of more participants is likely to mean that a broader spectrum of people are covered by the research and that there might be a greater variety of experiences and opinions emerging from the investigation. Indeed, under certain circumstances researchers can deliberately select participants who are very different in order to gather widely differing views and experiences on the topic of the interview.

But, does this really constitute a *group* interview? Where the interviewer remains the focal point of the communication it suggests that the interview is actually conducted with a series of individuals who happen to have been collected together at one time and in one place to suit the convenience of the researcher and his/her wish to boost the number of interviewees in the research. The participants are a group in so far as they are grouped together, but the researcher does not interact with participants as a group – only as individuals.

An alternative vision of the group interview is one that stresses the 'group' characteristics of the interaction during an interview. It sees the group interview as distinctive in the way that it can get the participants to respond as part of a group, rather than as individuals. The researcher's incentive for using a group interview, in this case, is not a quantitative one concerned with increased numbers and improved representativeness. It is, instead, a qualitative one concerned with the way that group discussions can be more illuminating. The group discussion allows participants to listen to alternative points of view. It allows members to express support for certain views and to challenge views with which they disagree. The group interview, in this sense, trades on group dynamics. It uses the social and psychological aspects of group behaviour to foster the ability of participants to get involved, speak their minds and reflect on the views of others.

Focus groups

Focus groups make particular use of group dynamics. They consist of small groups of people who are brought together by a 'moderator' (the researcher) to explore attitudes and perceptions, feelings and ideas about a specific topic. The three distinctive and vital points about focus groups are that:

- there is a *focus* to the session, with the group discussion being based on an item or experience about which all participants have similar knowledge;
- particular emphasis is placed on the *interaction within the group* as a means for eliciting information;
- the moderator's role is to *facilitate* the group interaction.

The focus

The discussion in a focus group is triggered by a 'stimulus'. The stimulus might be some shared experience that the participants bring to the session from their personal background. They might all share an occupation, all suffer a similar illness or, perhaps, all have watched a particular TV series. They will have this much at least in common. Alternatively, the stimulus can be something introduced by the moderator at the beginning of a session. It can take the form of a piece of merchandise, an advertisement or a short video that is shown at the beginning of a session as a way of stimulating discussion. Members are sometimes asked to interpret a particular photograph or to do a ranking exercise. Such kinds of moderator-introduced stimulus have emerged as common practice and are often regarded today as a crucial part of focus group activity.

Whatever the stimulus, however, its role is vital in the sense that it literally *focuses* the discussion by

• providing a topic with which all members of the group are familiar, and
• channelling the discussion onto something specific and concrete.

Group interaction

During a focus group session participants are encouraged to discuss the topic among themselves. This interaction helps the researcher to understand the reasoning behind the views and opinions that are expressed by group members. It provides the researcher with a method of investigating the participants' reasoning and a means for exploring underlying factors that might explain why people hold the opinions and feelings they do. As Morgan (2006: 121) puts it:

> [Focus group members] share their experiences and thoughts, while also comparing their own contributions to what others have said. This process of sharing and comparing is especially useful for hearing and understanding a range of responses on a research topic. The best focus groups thus not only provide data on *what* the participants think but also *why* they think the way they do.

Such sharing and comparing of personally held points of view can lead in either of two directions – both of which can be of value to the researcher. The group discussion can lead to some consensus with members of the group largely agreeing and arriving at some shared viewpoint. For some advocates of the focus group method this is the desired outcome because it presents the researcher with data on some collective opinion about a topic. Alternatively, the group discussion might serve to expose significant differences among group members in which case the researcher is presented with data about a range of opinions and feelings relating to the topic. Either way, the benefit of the discussion and interaction, questioning and reflection, is that it reveals the reasoning and underlying logic used by participants. It thus gives the researcher an insight into not only what people think, but also *why* they hold those views.

The role of the moderator

The moderator is responsible for organizing the focus group session; for selecting the members and arranging the venue at a time and place when all group members can attend. They will take responsibility for:

• creating a comfortable atmosphere for the discussion;
• introducing the stimulus;

- keeping the discussion on track, focused around the topic;
- encouraging participation from all members;
- ensuring there is no abuse or intimidation.

The moderator will also keep field notes relating to the discussion and, for the purposes of research, will make an audio recording of the talk. But the distinguishing feature of the moderator's role – the thing that separates it from that of an interviewer – is that during the session the moderator will encourage participants to talk with one another. Instead of being the focal point of interactions, posing the questions and dictating the sequencing of talk (as an interviewer does), the good moderator wants to stand back and let the group talk among themselves. In principle, the moderator *helps* the group rather than leads it.

> **Key point: when are focus groups particularly useful?**
>
> - **For understanding underlying motives and meanings that explain particular views and opinions;**
> - **For exploring new areas of research where the researcher quickly wants to gain a broad feel for the issues as they are perceived by particular groups of people;**
> - **For gauging the extent to which there is a fair level of agreement and shared views among a group of people in relation to a specific topic. This facet of focus groups has been used for developing questionnaire items;**
> - **For checking whether a particular item or experience evokes disagreement among members of a group or exposes a range of contrasting views. This facet of focus groups has been used for checking hypotheses.**

The size of focus groups

When deciding the size of a focus group there might seem to be good grounds for believing that 'bigger is better'. In principle, larger groups might seem to have advantages in terms of:

- collecting data from a wider cross-section of people (representativeness of the data);
- collecting data from more people from each session (convenience and economy).

Weighed against such potential advantages there are some practical considerations that tend to persuade social researchers to limit the size of their groups.

- Larger numbers are more difficult to schedule. Depending on the kind of people who are participating, it can prove quite a challenge for the researcher to set up a focus group at a place and time that is convenient for all group members. The more members there are the more difficult this becomes.
- Larger groups can become unwieldy and hard to control. The more participants there are the more likely it is that the group will fragment, with splinter groups starting to talk among themselves. The focus group is more likely to lose its focus with multiple groups and multiple discussions breaking out spontaneously.
- Larger groups cost more. Even gathering together a group of six to nine people can prove to be expensive. Market researchers and opinion pollsters who work in a commercial environment will probably have the resources to pay the expenses of focus group members (e.g. travel costs). Small-scale social researchers may not have such resources.
- Larger groups can inhibit contributions from less confident people. There is the danger that some voices will not be heard while more extrovert participants might dominate the discussion.
- Discussions within larger groups are more difficult to record. With increased numbers it becomes ever more difficult to capture the input from all participants and ever more difficult to identify exactly who is speaking at any one time. Transcribing the recording is made still more difficult by the way people interrupt and 'talk-over' one another during discussions.

> *Key point: the size of focus groups*
>
> It is generally recommended that focus groups should consist of between six and nine people. This allows for a fair range of opinions and experiences to be included among the participants. For practical purposes, however, focus groups sometimes consist of fewer than six people. *Mini-focus groups* of three or four people are used quite regularly in small-scale social research.

How long should a focus group last?

Typically, focus groups last about 1½ to 2 hours. They tend to last longer than one-to-one interviews mainly because there are more people involved and more opinions to be aired. Extra time is needed also to allow for the moderator to introduce the stimulus at the start of the session and to allow for any latecomers to join the group.

The selection of group members

There are practical factors affecting the selection of people to join a focus group. In the first instance, potential recruits need to be available: they need to live within reasonable travelling distance, be willing to devote a few hours of their time to help the research, and be able to attend at the time and date of scheduled focus group meetings.

They also need to be people who the researcher knows something about. Given the nature of focus groups, researchers generally use purposive sampling or possibly quota sampling as the basis for recruiting participants and this requires that, rather than choosing people on a random basis, participants are selected on the basis of some personal attribute that is relevant to the purposes of the research. They are selected on the basis of who they are and how this fits in with the topic of the research (for instance, a person who suffers from a particular ailment, a person who uses a particular mode of transport, a person who looks after an elderly relative, or a person who is the mother of young children).

It suits some researchers to select focus group members deliberately to get differences of opinion. Using a quota principle, the group membership can be manipulated to ensure that there is a *divergence* of views and experiences. So, for example, a focus group on the use of cycle lanes in large cities could be arranged to include a quota of cyclists and a quota of motorists on the assumption that cyclists and motorists will have contrasting perspectives on the topic. This use of quotas to set up confrontational discussions within a group, it should be said, is not very common. More normally, the use of quotas is intended simply to ensure that an appropriate range of opinions and experiences gets voiced during the group's discussion on the specific topic, with attention to quotas for specific ages, sex, income, etc. being used.

Other researchers tend to concentrate on the matter of *similarity* when it comes to the selection of participants. They place particular value on the selection of participants who all share some relevant attribute for the research. Where group members are chosen deliberately because they have some common interest or similarity it tends to be easier for the participants to talk openly about issues that they might otherwise feel are taboo or too embarrassing to talk about. Where there is any sensitivity surrounding the topic, the advantages of selecting participants who share relevant circumstances are fairly obvious. Topics such as obesity, impotence, child abuse, sexual harassment and bullying illustrate the point in an extreme way; clearly the researcher would need to pay careful attention to the choice of participants if the session was to stand much chance of having an open and worthwhile discussion.

Sometimes, focus group members will be strangers who have never met before and, as strangers, it might take some time and encouragement from the moderator to get the participants to 'open-up' and speak freely about themselves and their opinions. Other times, they might already know one another. Indeed, a recruitment strategy that is preferred by some researchers is to invite people who are already members of an *existing group*. Not only does this overcome the problem of 'breaking the ice' it has other benefits as well. For one thing, it makes the focus group easier to arrange. It is more straightforward to make contact and arrange a time for the meeting with an existing group who might already have scheduled meetings planned well in advance. Another advantage is that the researcher can tap into a group with a ready-made interest in the area of the investigation. Special interest groups, support groups, clubs, local associations and the like can provide a rich source for focus groups that are tailored to the needs of the research.

Ethics, trust and confidentiality

To enable a full, frank and free-flowing discussion there needs to be a reasonable degree of *trust* operating among members of the focus group. If participants are suspicious, or if they feel threatened, they are less likely to speak during a session. And when they do contribute the chances are that they will be less open and honest about their true feelings and experiences. The success of a focus group, therefore, depends on establishing a climate of trust within the group, and it is a key part of the role of the moderator to foster a situation in which participants feel at ease and sufficiently comfortable in the company of the other group members to express themselves freely.

One ingredient here is *confidentiality*. Group members need to feel assured that if they express a personal feeling or reveal some aspect of their personal life during the discussion that such information will be treated as confidential by the group. What is said by individuals during the focus group session ought to remain private and not get disclosed publicly by other members of the group. This is important because, given the nature of focus group discussions, individuals can sometimes 'open up' about a private, embarrassing or sensitive aspect of their life – possibly getting swept along on the wave of empathy with other members, or even in a passionate attempt to argue against the point being made by someone else in the group. Such revelations arising during the cut and thrust of a group discussion might not be something the member would want repeated outside the context of the group. It could be something that, upon reflection in the cool light of the following day, they wish they had not said.

There needs to be mutual trust on this point, with focus group members respecting each other's words as confidential. But this raises an interesting point relating to research ethics. Whereas the researcher might be expected to operate in accord with established research ethics and be duty bound to treat the data as confidential, volunteers who are recruited to participate in a focus group might not be aware of such an ethical position. It is part of the facilitator's role, therefore, to establish that all group members need to honour the requirement to treat the discussion as confidential. This should be explicitly stated by the facilitator as part of the formalities at the beginning of the session and reiterated as a reminder to group members at the end of the session.

Link up with **Research ethics, pp. 141–51**

The interviewer effect

Personal identity

Research on interviewing has demonstrated fairly conclusively that people respond differently depending on how they perceive the person asking the questions. In particular, the *sex*, the *age* and the *ethnic origins* of the interviewer have a bearing on the amount of information people are willing to divulge and their honesty about what they reveal. The data, in other words, are affected by the personal identity of the researcher. This point applies whether the interview is conducted face to face or online. In the case of online interviews, although interviewees might not be able to see the interviewer their *perception* of the person who is collecting the data can still influence their willingness to divulge information.

The impact of the researcher's personal identity, of course, will depend on who is being interviewed. It is not, strictly speaking, the identity in its own right that affects the data, but what the researcher's identity means as far as the person being interviewed is concerned. *Interviewees, and interviewers come to that, have their own preferences and prejudices, and these are likely to have some impact on the chances of developing rapport and trust during an interview.*

The effect of the researcher's identity, in practice, will also depend on the nature of the topic being discussed. On sensitive issues or on matters regarded as rather personal, the interviewer's identity assumes particular importance. If the research is dealing with religious beliefs, with earnings, with sexual relationships, with personal health or any of a host of similar issues, the sex, age and ethnicity of the interviewer in relation to the sex, age and ethnicity of the interviewee is very likely to influence the nature of the data that emerge – their fullness and their honesty. On some questions people can be embarrassed. They can feel awkward or defensive. Whenever this is the case, there is the possibility that interviewees might supply answers which they feel fit in with what the researcher expects from them – fulfilling the perceived expectations of the researcher. Or the answers might tend to be tailored to match what the interviewee suspects is the researcher's point of view, keeping the researcher happy. Either way, the quality of the data suffers.

From the perspective of the small-scale project researcher there is a limit to what can be done about this. Although interviews conducted over the Internet, and to a lesser extent interviews conducted by phone, do provide some possibilities for disguising who we are, there are definite limits to the extent that researchers can disguise their 'self' during face-to-face interviews. We bring to such interviews certain personal attributes which are 'givens' and which cannot be altered on a whim to suit the needs of the research interview. *Our sex, our age, our ethnic origin, our accent, even our occupational status, all are aspects of our 'self' which, for practical purposes, cannot be changed.* We can make efforts to be polite and punctual, receptive and neutral, in order to encourage the right climate for an interviewee to feel comfortable and provide honest answers. What we cannot do is change these personal attributes.

> **Key point: the interviewer effect**
>
> - What are the social status, educational qualifications and professional expertise of the people to be interviewed, and how do these compare with my own? Is this likely to affect the interviewer-interviewee relationship in a positive or negative manner?
> - Is there likely to be an age gap between myself and the interviewee(s) and, if so, how might this affect the interview?
> - In relation to the topic being researched, will interviewing someone of the opposite sex or a different ethnic group have an impact on their willingness to answer questions openly and honestly?

Self-presentation

Conventional advice to researchers has been geared to minimizing the impact of researchers on the outcome of the research by having them adopt a passive and neutral stance. The idea is that the researcher:

- presents himself or herself in a light which is designed not to antagonize or upset the interviewee (conventional clothes, courtesy, etc.);
- remains neutral and non-committal on the statements made during the interview by the interviewee.

Passivity and neutrality are the order of the day. The researcher's 'self', adopting this approach, is kept firmly hidden beneath a cloak of cordiality and receptiveness to the words of the interviewee. To a certain degree, this is sound advice. The researcher, after all, is there to listen and learn, not to preach. The point is to get the interviewee to open up, not to provoke hostility or put the interviewee on the defensive.

Personal involvement

One line of reasoning argues that a cold and calculating style of interviewing reinforces a gulf between the researcher and the informant, and does little to help or empower the informant. Now, if the aims of the research are specifically to help or empower the people being researched, rather than dispassionately learn from them, then the approach of the interviewer will need to alter accordingly (Oakley, 1981). Under these circumstances, the researcher will be inclined to show emotion, to respond with feeling and to engage in a true dialogue with the interviewee. The researcher will become fully involved as a person with feelings, with experiences and with knowledge that can be shared with the interviewee. A word of warning, though. This style of interviewing remains 'unconventional', and the researcher needs to be confident and committed to make it work. The researcher also needs to feel sure that his or her audience understand and share the underlying logic of the approach rather than expecting the researcher to adopt the cool and dispassionate stance.

Internet interviews and online focus groups

It is possible to use the Internet to conduct interviews and run focus groups. The Internet interview, at its simplest, consists of an exchange of email correspondence. Alternatively, it can be conducted through 'bulletin boards', 'chat rooms' or messaging services such as offered by Yahoo! or MSN Messenger. Chat rooms allow messages to be sent back and forth, in turn, as in a conversation. To this extent, chat rooms provide synchronous communication in 'real time'. Connection is made through an Internet service provider (ISP) and normally involves a process of registering when first joining. On entering a chat room a newcomer will normally wait and watch from the sidelines as the participants exchange messages. This is known as 'lurking'. It allows the newcomer to get a feel for the discussions that are going on before joining in with something relevant and constructive. Bear in mind the fact that any comment that is written to a chat room becomes visible to anyone (across the world) who happens to be visiting the chat room at that time. Any of these can reply to you. The reply, again, is public. However, chat rooms also allow individuals to communicate with one another on a one-to-one basis where others will not see the messages. This is known as 'whispering'.

A form of interviewing can also be conducted using mailing lists. Mailing lists operate through an automated email program that, when it receives a message, simply forwards that message on to the email addresses of all the subscribers to the list. The mailing list contains email addresses for those who share an interest in specific topics or items. Some lists are moderated, some are not. And some list servers keep on file all the messages that are posted – thus being able to trace, and deter, the sending of messages that are rude, offensive or inappropriate for the specific list.

Bulletin boards or Newsgroups have become a readily accessible resource for researchers, who can identify, and make contact with, special interest groups on just about any imaginable topic. Subscribing to a newsgroup is much like putting yourself on a mailing list to receive news and information about a particular item of special interest. When subscribers log on to a particular group they automatically get sent the messages that have been posted by other members. Although they appear much like email, newsgroups rely on sites maintained on a server computer, with different software being used to make the system operate. To add a contribution to the newsgroup, users send a message much as they would on email. And, as with email, the communication is 'asynchronous' – not in 'real time'. Some newsgroups are moderated – others are not.

From the researcher's point of view, the use of bulletin boards or newsgroups has some distinct benefits:

- The responses do not depend on who happens to be visiting the site at any one specific moment (an advantage over the use of chat rooms).
- The responses tend to come from those with a strong interest in the topic. Newsgroups tend to be information-based forums, compared with the more social nature of chat rooms, and have a more serious side to them that means members might be better disposed to assisting researchers.
- The responses are likely to reflect a 'considered opinion' rather than an instant 'off-the-cuff' remark, since the respondent has time to reflect on the issue.
- It is possible to trace archive material that records past discussions – often over several years.

There is, however, a significant component of the conventional interview that is missing when using the Internet. There is a *loss of visual clues*. The interviewer and the interviewee cannot see one another (unless there is a video-conferencing link). There can also be a *considerable time gap* between the question and the answer – more than would normally be associated with a face-to-face interview. At one level, these two features of Internet interviews can be regarded as an impediment to the collection of data. The absence of visual clues prevents the interviewer from picking up on important facial expressions and other non-verbal communication that could be valuable for understanding the interviewee's thoughts. The time lapse can stultify the flow of interaction, depriving the interview of its natural qualities.

The other side of the coin, as advocates of Internet interviewing point out, is that these features of Internet interviews can reduce the *interviewer effect*. They can:

- Reduce the culture and gender effects of interaction. The absence of visual clues means that what is stated by the interviewees is less likely to be affected by status factors linked to the respective age, sex, ethnicity, accent and social class of the interviewer and the interviewee. It acts as an 'equalizer' in terms of the communication.
- Overcome embarrassment on some topics. The lack of face-to-face contact helps to make the interviewee less uncomfortable when responding to questions on sensitive topics. The contact, being less 'personal', is likely to be less embarrassing when covering issues where factors like the interviewer's sex and age might otherwise affect the response.
- Allow interviewees time for reflection on and consideration of the question.

The quality of their answers might be improved as a result of them having time to think through the issues.

Online focus groups

Online focus groups can be conducted using chat rooms or messaging services (or by using specialist conferencing software, although this can be expensive and technically complex). The use of chat rooms or messaging services allows the focus groups to be conducted 'remotely' rather than in the conventional face-to-face manner, retaining the element of direct interaction between group members as ideas and information get exchanged in 'real time' (see Bloor *et al.*, 2001). As with interviews, there are advantages in terms of costs and the prospect of bringing people together who would not otherwise be able to operate as a group because they are geographically dispersed. It is also possible to use newsgroups, bulletin boards or even email to conduct versions of a focus group. The use of such 'non-real-time' communication has the advantage that it extends still further the range of people who can participate in a group. It overcomes time zone differences to allow interaction between focus group members who may live in different continents across the globe. The downside to this is that because these versions operate in 'non real time' the focus groups inevitably lose some of the spontaneity of group interaction between members that is a feature of the dynamics of face-to-face focus groups.

Online focus groups, whether operating in real time or non real time, also exacerbate the problem inherent to ordinary focus groups concerning confidentiality and the privacy of statements that are made as part of the focus group discussion. The researcher needs to prevent personal information given during a focus group meeting from being disclosed by other members of the group to anyone outside the group.

Planning and preparation for face-to-face interviews

The topics for discussion

With the use of unstructured interviews, it might be argued that the researcher should not have preconceived ideas about the crucial issues and direction the interview should take. In practice, however, it is not very often that researchers operate at the extreme end of the continuum with unstructured interviews. In the vast majority of cases, researchers approach an interview with some agenda and with some game-plan in mind. In such cases it would be tempting fate to proceed to a research interview without having devoted considerable time to thinking through the key points that warrant attention. This does not necessarily mean that the researcher needs to have a rigid framework of questions and issues in mind – though this will be the case when using structured interviews. It does mean that there is likely to be more benefit from the interview if he or she is well informed about the topic and has done the necessary homework on the issues that are likely to arise during the interview.

Choice of informants

In principle, there is nothing to stop researchers from selecting informants on the basis of random sampling. In practice, though, this is unlikely to happen. Interviews are generally conducted with lower numbers than would be the case with questionnaire surveys, and this means that the selection of people to interview is more likely to be based on non-probability sampling. People tend to be chosen deliberately because they have some special contribution to make, because they have some unique insight or because of the position they hold. It is worth emphasizing, though, that there is no hard and fast rule on this. It depends on whether the overall aim of the research is to produce results which are generalizable (in which case the emphasis will be on choosing a representative sample of people to interview) or the aim is to delve in depth into a particular situation with a view to exploring the specifics (in which case the emphasis will be on choosing key players in the field).

In the case of group interviews, researchers can decide to select interviewees in order to get a cross-section of opinion within the group, or, perhaps, to ensure that group members hold opposing views on the topic for discussion.

Authorization

In many, if not most, research situations it will be necessary to get approval from relevant 'authorities'. This will be necessary in any instance of research where the people selected to participate in the interviews are either:

- working within an organization where they are *accountable to others* higher up the chain of command;
- or potentially vulnerable, and therefore *protected by responsible others* – the young, the infirm and some other groups are under the protection of others whose permission must be sought (e.g. school children).

Organizations, authorities and Internet moderators who grant permission will wish to be persuaded that it is *bona fide* research, and they will also be influenced by the personal/research credentials of the researcher. Letters of contact, therefore, should spell out the range of factors which will *persuade the organization or authority that the researcher is both (a) trustworthy and (b) capable*. Research which can call on suitable referees or which will be conducted under the auspices of a suitable organization (e.g. a university) is at an advantage for these.

To emphasize what ought to be obvious, such authorization to conduct the interviews must be gained *before* the interviews take place.

Arranging the venue

In the case of face-to-face interviews, securing an agreement to be interviewed is often easier if the prospective interviewee is *contacted in advance*. This also allows both parties to arrange a mutually convenient time for the interview. At this point, of course, the researcher will probably be asked how long the interview will take, and should therefore be in a position to respond. It is most unlikely that busy people will feel comfortable with a suggestion that the interview will 'take as long as it takes'. The researcher needs to make a bid for an *agreed length of time* whether it be 15 minutes, half an hour, 45 minutes or an hour.

Where a face-to-face interview takes place 'on site' the researcher cannot always control events as they might want. This means there is an added danger that things can go wrong. Through whatever means, though, the researcher needs to try to get a *location for the interview* which will not be disturbed, which offers privacy, which has fairly good acoustics and which is reasonably quiet. This can prove to be a pretty tall order in places like busy organizations, schools, hospitals and so on. But at least the desirability of such a venue should be conveyed to the person arranging the interview room.

Within the interview room, it is important to be able to set up the *seating arrangements* in a way that allows comfortable interaction between the researcher and the interviewee(s). In a one-to-one interview the researcher should try to arrange seating so that the two parties are at a 90 degree angle to each other. This allows for eye contact without the confrontational feeling arising from sitting directly opposite the other person. With group interviews, it is important to arrange the seating to allow contact between all parties without putting the researcher in a focal position and without hiding individuals at the back of the group or outside the group.

Interview skills

The good interviewer needs to be attentive. This may sound obvious, but it is all too easy to lose the thread of the discussion because the researcher needs to be monitoring a few other things while listening closely to what the informant has to say: writing the field notes, looking for relevant non-verbal communication, checking that the recorder is working.

The good interviewer is sensitive to the feelings of the informant. This is not just a matter of social courtesy, though that is certainly a worthy aspect of it. It is also a skill which is necessary for getting the best out of an interview. Where the interviewer is able to empathize with the informant and to gauge the feelings of the informant, they will be in a better position to coax out the most relevant information.

The good interviewer is able to tolerate silences during the talk, and knows when to shut up and say nothing. Anxiety is the main danger. Fearing that the interview might be on the verge of breaking down, the researcher can feel the need to say something quickly to kick-start the discussion. Worrying about cramming in every possible gem of wisdom in the allotted time, the interviewer can be inclined to rush the informant on quickly to the next point. But, most of all, feeling uncomfortable when the conversation lapses into silence, the interviewer can be all too quick to say something when a more experienced interviewer would know that the silence can be used as a wonderful resource during interviews (see below).

The good interviewer is adept at using prompts. Although silences can be productive, the interviewer needs to exercise judgement on this. There are times during an interview when the researcher might feel that it is necessary to spur the informant to speak. Listed below are some examples of how this can be done. What the examples share is a degree of subtlety. It is not normally acceptable for research interviewers to *demand* that the informant answers the questions. Research interviews are not police interviews. The idea is to nudge the informant gently into revealing their knowledge or thoughts on a specific point.

The good interviewer is adept at using probes. There are occasions during an interview when the researcher might want to delve deeper into a topic rather than let the discussion flow on to the next point. An informant might make a point in passing which the researcher thinks should be explored in more detail. Some explanation might be called for, or some justification for a comment. Some apparent inconsistency in the informant's line of reasoning might be detected, an inconsistency which needs unravelling. Examples of how this can be done are listed below. Again, they attempt to be subtle and avoid an aggressive stance.

The good interviewer is adept at using checks. One of the major advantages of interviews is that they offer the researcher the opportunity to check that he or she has understood the informant correctly. As an ongoing part of the normal talk during interviews, the researcher can present a summary of what they think the informant has said, which the informant can then confirm as an accurate understanding, or can correct it if it is felt to be a misunderstanding of what has been said. Such checks can be used at strategic points during the interview as a way of concluding discussion on one aspect of the topic.

With focus groups, the good researcher manages to let everyone have a say. It is vital to avoid the situation where a dominant personality hogs the discussion and bullies others in the group to agree with his or her opinion.

The good interviewer is non-judgemental. As the researcher enters the interview situation they should, as far as is possible, suspend personal values and *adopt a non-judgemental stance* in relation to the topics covered during the interview. This means not only biting your lip on occasion, but also taking care not to reveal disgust, surprise or pleasure through facial gestures. The good researcher must also *respect the rights of the interviewee*. This means accepting if a person simply does not wish to tell you something and knowing when to back off if the discussion is beginning to cause the interviewee particular embarrassment or stress. This is a point of personal sensitivity and research ethics.

Key point: tactics for interviews – prompts, probes and checks

Remain silent	(prompt)
Repeat the question	(prompt)
Repeat the last few words spoken by the interviewee	(prompt)
Offer some examples	(prompt)
Ask for an example	(probe)
Ask for clarification	(probe)
Ask for more details	(probe)
Summarize their thoughts	(check)

('So, if I understand you correctly . . .
What this means, then, is that . . .')

Conducting the interview

In the intensity of a research interview it is not easy to attend to all the points that should be remembered and, in any case, interviews are 'live' events which require the interviewer to adjust plans as things progress. Nevertheless, there are some pretty basic formalities that need to be observed. There are also a number of skills the researcher should exercise and, despite the fluid nature of interviews, it is worth spelling out a list of things that go towards a good interview.

Introduction and formalities

At the beginning there should be the opportunity to say 'Hello', to do some introductions, to talk about the aims of the research and to say something about the origins of the researcher's own interest in the topic. During the initial phase, there should also be confirmation that you have permission to record the discussion and reassurances about the confidentiality of comments made during the interview. The aim is to set the tone for the rest of the interview – normally a relaxed atmosphere in which the interviewee feels free to open up on the topic under consideration. *Trust* and *rapport* are the keywords.

During the pre-interview phase, the interviewer should do two other things:

- prepare the recording equipment;
- as far as possible, arrange the seating positions to best advantage.

Starting the interview

The first question takes on a particular significance for the interview. It should offer the interviewee the chance to settle down and relax. For this reason it is normally good practice to *kick off with an 'easy' question*: something on which the interviewee might be expected to have well formulated views and something that is quite near the forefront of their mind. Two tactics might help here.

- Ask respondents, in a general way, about themselves and their role as it relates to the overall area of the interview. This allows the researcher to collect valuable *background information about informants* while, at the same time, letting informants start off by covering familiar territory.
- *Use some 'trigger' or 'stimulus' material*, so that the discussion can relate to something concrete, rather than launch straight into abstract ideas.

Monitoring progress

During the interview, the researcher should keep a discreet eye on the time. The good researcher needs to wind things up within the allotted time and will have covered most of the key issues during that time. While doing this, the good interviewer also needs to attend to the following things during the progress of the interview itself.

- *Identify the main points being stated by the interviewee* and the priorities as expressed by the interviewee. With focus groups, what consensus is emerging about the key points?
- Look for the underlying logic of what is being said by the informant. *The interviewer needs to 'read between the lines'* to decipher the rationale lying beneath the surface of what is being said. The interviewer should ask 'What are they really telling me here?' and, perhaps more significantly, 'What are they *not* mentioning?'
- *Look for inconsistencies* in the position being outlined by the interviewee. If such inconsistencies exist, this does not invalidate their position. Most people have inconsistencies in their opinions and feelings on many topics. However, such inconsistencies will be worth probing as the interview progresses to see what they reveal.

- Pick up clues about whether the informant's answers involve an element of *boasting* or are answers intended to *please the interviewer*.
- *Be constantly on the look out for the kind of answer that is a 'fob-off'*.
- *Get a feel for the context* in which the discussion is taking place. The priorities expressed by the interviewee might reflect events immediately prior to the interview, or things about to happen in the near future. They might be 'issues of the moment', which would not assume such importance were the interview to be conducted a few weeks later. The researcher needs to be sensitive to this possibility and find out from the interviewee if there are events which are influencing priorities in this way.
- Keep a suitable level of eye contact throughout the interview and *make a note of non-verbal communication* which might help a later interpretation of the interview talk.

Finishing the interview

Interviews can come to an end because the interviewee has run out of things to say and the interviewer cannot elicit any more information from the person. This is not a good state of affairs unless the interview has no outside time limit. It is better for the interview to come to a close in some orderly fashion guided by the interviewer. Having kept an eye on the time, and having ensured that most of the required areas for discussion have been covered, the interviewer should draw events to a close making sure that:

- the interviewee is invited to raise any points that they think still need to be covered and have not been covered so far;
- the interviewee is thanked for having given up the time to participate in the interview.

Recording the interview

The researcher wishing to capture the discussion that happens during the interview can rely on memory. However, the human memory is rather unreliable as a research instrument. As psychologists tell us, human memory is prone to partial recall, bias and error. Interviewers, instead, can call on other more permanent records of what was said.

Field notes

Under certain circumstances researchers will need to rely on field notes written soon after the interview or actually during the interview. Sometimes interviewees will decline to be recorded. This means that what was actually said will always remain a matter of recollection and interpretation. There will never be an objective record of the discussion. This suits the needs of certain interviewees, particularly where the discussion touches on sensitive issues, commercially, politically or even personally. Notes taken during the interview, however, offer a compromise in such situations. The interviewer is left with some permanent record of their interpretation of what was said, and can refer back to this at various later stages to refresh the memory. The notes also act as some form of permanent record. However, from the interviewee's point of view, it is always possible to deny that certain things were said and to argue that the researcher might have 'misinterpreted' a point should the interviewee wish to dissociate him/herself from the point at some later date. A crucial advantage of taking field notes at an interview, however, is that they can fill in some of the relevant information that a recording alone might miss. Field notes can cover information relating to the context of the location, the climate and atmosphere under which the interview was conducted, clues about the intent behind the statements and comments on aspects of non-verbal communication as they were deemed relevant to the interview.

> **Key point: field notes**
>
> Field notes need to be made during the interview itself or, if this is not feasible, as soon afterwards as possible. They need to be made while events are fresh in the mind of the interviewer.

Audio recording

In practice, most research interviewers rely on *audio recordings backed up by written field notes*. Initially, interviewees can feel rather inhibited by the process of recording but most participants become more relaxed after a short while. When used sensitively, audio recording does not pose too much of a disturbance to interview situations, and it has certain clear benefits. Audio recordings offer a permanent record and one that is fairly complete in terms of the speech that occurs. They also lend themselves to being checked by other researchers. However, the downside is that they capture only speech, and miss non-verbal communication and other contextual factors. Video recordings, for their part, capture non-verbal as well as verbal communications and offer a more complete record of events during the interview. And, as with audio recordings, they provide a permanent record that can be checked by other researchers. The use of video recordings, however, tends to be the exception rather than the rule. It is not the cost factor that explains this because video equipment is not particularly expensive. Generally, it is the intrusiveness of video recordings that deters researchers from using them. For practical purposes, most interviewers would consider that audio recordings provide sufficient data, data that are good enough for the purpose of research, and that benefits gained through the video recording of an interview are outweighed by the extra disruption that video recording brings to the setting.

Equipment

It is a cardinal sin to start an interview without having thoroughly checked out the equipment. This sounds obvious, but in the run-up to an interview it is all too easy to overlook such a basic chore. Remember, an interview is a one-off situation. If the equipment fails you can hardly expect the interviewee to run through the whole discussion again!

Hard and fast advice on equipment is difficult to give, because technological advances can make such advice quickly out of date. What can be said at a general level is that the researcher should:

- use equipment which is good enough to supply adequate sound (or visual) reproduction;
- be certain that the equipment is functioning well before the interview;
- have a reliable power source plus back-up in case of emergency;
- choose storage devices that have enough memory, or last long enough, to cover the planned duration of the interview without the need to 'reload' the recorder.

Transcribing audio recordings of interviews

There might be a temptation to regard transcribing audio recordings as a straightforward process. In practice, researchers soon find that it is not. First of all, it is very time-consuming. For every hour of talk on an audio recording it will take several more to transcribe it. The actual time will depend on the clarity of the recording itself, the availability of transcription equipment and the typing speed of the researcher. When you are planning interview research, it is important to bear this in mind. From the point of view of the project researcher, the process of transcribing needs to be recognized as a substantial part of the method of interviewing and not to be treated as some trivial chore to be tagged on once the real business of interviewing has been completed.

The process of transcription is certainly laborious. However, it is also a very valuable part of the research, because it brings the researcher 'close to the data'. The process brings the talk to life again, and is a real asset when it comes to using interviews for qualitative data. Added to this, the end-product of the process provides the researcher with a form of data that is far easier to analyse than the audio recording in its original state.

> **Key point: transcription is time consuming**
> The transcription of audio recordings is a time-consuming activity. For every one hour of interview recording it generally takes two to three hours of work to transcribe the talk into text.

Annotations

When transcribing an audio recording, the researcher should put informal notes and comments alongside the interviewee's words. These annotations can be based on the memories that come flooding back during the process of transcribing. They should also draw on field notes taken during the interview or notes made soon afterwards about the interview. They should include observations about the ambience of the interview and things like gestures, outside interferences, uncomfortable silences or other feelings that give a richer meaning to the words that were spoken. These annotations should be placed in a special column on the page.

Line numbering and coding

To locate different parts of the transcript and to help navigate through to particular points in it, each line in the transcript should ideally have a unique line number by which to identify it. Qualitative data analysis software always includes a facility to do this, but it is also easily accomplished using basic word processing software such as MS Word. The page layout for the transcript should include a reasonable amount of clear space on which to write notes and there should be a wide margin on the side of the page that can be used later for coding and classifying the data and for writing notes. Qualitative data analysis software allows this automatically.

Problems of transcription

The transcription of audio recordings is not a straightforward mechanical exercise in which the researcher simply writes down the words that are spoken by research participants. In practice, it can be quite challenging, and there are three main reasons for this.

- *The recorded talk is not always easy to hear.* Especially with group interviews, but also with one-to-one versions, there can be occasions when more than one person speaks at the same time, where outside noises interfere or where poor audio quality itself makes transcribing the words very difficult. There is a fine dividing line here between the need to ditch these parts of the interview records and disregard them as worthwhile data, and the need to exercise some reasonable interpretation about what was actually said.

Interview transcripts: an example

Line of the transcript		Code for the content	Notes
↓		↓	↓
46	*Interviewer:* Do you feel under pressure to drink		
47	when you go out with your mates because they		
48	are drinking?		
49			*James looked*
50	*James:* Yeh, but it's not always . . . (*untranscribable*)		*annoyed as Elise*
51			*and Gordon*
52	*Elise:* . . . it's worse with the lads, I think, because . . .		*talked over him.*
53			
54	*Gordon:* . . . I was on holiday, and I don't like beer,		
55	and all my friends were drinking. I was drinking		
56	half a glass and I thought I can stick that out	08	
57	because I don't like it at all. I was drinking it and		
58	thinking this is horrible, just to look like one of		*Gordon says later*
59	the crowd, because I felt a bit left out. My		*that he drinks*
60	brother came up to me in front of the crowd		*beer regularly*
61	and said 'Gordon you don't like lager!' So all my	15	*now.*
62	friends found out, and they said 'Look, we		
63	understand if you don't like it' – and some of		
64	the people there were just like me, they didn't		
65	like it.		

Part of the transcript of a group interview conducted with 15–16-year-olds about peer pressure and alcohol consumption. The names have been changed.

Notice how, typical of a group interview, more than one person is trying to talk at once. Elise cuts across James, and then gets interrupted in turn by Gordon, who manages to hold the spotlight for a moment or two. When more than one person is talking at a time it makes transcription difficult, because it is hard to capture on tape what is being said. It tends to become something of a cacophony.

- *People do not always speak in nice finite sentences*. Normally, the researcher needs to add punctuation and a sentence structure to the talk, so that a reader can understand the sequence of words. The talk, in a sense, needs to be reconstructed so that it makes sense in a written form. This process takes time – and it also means that the crude data get cleaned up a little by the researcher so that they can be intelligible to a readership who were not present at the time of the recording.
- *Intonation, emphasis and accents used in speech are hard to depict in a transcript*. There are established conventions which allow these to be added to a written transcript, but the project researcher is unlikely to be able to devote the necessary time to learn these conventions. The result is that transcripts in small-scale research are generally based on the words and the words alone, with little attempt to show intonation, emphasis and accents. Nor are

pauses and silences always reported on a transcript. The consequence is that, in practice, the data are stripped of some of their meaning.

> **Key point: transcription**
>
> Transcription is not a mechanical process of putting audio-recorded talk into written sentences. The talk needs to be 'tidied up' and edited a little to put it in a format on the written page that is understandable to the reader. Inevitably, it loses some authenticity through this process.

Link up with **Qualitative data analysis, Chapter 14**

Representing the data: the use of interview extracts in research reports

Extracts from transcripts can be used to good effect in social research. For one thing, they can be interesting in their own right, giving the reader a flavour of the data and letting the reader 'hear' *the points as stated by the informants*. For another, they can be used as a *piece of evidence* supporting the argument that is being constructed in the report by the researcher. It is very unlikely, however, that an extract from an interview transcript can be presented as proof of a point. There are two reasons for this.

* *The significance of extracts from transcripts is always limited by the fact that they are, to some extent, presented out of context.* Extracts, as the very word itself suggests, are pieces of the data that are plucked from their context within the rest of the recorded interview. This opens up the possibility that the quote could be taken 'out of context'. Everyone knows the danger of being quoted out of context. The meaning of the words is changed by the fact that they are not linked to what came before and what was said after. The shrewd researcher will try to explain to the reader the context within which the extract arose but, inevitably, there is limited opportunity to do this in research reports.
* *The process of selecting extracts involves a level of judgement and discretion on the part of the researcher.* The selection of which parts of the transcript to include is entirely at the discretion of the researcher, and this inevitably limits the significance which can be attached to any one extract. It is an editorial decision which reflects the needs of the particular research report. How does the reader know that it was a fair selection, representative of the overall picture?

As a result, in the vast majority of reports produced by project researchers extracts will serve as illustrations of a point and supporting evidence for an argument – nothing more and nothing less. It is important that the project researcher is aware of this when using extracts, and avoids the temptation to present quotes from interviewees as though they stand in their own right as unequivocal proof of the point being discussed.

Having made this point, there are some things the researcher can do to get the best out of the extracts that are selected.

- Use quotes and extracts verbatim. Despite the points above about the difficulty of transcribing recordings, the researcher should be as literal as possible when quoting people. Use the exact words.
- Change the names to ensure anonymity (unless you have their explicit permission to reveal the person's identity).
- Provide some details about the person you are quoting, without endangering their anonymity. The general best advice here is to provide sufficient detail to distinguish informants from one another and to provide the reader with some idea of relevant background factors associated with the person, but to protect the identity of the person you quote by restricting how much information is given (e.g. teacher A, female, school 4, geography, mid-career).
- Try to give some indication of the context in which the quotation arose. Within the confines of a research report, try to provide some indication of the context of the extract so that the meaning *as intended* comes through. As far as it is feasible, the researcher should address the inevitable problem of taking the extract 'out of context' by giving the reader some guidance on the background within which the statement arose.

The validity of interview data: how do you know the informant is telling the truth?

This is a crucial question facing the researcher who uses interview data. When the interview is concerned with gathering information of a factual nature, the researcher can make some checks to see if the information is broadly corroborated by other people and other sources. When the interview concerns matters such as the emotions, feelings and experiences of the interviewee, it is a lot more difficult to make such checks. Ultimately, there is no absolute way of verifying what someone tells you about their thoughts and feelings. Researchers are not 'mind readers'. But there are still some practical checks researchers can make to gauge the credibility of what they have been told. It should be stressed, though, that these are not watertight methods of detecting false statements given during interviews. They are practical ways of helping the researcher to avoid being a gullible dupe who accepts all that he or she is told at face value. They help the researcher to 'smell a rat'. By the same token, if the following checks are used, the researcher can have greater confidence in the interview data, knowing that some effort has been made to ensure the validity of the data.

Check the data with other sources

The researcher should make efforts to corroborate the interview data with other sources of information on the topic. *Triangulation* should be used. Documents and observations can provide some back-up for the content of the interview, or can cast some doubt on how seriously the interview data should be taken. Interview content can even be checked against other interviews to see if there is some level of consistency. The point is that interview data should not be taken at face value if it is at all possible to confirm or dispute the statements using alternative sources.

Link up with **Triangulation, pp. 134–9**

Checking the transcript with the informant

Where possible, the researcher should go back to the interviewee with the transcript to check with that person that it is an accurate statement. Now, of course, checking for accuracy is not strictly what is going on here. Unless the interviewer also sends a copy of the recording, the interviewee has no way of knowing if what appears on the transcript is actually what was said. The point of the exercise is more to do with 'putting the record straight'. If the researcher is solely concerned with gathering facts from the interview, this is an opportunity to ensure that the facts are correct and that the interviewer has got the correct information. That is a nice safeguard. If, alternatively, the interview is concerned with a person's emotions, opinions and experiences, the exercise invites the interviewee to confirm that what was said at the time of the interview was what was really meant, and not said 'in the heat of the moment'. Either way, there is an initial check on the accuracy of the data.

Check the plausibility of the data

Some people are interviewed specifically because they are in a position to know about the things that interest the researcher. The 'key players' are picked out precisely because they are specialists, experts, highly experienced – and their testimony carries with it a high degree of credibility. This is not necessarily the case with those chosen for interview on some other grounds. When assessing the credibility of information contained in an interview, the researcher needs to gauge how far an informant might be expected to be in possession of the facts and to know about the topic being discussed. The researcher should ask if it is reasonable to suppose that such a person would be in a position to comment authoritatively on the topic – or is there a chance that they are talking about something of which they have little knowledge?

Look for themes in the transcript(s)

Where possible, avoid basing findings on one interview – look for themes emerging from a number of interviews. Where themes emerge across a number of interviews, the researcher does not have to rely on any one transcript as the sole source of what is 'real' or 'correct'. A recurrent theme in interviews indicates that the idea/issue is something which is shared among a wider group, and therefore the researcher can refer to it with rather more confidence than any idea/issue which stems from the words of one individual.

Advantages of interviews

- *Depth of information.* Interviews are particularly good at producing data which deal with topics in depth and in detail. Subjects can be probed, issues pursued and lines of investigation followed over a relatively lengthy period.
- *Insights.* The researcher is likely to gain valuable insights based on the depth of the information gathered and the wisdom of 'key informants'.
- *Equipment.* Interviews require only simple equipment and build on conversation skills which researchers already have.
- *Informants' priorities.* Interviews are a good method for producing data based on informants' priorities, opinions and ideas. Informants have the opportunity to expand their ideas, explain their views and identify what *they* regard as the crucial factors.
- *Flexibility.* As a method for data collection, interviews are probably the most flexible. Adjustments to the lines of enquiry can be made during the interview itself. Interviewing allows for a developing line of enquiry.
- *High response rate.* Interviews are generally prearranged and scheduled for a convenient time and location. This ensures a relatively high response rate.
- *Validity.* Direct contact at the point of the interview means that data can be checked for accuracy and relevance as they are collected. In the case of Internet interviews, there is also the elimination of errors at the data entry stage. The researcher is no longer faced with passages in a tape-recorded interview where voices cannot be heard clearly and where there is consequently some doubt about what was actually said. Using the Internet, interview responses come in the form of text – text constructed directly by the interviewee. This eliminates inaccuracies in the data arising from the process of transcription.

- *Therapeutic.* Interviews can be a rewarding experience for the informant. Compared with questionnaires, observation and experiments, there is a more personal element to the method, and people tend to enjoy the rather rare chance to talk about their ideas at length to a person whose purpose is to listen and note the ideas without being critical.

Disadvantages of interviews

- *Time-consuming.* Analysis of data can be difficult and time-consuming. Data preparation and analysis is 'end-loaded' compared with, for instance, questionnaires which are pre-coded and where data are ready for analysis once they have been collected. The transcribing and coding of interview data is a major task for the researcher which occurs after the data have been collected.
- *Data analysis.* The interview method tends to produce *non-standard responses*. Semi-structured and unstructured interviews produce data that are not pre-coded and have a relatively open format.
- *Reliability.* The impact of the interviewer and of the context means that consistency and objectivity are hard to achieve. The data collected are, to an extent, unique owing to the specific context and the specific individuals involved. This has an adverse effect on *reliability*.
- *Interviewer effect.* The data from interviews are based on what people say rather than what they do. The two may not tally. What people say they do, what they say they prefer and what they say they think cannot automatically be assumed to reflect the truth. In particular, interviewee statements can be affected by the identity of the researcher. Internet interviews, with their lack of visual and verbal clues, can go a long way towards avoiding this problem. The absence of visual and verbal clues, some researchers argue, democratizes the research process by equalizing the status of researcher and respondent, lowering the status differentials linked with sex, age, appearance and accent, and giving the participant greater control over the process of data collection. The lack of such clues, equally, can help to overcome embarrassment on topics and allow the respondent to open up in a way that is unlikely to happen in the physical presence of a researcher.
- *Inhibitions.* In the case of face-to-face interviews, the audio recorder (or video recorder) can inhibit the informant. Although the impact of the recording device tends to wear off quite quickly, this is not always the case. The interview is an artificial situation (as, of course, are experiments) where people are speaking for the record and on the record, and this can be daunting for certain people.
- *Invasion of privacy.* Tactless interviewing can be an invasion of privacy and/or upsetting for the informant. While interviews can be enjoyable, the

other side of the coin is that the personal element of being interviewed carries its own kinds of dangers as well.

- *Resources*. With face-to-face interviews the *costs* of interviewer's time and travel can be relatively high, particularly if the informants are geographically dispersed.

Checklist for the use of interviews

When undertaking survey research you should feel confident about answering 'yes' to the following question: ☑

1 Have field notes been written to provide supplementary information about the interaction during the interview?   ☐

2 Have relevant details been collected about the context within which the interviews took place (location, prior events, ambience, etc.)?   ☐

3 Has consideration been given to the effect of the recording equipment on the openness with which informants replied?   ☐

4 During the interviews was the discussion monitored appropriately in terms of:
   - informants' key points?   ☐
   - reading between the lines of what was said?   ☐
   - trying to identify any inconsistencies?   ☐
   - being aware of the 'fob-off' answer?   ☐
   - looking for boastful or exaggerated answers?   ☐
   - looking for answers intended simply to please the interviewer?   ☐

5 During the interviews were prompts, probes and checks used to gain worthwhile, detailed insights?   ☐

6 Has consideration been given to the way the researcher's self identity might have affected the:
   - interaction during the interview?   ☐
   - interpretation of the data?   ☐

7 In the case of interviews conducted via the Internet, has consideration been given to the impact of Internet research in terms of the:
   - loss of visual clues during the interaction?   ☐
   - use of non-real-time communication?   ☐

8 Has informed consent been obtained from interviewees and relevant authorities?   ☐

9 Have all documents and recordings been stored securely, with appropriate measures to protect the confidentiality of the data?   ☐

© M. Denscombe, *The Good Research Guide*. Open University Press.

11

Observation

*The nature of observational research • Perception and observation •
Systematic observation and observation schedules • Creating an
observation schedule • Retaining the naturalness of the setting •
Advantages of systematic observation • Disadvantages of systematic
observation • Checklist for the use of observation schedules • Participant
observation • What to observe, what to record • Self, identity and
participant observation • Advantages of participant observation •
Disadvantages of participant observation • Checklist for participant
observation*

The nature of observational research

Observation offers the social researcher a distinct way of collecting data. It
does not rely on what people *say* they do, or what they *say* they think. It is
more direct than that. Instead, it draws on the direct evidence of the eye to
witness events first hand. It is based on the premise that, for certain purposes,
it is best to observe what actually happens.

There are essentially two kinds of observation research used in the social
sciences. The first of these is *systematic* observation. Systematic observation has
its origins in social psychology – in particular the study of interaction in settings such as school classrooms (Croll, 1986; Flanders, 1970 and Simon and
Boyer, 1970). It is normally linked with the production of quantitative data
and the use of statistical analysis. The second is *participant* observation. This is
mainly associated with sociology and anthropology, and is used by researchers
to infiltrate situations, sometimes as an undercover operation, to understand
the culture and processes of the groups being investigated. It usually produces
qualitative data.

These two methods might seem poles apart in terms of their origins and their use in current social research, but they share some vital characteristics.

- *Direct observation.* The obvious connection is that they both rely on direct observation. In this respect they stand together, in contrast to methods such as questionnaires and interviews, which base their data on what informants tell the researcher, and in contrast to documents where the researcher tends to be one step removed from the action.
- *Fieldwork.* The second common factor is their dedication to collecting data in real life situations – out there in the field. In their distinct ways, they both involve fieldwork. The dedication to fieldwork immediately identifies observation as an *empirical* method for data collection. As a method, it requires the researcher to go in search of information, first hand, rather than relying on secondary sources.
- *Natural settings.* Fieldwork observation – distinct from laboratory observations – occurs in situations which would have occurred whether or not the research had taken place. The whole point is to observe things as they normally happen, rather than as they happen under artificially created conditions such as laboratory experiments. There is a major concern to avoid disrupting the *naturalness of the setting* when undertaking the research. In this approach to social research, it becomes very important to minimize the extent to which the presence of the researcher might alter the situation being researched.
- *The issue of perception.* Systematic observation and participant observation both recognize that the process of observing is far from straightforward. Both are acutely sensitive to the possibility that researchers' perceptions of situations might be influenced by personal factors and that the data collected could thus be unreliable. They tend to offer very different ways of overcoming this, but both see it as a problem that needs to be addressed.

Perception and observation

Two researchers looking at the same event ought to have recorded precisely the same things. Or should they? Using common sense, it might seem fairly obvious that, as long as both researchers were present and able to get a good vantage point to see all that was happening, the records of the events – the data – should be identical. Yet in practice this might not be the case. It is possible that the two researchers will produce different records of the thing they jointly witnessed.

Why should this be the case? Obviously, the competence of each individual researcher is a factor which has to be taken into consideration. The powers of observation, the powers of recall and the level of commitment of individual researchers will vary, and this will have an effect on the observational data that are produced.

The variation in records also reflects psychological factors connected to memory and perception. Obviously, the research information on this area is vast but, as far as the use of observation as a research method is concerned, there are three things which are particularly important that emerge from the work of psychologists on these topics.

First, they point to the frailties of human memory and the way that we cannot possibly remember each and every detail of the events and situations we observe. Basically, we forget most of what we see. But what we forget and what we recall are not decided at random. There is a pattern to the way the mind manages to recall certain things and forget others. There is *selective recall*.

Second, they point to the way the mind filters the information it receives through the senses. It not only acts to reduce the amount of information, it also operates certain 'filters' which let some kinds of information through to be experienced as 'what happened', while simultaneously putting up barriers to many others. There is *selective perception*.

Third, they point to experiments which show how these filters not only let in some information while excluding the rest, but also boost our sensitivity to certain signals depending on our emotional and physical state, and our past experiences. What we experience can be influenced to some extent by whether we are, for instance, very hungry, angry, anxious, frustrated, prejudiced, etc. What we experience is shaped by our feelings at the moment and by the emotional baggage we carry around with us as a result of significant things that have happened to us during our lifetime. These things account for *accentuated perception*.

The selection and organization of stimuli, then, is far from random. In fact, there is a tendency to highlight some information and reject some other, depending on:

- *Familiarity*. We tend to see what we are *used* to seeing. If there is any ambiguity in what is being observed, we tend to interpret things according to frequent past experiences.
- *Past experiences*. Past experience 'teaches' us to filter out certain 'nasty' stimuli (avoidance learning) or exaggerate desirable things.
- *Current state*. Physical and emotional states can affect what is perceived by researchers. Physiological states such as hunger and thirst can influence the way we interpret what we 'see'. Emotions, anxieties and current priorities can likewise alter our perceptions.

Without delving too deeply into the psychology of perception, it is easy to appreciate that, as human beings, researchers do not simply observe and record the events they witness in some mechanical and straightforward fashion. Evidence in relation to memory and perception indicates that the mind acts as an intermediary between 'the world out there' and the way it is experienced by the individual. There is almost inevitably *an element of interpretation.*

Systematic observation and observation schedules

The psychology of memory and perception explains why the facts recorded by one researcher are very likely to differ from those recorded by another, and why different observers can produce different impressions of the situation. However, all this is rather worrying when it comes to the use of observation as a method for collecting data. It suggests that the data are liable to be inconsistent between researchers – too dependent upon the individual and the personal circumstances of each researcher. It implies that different observers will produce different data.

It is precisely this problem which is addressed by systematic observation and its use of an *observation schedule.* The whole purpose of the schedule is to minimize, possibly eliminate, the variations that will arise from data based on individual perceptions of events and situations. Its aim is to provide a framework for observation which *all* observers will use, and which will enable them to:

- be alert to the same activities and be looking out for the same things;
- record data systematically and thoroughly;
- produce data which are consistent between observers, with two or more researchers who witness the same event recording the same data.

To achieve these three aims, observation schedules contain a list of items that operate something like a checklist. The researcher who uses an observation schedule will monitor the items contained in the checklist and make a record of them as they occur. All observers will have their attention directed to the same things. The process of systematic observation then becomes a matter of measuring and recording how many times an event occurs, or how long some event continues. In this way, there will be a permanent record of the events which should be consistent between any researchers who use the schedule, because *what* is being observed is dictated by the items contained in the schedule. When researchers are properly trained and experienced, there should be what is called high 'inter-observer' reliability.

The value of findings from the use of an observation schedule will depend, however, on how appropriate the items contained in the schedule are for the situation. Precise measurements of something that is irrelevant will not advance the research at all. It is imperative, for this reason, that the items on the schedule are carefully selected. The findings will only be worth something if the items can be shown to be appropriate for the issues being investigated, and for the method of observation as well.

Creating an observation schedule

Literature review

Initially, the possible features of the situation which might be observed using a schedule can be identified on the basis of a literature review. Such a literature review will present certain things as worthy of inclusion, and should allow the researcher to prioritize those aspects of the situation to be observed. It would be nice to have a huge number of items in the schedule, but this is not practical. Researchers are limited by the speed and accuracy with which it is possible to observe and record events they witness. So the items for inclusion need to be restricted to just the *most* significant and *most* relevant, because it is simply not feasible to include everything. Previous research and previous theories provide the key to deciding which features of the situation warrant the focus of attention.

Types of events and behaviour to be recorded

Observers can measure what happens in a variety of ways. The choice will depend on the events themselves and, of course, the purpose to which the results will be put. Observations can be based on:

- *Frequency of events.* A count of the frequency with which the categories/items on the observation schedule occur.
- *Events at a given point in time.* At given intervals (for instance, 25 seconds) the observer logs what is happening at that instant. This might involve logging numerous things which happen simultaneously at that point.
- *Duration of events.* When instances occur they are timed, so that the researcher gets information on the total time for each category, and when the categories occurred during the overall time-block for the period of observation.
- *Sample of people.* Individuals can be observed for predetermined periods of time, after which the observer's attention is switched to another person in a rota designed to give representative data on all those involved in the situation.

Suitability for observation

When the items for inclusion in the schedule are being selected there are seven conditions that need to be met. The things to be observed need to be:

- *Overt.* First and foremost, items should entail *overt behaviour* which is observable and measurable in a direct manner. Things like attitudes and thoughts need to be inferred by the researcher, and are not observable in a direct manner.
- *Obvious.* They should require a minimum of interpretation by the researcher. The researcher should have little need to decipher the action or fathom out whether an action fits one or another category.
- *Context independent.* Following from the point above, this means that the context of the situation should not have a significant impact on how the behaviour is to be interpreted.
- *Relevant.* They should be the most relevant indications of the thing to be investigated. It is important that the researcher chooses only valid indicators, things that are a good reflection of the things being studied.
- *Complete.* They should cover all possibilities. Care needs to be taken to ensure, as far as is possible, that the categories on the observation schedule cover the full range of possibilities and that there are not gaps which will become glaringly evident once the observation schedule is used in the field.
- *Precise.* There should be no ambiguity about the categories. They need to be defined precisely and there should be no overlap between them. There should be the most *relevant indicators* of the thing being investigated.
- *Easy to record.* They should occur with *sufficient regularity and sequence* for the observer to be able to log the occurrences accurately and fruitfully. If the category is something that is relatively rare, it will prove frustrating and wasteful of time to have a researcher – pen poised – waiting, waiting, waiting for something to happen. And if, like buses, the events then all come at once, the observer might well find it impossible to log all instances. There is a practical consideration here which affects the categories to be observed. (Choose one-at-a-time events, avoid simultaneously occurring events.)

Sampling and observation

When deciding what thing is to be observed, the researcher also needs to make a strategic decision concerning the kind of *sampling* to be used. Researchers using systematic observation generally organize their research around set time-blocks of observation in the field. For example, these might be one-hour chunks of time *in situ.* These time-blocks themselves need to be chosen so as to avoid any bias and to incorporate a representative sample of the thing in question. So, if the research were to be observations of inter-action in school classrooms, the researcher would need to ensure that the research occurred across the full school week, the full school day and a cross-section of subjects. To confine observations to Friday afternoons, or to one subject such as history, would not provide an accurate picture across the board.

Example of an observation schedule

For the purposes of illustration, consider an observation schedule intended for use in art classes in a secondary school. The art classes are the 'situation' for which the observation schedule needs to be designed. Its 'purpose' is to measure the amount of lesson time wasted by students queuing to clean their paint brushes in the sink. Its aim might be to provide quantitative, objective data in support of the art teacher's bid for resources to have a second sink installed in the art classroom. The simple observation schedule to be used in this context could take the following format.

Location: School A
Date: 28 April
Time: 11 a.m. to 12 noon

Identity of student	Student starts queuing	Student arrives at sink	Queuing time
Student Ann	11.15	11.15	0
Student Tom	11.15	11.18	3
Student David	11.15	11.20	5
Student Diane	11.16	11.23	7
Student Tony	11.17	11.24	7
Student Eileen	11.19	11.26	7
Student			
Student			
Student			

In this example, a decision has been made to record the duration of the event: queuing time. It would have been possible to record the number of occasions that students in the class queued, or to have noted at intervals of say 30 seconds over a one-hour period how many students were queuing at that moment. These would have provided slightly different kinds of results. If we were concerned with how queuing interrupted the concentration of students on a task it would have been more appropriate to record the frequency. Had the aim been to look at bottlenecks in the queuing, time sampling would have allowed the ebb and flow of students to the sink to be shown quite clearly. When the aim is to support the claim that students' time is wasted in queues for the sink, it is appropriate to record the total time spent in the queue.

The item in this example is suitably straightforward to observe. We would presume that standing in line is an obvious and observable form of behaviour and that, despite some occasions when students might not be solely concerned with getting their paint brushes clean when they join the queue (they might be socializing or wasting time deliberately), standing in line offers a fairly valid indicator of the thing that is of interest to the researcher: time wasted queuing.

The same applies to the selection of *people* for inclusion in the study. To get a representative picture of the event or situation, the use of systematic observation can involve a deliberate selection of people to be observed, so that there is a cross-section of the whole research population. In the case of observation in a school classroom, for example, the researcher could identify in advance a sample according to the sex and ability of students, thus ensuring that the observations that take place are based on a representative sample.

Recording contextual factors

Precisely because the use of an observation schedule has the tendency to decontextualize the things it records, more advanced practice in this area has made a point of insisting that researchers collect information about relevant background matters whenever they use a schedule (Galton *et al.*, 1980). Such background information helps to explain the events observed, and should be logged with the schedule results to help the observer understand the data he or she has collected.

Retaining the naturalness of the setting

With systematic observation, the issue of retaining the naturalness of the setting hinges on the prospect of the researcher fading into the background and becoming, to all intents and purposes, invisible. At first this might seem an implausible thing. Armed with a clipboard and pen, and looking like a 'time and motion' researcher, it would seem unlikely that such systematic observation could avoid disrupting the events it seeks to measure. However, those who engage in this style of research report that it is indeed possible to 'merge into the wallpaper' and have no discernible impact. They stress that to minimize the likelihood of disruption researchers should pay attention to three things:

- *Positioning*. Unobtrusive positioning is vital. But the researcher still needs to be able to view the whole arena of action.

- *Avoiding interaction.* The advice here is to be 'socially invisible', not engaging with the participants in the setting if at all possible.
- *Time on site.* The experience of systematic observers assures them that the longer they are 'on site', the more their presence is taken for granted and the less they have any significant effect on proceedings.

Link up with **Observer effect, p. 53**

Advantages of systematic observation

- *Direct data collection.* It directly records what people do, as distinct from what they say they do.
- *Systematic and rigorous.* The use of an observation schedule provides an answer to the problems associated with the selective perception of observers, and it appears to produce *objective* observations. The schedule effectively eliminates any bias from the current emotions or personal background of the observer.
- *Efficient.* It provides a means for collecting substantial amounts of data in a relatively *short timespan.*
- *Pre-coded data.* It produces quantitative data which are pre-coded and ready for analysis.
- *Reliability.* When properly established, it should achieve high levels of inter-observer reliability in the sense that two or more observers using a schedule should record very similar data.

Disadvantages of systematic observation

- *Behaviour, not intentions.* Its focus on overt behaviour describes what happens, but not *why* it happens. It does not deal with the intentions that motivated the behaviour.
- *Oversimplifies.* It assumes that overt behaviours can be measured in terms of categories that are fairly straightforward and unproblematic. This is premised on the idea that the observer and the observed share an understanding of the overt behaviour, and that the behaviour has no double meaning, hidden meaning or confusion associated with it. As such, systematic observation has the in-built potential to oversimplify; to ignore or distort the subtleties of the situation.
- *Contextual information.* Observation schedules, by themselves, tend to miss contextual information which has a bearing on the behaviours recorded. It is not a holistic approach.

- *Naturalness of the setting.* Despite the confidence arising from experience, there remains a question mark about the observer's ability to fade into the background. Can a researcher with a clipboard and observation schedule really avoid disrupting the naturalness of the setting?

Checklist for the use of observation schedules

When using observation schedules you should feel confident about answering 'yes' to the following questions: ☑

1 Has the observation schedule been piloted? ☐

2 Have efforts been made to minimize any disturbance to the naturalness of the setting caused by the presence of the observer? ☐

3 Do the planned periods for observation provide a representative sample (time, place, context)? ☐

4 Are the events/behaviour to be observed:
- (a) sufficiently clear-cut and unambiguous to allow reliable coding? ☐
- (b) the most relevant indicators for the purposes of the research? ☐

5 Is the schedule complete (incorporating all likely categories of events/behaviour)? ☐

6 Do the events/behaviour occur regularly enough to provide sufficient data? ☐

7 Does the schedule avoid multiple simultaneous occurrences of the event/behaviour which might prevent accurate coding? ☐

8 Is the kind of sampling (event/point/time) the most appropriate? ☐

9 Is there provision for the collection of contextual information to accompany the schedule data? ☐

© M. Denscombe, *The Good Research Guide*. Open University Press.

Participant observation

A classic definition of participant observation spells out the crucial characteristics of this approach, and the things which distinguish it from systematic
observation.

> By participant observation we mean the method in which the observer
> participates in the daily life of the people under study, either openly in the
> role of researcher or covertly in some disguised role, observing things that
> happen, listening to what is said, and questioning people, over some
> length of time.
>
> (Becker and Geer, 1957: 28)

As Becker and Geer indicate, the participant observer can operate in a completely covert fashion – like an undercover agent whose success depends on
remaining undetected, whose purpose remains top secret. If no one knows
about the research except the researcher, the logic is that no one will act in
anything but a normal way. Preserving the *naturalness of the setting* is the key
priority for participant observation. The principal concern is to minimize disruption so as to be able to see things as they normally occur – unaffected by
any awareness that research is happening.

Another priority is to gain information about cultures or events which
would remain hidden from view if the researcher were to adopt other
methods. Such information could remain hidden for two reasons. Those
involved in the culture or event could deliberately hide or disguise certain
'truths' on occasions when they are 'under the microscope'. In this case, covert
participant observation reveals such events by doing the research secretly.
Nothing will get hidden. The 'participant observer' will be able to see everything – the real happenings, warts and all. Alternatively, aspects of the culture/
events could remain hidden because researchers using other methods would
remain unaware of them. In this case, participant observation discloses things
through the researcher's *experience* of participating in the culture or event.
Only by experiencing things from the insider's point of view does the
researcher become aware of the crucial factors explaining the culture or event.
With participant observation the aim is to get *insights* into cultures and events
– insights only coming to one who experiences things as *an insider*.

The nature of participant observation also allows the researcher to place
greater *emphasis on depth* rather than breadth of data. In principle, participant
observation can produce data which are better able than is the case with other
methods to reflect the detail, the subtleties, the complexity and the intercon-
nectedness of the social world it investigates. In the spirit of anthropology,
cultures and events are subject in the first instance to *detailed study*. Attention
is given to intricate details of the social world being studied, and on the

routine as well as the special and the extraordinary. Emphasis is placed on *holistic* understanding, in which the individual things being studied are examined in terms of their relationships with other parts, and with the whole event or culture. And, in similar vein, things are examined in relation to their *context*. In those respects, participant observation scores highly in terms of the *validity* of the data.

Link up with **Ethnography, Chapter 4**

However, the participant observer role need not involve this total immersion. There are versions of participant observation in which the participation element is rather different. Participation, in this sense, means 'being there' and 'in the middle of the action'. One possibility here is that the researcher's role as an observer is still kept secret. Particularly when contemplating fieldwork in more salacious settings, this strategy can be very valuable (Humphreys, 1970). O'Connell Davidson (1995), studying the working practices of a prostitute, acted occasionally as a receptionist for Madame Desirée, thus allowing her to be part of the normal scene but also allowing a judicious distance from the heart of the action.

Another possibility involves hanging out with a group rather than becoming a member of that group. And this can allow the researcher to be open about their purpose – to get consent for the research – in a way that is denied to the total version of participant observation. Of course, the downside of this is that the presence of the researcher can serve to disrupt the naturalness of the setting.

There are numerous variations which have been used that tinker with the extent of total participation and the extent of open observation, but the essential notion of participant observation revolves around the three possibilities:

- *Total participation*, where the researcher's role is kept secret. The researcher assumes the role of someone who normally participates in the setting. Consent cannot be gained for the research, which poses ethical problems.
- *Participation in the normal setting*, where the researcher's role may be known to certain 'gatekeepers', but may be hidden from most of those in the setting. The role adopted in this type of participant observation is chosen deliberately to permit observation without affecting the naturalness of the setting, but it also allows the researcher to keep a distance from the key group under study. This distance might be warranted on the grounds of propriety, or the researcher lacks the personal credentials to take on the role in question.
- *Participation as observer*, where the researcher's identity as a researcher is openly recognized – thus having the advantages of gaining informed consent from those involved – and takes the form of 'shadowing' a person or group through normal life, witnessing first hand and in intimate detail the culture/events of interest.

What to observe, what to record

Starting fieldwork

The researcher should not enter the field with pre-established hypotheses to be tested. The researcher is *there to learn about the situation*. The longer the researcher is able to spend 'on site' the better, because the longer he or she is part of the action the more can be learnt about the situation. Good participant observation demands that the researcher devotes *considerable time* to the field-work. This is not a hit and run research method. Time on site is needed to gain trust, to establish rapport and foster insights, insights that are the trade mark of participant observation as a research method.

Then there is the question of what to observe during the time on site. The researcher should start out being fairly non-selective in terms of what he or she observes. Before anything else, the participant observer should aim to *get an 'overall feel' for the situation*, and to do this he or she should engage in what can be termed 'holistic observation'.

Of course, getting a general feel for the setting, while it is valuable as a background scene-setting device, is really a prelude to more *focused observa tions*. As things emerge which appear to have particular significance or interest, observation will shift from the broad canvas of activity in the setting towards specific areas. Things which emerge as important, strange or unusual invite closer scrutiny.

Following from focused observations, the researcher might be able to undertake *special observations* which concentrate on aspects of the setting in which there appear to be things which are unexpected or contradictory. Attention can be focused upon things that, according to the observer's common sense, ought not to happen.

Finally, observations can try to *identify issues and problems* which participants themselves regard as crucial. The point is to observe instances which indicate how members of the setting see things – *their* views, beliefs and experiences.

Making field notes

The fieldwork researcher needs to translate the observations into some permanent record at the very earliest opportunity. This might be 'field notes' in the form of written records or tape-recorded memos. Whatever the form, the researcher doing fieldwork needs to develop a strategy for writing up field notes as soon as possible after the observation.

The need to do so stems from two things. First, the human memory is not only selective, but also frail. It is so easy to forget things, particularly the minor incidents and passing thoughts, if field notes are delayed for a matter of days, let alone weeks. *Field notes are urgent business*. The researcher needs to build into the research some provision to make the field notes on a regular and prompt basis. The second factor involved here is the general need to take field notes outside the arena of action. To take field notes while engaging in the action as a participant, to state the obvious, would be (a) to disrupt the naturalness of the setting and (b) to disclose the researcher's role as observer. As a general rule, then, participant observers need to establish occasions during fieldwork, or very soon afterwards, when they can make field notes in private and unknown to those being observed. The simplest strategy is to write up the field notes as soon as you get home – assuming that home is separate from the field being studied.

Ethics

Participant observation can pose particular ethical problems for the researcher. If 'total' participation is used, then those being studied will not be aware of the research or their role in it. They can hardly give 'informed consent'. The justification for such covert research cannot depend on consent, but draws instead on two other arguments. First, if it can be demonstrated that none of those who were studied suffered as a result of being observed, the researcher can argue that certain ethical standards were maintained. Second, and linked, if the researcher can show that the identities of those involved were never disclosed, again there is a reasonable case for saying that the participant observation was conducted in an ethical manner.

Whichever variant of participant observation is used, there is the possibility that confidential material might 'fall into the hands' of the researcher. Now, while this is true of most research methods, its prospects are exacerbated with the use of participant observation, owing to the closeness and intimacy of the researcher's role *vis-à-vis* those being researched. Confidential material might be disclosed inadvertently by someone who does not know the research interest of the participant. Or, possibly even more problematic, things might get revealed as a result of the trust and rapport developed between the researcher and those being observed. This could be true for any of the variants of participant observation. The ethical problem is whether to use such material and how to use it. And here the guidelines are quite clear: (a) any use of the material should ensure that no one suffers as a result, and (b) any use of the material should avoid disclosing the identities of those involved. Any departure from these guidelines would need very special consideration and justification.

Self, identity and participant observation

Equipment for research: the 'self'

One of the attractions of participant observation is that it hinges on the researcher's 'self', and does not call on much by the way of technical back-up in the form of gadgets or software. Nor does it tend to produce data that call for statistical analysis. *The key instrument of participant observation methods is the researcher as a person.*

This suggests that there is little in the way of 'entry costs' to act as a deterrent. Equipment costs are very low. There might appear to be no need for training (though this, of course, would be a fallacy). The researcher, it might seem, can jump right into the fieldwork and get on with it. However, as we see in the next sections, this dependence on the 'self' is not altogether a straightforward advantage.

Access to settings

Access is not necessarily a matter of getting approval from relevant authorities or getting a 'gatekeeper' to help open doors to the necessary contacts and settings. As well as these, when engaging in the total version of participant observation there is a special, peculiar issue affecting access. If the researcher is to adopt a role in the setting then he or she needs to have the *necessary credentials* – both personal and qualifications.

To operate 'under cover' in a setting it is obvious that the researcher should not stand out like a sore thumb. Depending on the situation, this can effectively exclude many researchers from many roles. The age factor will bar most (all?) researchers from using participant observation to investigate student cultures in schools. Observing the setting as a teacher is a more likely prospect. Sex will offer other barriers. Male researchers will be hard pushed to use total participant observation for the study of, for example, cocktail waitresses. Observing as a barman in the setting is a more likely prospect. Black researchers will find it exceptionally difficult to infiltrate the Ku Klux Klan. The biological factors place severe constraints on access to situations. Skills and qualifications provide another barrier. To participate in the sense of adopting a role it is necessary to have the necessary skills and qualifications associated with that group. As Polsky (1967) points out, his study of pool hall hustling was only possible as a participant observer because – through a 'misspent youth' – he was already something of an accomplished pool player himself. The would-be researcher, however, might be reluctant or unable to achieve such a skill specifically for the purpose of a piece of research. Following the logic here, there are many, many roles which the researcher will be unable to adopt – from brain surgeon to tree surgeon – because of a lack of credentials.

Selecting a topic

In view of the constraints on access and the potential hazards of doing field-work as a full participant, there are two things which emerge that have a direct bearing on the selection of a topic.

*   To a large extent, researchers who do participant observation have their topic selected for them on the basis of their pre-existing personal attributes. The 'choice' is rarely much of a free choice. The researcher's self – age, sex, ethnicity, qualifications, skills, social background and lifestyle – tends to direct the possibilities and provide *major constraints on the roles that can be adopted*.
*   While it is arguably the most revealing and sensitive of research methods in the social sciences, it is also very demanding. *It is not a soft option*. The level of commitment needed for full participant observation can be far more than that demanded by other methods – commitment in terms of researcher's time and the degree to which the act of research invades the routine life of the researcher.

It is not surprising, then, that many of the fascinating studies emerge as 'one-offs' in which researchers have explored an area of social life for which they are uniquely qualified to participate through their own past experience. It is far more unusual to find examples where researchers have been deliberately employed to infiltrate a group (e.g. Festinger *et al.*, 1956) or where researchers have consciously adopted a role which is alien to them and which involves danger and discomfort (e.g. Griffin, 1962).

Another consequence of the restrictions to full participation is the decision of many social researchers to opt for the version of participant observation which is not 'total participation'. Participation in the setting and participation as observer offer approaches which side-step some of the dangers of total participation and offer a more palatable experience for the researcher on many occasions (e.g. O'Connell Davidson, 1995; Humphreys, 1970; Whyte, [1943] 1981).

Going native

If the researcher has the necessary credentials and personal resources to gain access as a participant observer, they are then faced with the need to operate at two levels while in the setting. The success of participant observation relies on the researcher's ability, at one and the same time, to be a member of the group being studied *and* to retain a certain detachment which allows for the research observation aspect of the role. It is vital, in this respect, that the researcher does not lose sight of the original purpose for being there and does not get engulfed by the circumstances or swallowed up. The success of participant observation depends on being able to walk a tightrope between the involvement and passion associated with full participation and the cool detachment associated with research observation. If the researcher's self gets lost, this is rather like an anthropologist forgetting all about their research and settling down to live out their days as a member of the 'tribe' that they had originally set out to study: '*going native*'.

> Going native is an objectionable term, deservedly, for an objectionable phenomenon. It means over-identifying with the respondents, and losing the researcher's twin perspective of her own culture and, more importantly, of her 'research' and outlook.
>
> (Delamont, 1992: 34)

Dangers of fieldwork

Doing participant observation can be dangerous. First, there is *physical danger*. As Lee (1995) points out, being physically injured while doing fieldwork is fairly unlikely but, depending on the circumstances, cannot be ignored as a possibility. It is a potential built into some forms of fieldwork. Danger lurks for anthropologists who travel in remote regions with inhospitable climates and treacherous terrains. In the early years of the century, evidently, there were instances where anthropologists were actually killed by the people they were studying (Howell, 1990). Danger lurks for political scientists who operate in unstable societies where the rule of law is tenuous and civilians can get caught up in factional disputes. Danger lurks for sociologists and ethnographers when they make contact with groups whose activities are on the margins of, or even outside, the law. As they tap into the underworlds of drugs, prostitution, football hooligans, bikers, religious sects and the like, they take a risk.

Imagine, for the sake of illustration, that a researcher sees the need to investigate the culture surrounding the use of hard drugs by young people. The use of a participant observation approach would seem well suited to such a study. After all, the 'reality' of how, when and why hard drugs are used is hardly likely to emerge by using questionnaires or experiments. Interviews might be useful, but there is a *prima facie* case for participant observation as the method best suited to this particular issue. Provided that a researcher can overcome the first hurdle – to 'look the part' – the fieldwork then involves a range of dangers. There is actual physical danger. This is not just a reference to the prospect of getting mugged or assaulted, or of retribution if the cover is blown at some stage. There is also the danger posed by the lifestyle itself and the impact on health of a changed diet and changed accommodation. Changing lifestyle carries its own hazards. Of course, if the researcher were to become dependent on the use of hard drugs, the health consequences could be far more dramatic.

The fieldwork could involve a second danger: *legal prosecution*. Being 'part of the scene' when hard drugs are around immediately puts the researcher at risk of prosecution. There are no special immunities afforded to social researchers.

The researcher who chooses to engage in such fieldwork might also jeopardize his or her social well-being. The 'other' life he or she is called upon to live for the purposes of the research can have an adverse effect on domestic life, on relationships with others and on commitments to do with work and leisure which make up the 'normal' life of the researcher. *The researcher, in effect, needs to sustain two lifestyles*, and these may not be compatible. Being away from home, being out late and doing fieldwork at 'unsocial' hours can tax the patience of the nearest and dearest. (Let alone what the researcher does while in the field!)

Finally, there is the psychological danger resulting from the dual existence demanded of fieldwork such as this. The lifestyle, at its worst, can have something of a traumatic effect on the researcher, or can have a lasting or permanent effect on the researcher's personality.

> **Key point: dangerous fieldwork**
>
> 'Researchers often work in settings made dangerous by violent conflict, or in situations where inter-personal violence and risk are commonplace. Indeed, in many cases it is the violence itself, or the social conditions and circumstances that produce it, that actively compel attention from the social scientist.' (Lee, 1995: 1)

Advantages of participant observation

- *Basic equipment.* Participant observation uses the researcher's 'self' as the main instrument of research, and therefore requires little by way of technical/statistical support.
- *Non-interference.* It stands a better chance of retaining the naturalness of the setting than other social research methods.
- *Insights.* It provides a good platform for gaining rich insights into social processes and is suited to dealing with complex realities.
- *Ecological validity.* The data produced by participant observation has the potential to be particularly context sensitive and ecologically valid.
- *Holistic.* Participant observation studies offer holistic explanations incorporating the relationships between various factors.
- *Subjects' points of view.* As a method of social research, participant observation is good for getting at *actors' meanings* as they see them.

Disadvantages of participant observation

- *Access*. There are limited options open to the researcher about which roles to adopt or settings to participate in.
- *Commitment*. Participant observation can be a very demanding method in terms of personal commitment and personal resources.
- *Danger*. Participant observation can be potentially hazardous for the researcher; physically, legally, socially and psychologically risky.
- *Reliability*. Dependence on the 'self' of the researcher and on the use of field notes as data leads to a lack of verifiable data. Reliability is open to doubt. Because participant observation relies so crucially on the researcher's 'self' as the instrument of research, it becomes exceedingly difficult to repeat a study to check for reliability. The dependence on field notes for data, constructed (soon) after fieldwork and based on the researcher's recollections of events, does little to encourage those who would want to apply conventional criteria for reliability to this method.
- *Representativeness of the data*. There are problems of generalizing from the research. The focal role of the researcher's 'self' and the emphasis on detailed research of the particular setting opens participant observation to the criticism that it is difficult to generalize from the findings. In one sense, this might hold water as a valid criticism. After all, the situations for research using participant observation are not selected on the grounds of being representative. As we have seen, they tend to be chosen on the basis of a mixture of availability and convenience. However, it might be argued that it is inappropriate to apply standard criteria of reliability and generalizability to this method.
- *Deception*. When researchers opt to conduct full participation, keeping their true identity and purpose secret from others in the setting, there are *ethical problems* arising from the absence of consent on the part of those being observed, and of deception by the researcher.

Checklist for participant observation

When undertaking participant observation you should feel confident about answering 'yes' to the following questions: ☑

1 Is it clear which type of participant observation was used (total participation, participation in normal setting, participation as observer)? ☐

2 Is there evidence that the participant observation did not disturb the naturalness of the setting? ☐

3 Has consideration been given to the ethics of the fieldwork (secrecy, consent, confidentiality)? ☐

4 Has the influence of the researcher's self-identity been examined in terms of:
   (a) the choice of fieldwork situation? ☐
   (b) access to the setting? ☐
   (c) the perception of events and cultures? ☐

5 Was sufficient time spent in the field:
   (a) to allow trust and rapport to develop? ☐
   (b) to allow detailed observations and an in-depth understanding of the situation (detail, context, interconnections)? ☐

6 Does the participant observation allow insights to events and meanings that would not be possible using other methods? ☐

7 Were field notes made at the time or soon after participating in the field? ☐

© M. Denscombe, *The Good Research Guide*. Open University Press.

12

Documents

Kinds of documentary data

Documents can be treated as a source of data in their own right – in effect an alternative to questionnaires, interviews or observation. The documentary sources identified below are *written* sources. There are, though, alternative types of documents for research, which take the form of visual sources (pictures, artefacts) and even sounds (music). These also constitute some form of 'document' which has a value for research but, because they are used relatively rarely within the social sciences, the initial comments in this chapter are restricted to written forms of documents.

Government publications and official statistics

At first glance government publications and official statistics would seem to be an attractive proposition for the social researcher. They would appear to provide a documentary source of information that is:

- *Authoritative*. Since the data have been produced by the state, employing large resources and expert professionals, they tend to have *credibility*.
- *Objective*. Since the data have been produced by officials, they might be regarded as *impartial*.
- *Factual*. In the case of the statistics, they take the form of numbers that are

amenable to computer storage/analysis, and constitute 'hard facts' around which there can be no ambiguity.

It is not surprising, then, that in the Western world government publications and official statistics have come to provide a key source of documentary information for social scientists. However, the extent to which such documents can live up to the image of being authoritative, objective and factual depends very much on the data they contain (see below).

Newspapers and magazines

The 'press' provides a potentially valuable source of information for research purposes. One reason for this is that newspapers and magazines can supply good, up-to-date information. In this case, the value of the newspaper or magazine for the research will stem from one or a combination of:

- the expertise of the journalists;
- the specialism of the publication;
- the insider information which the correspondents can uncover.

So, for example, in the UK, business researchers might use *The Economist* or the *Financial Times* for these reasons. Of course, the discerning researcher will also realize that there are plenty of newspapers and magazines whose contents should not be relied upon to reflect anything approaching an objective account of real events!

Records of meetings

The bureaucratization of industrial society has created a wealth of documentation in relation to administration, policy, management, finance and commerce. These provide an abundant source of data for social researchers in whatever field they operate.

The purpose of most such documentation is to enhance accountability. The records which are kept of meetings (minutes), the records kept of transactions, the records kept of finances, etc. are kept in principle so that people and institutions can be held accountable for their actions. This means that the records need to have two qualities, both of which happen to be of particular value for research.

- First, they need to contain a fairly *systematic picture of things that have happened*. These might be decisions of a committee or transfers of money between accounts. Whatever the records, though, the principle behind them is that they provide a detailed and accurate picture of what took place. They have got to make events sufficiently transparent for the readers to comprehend what took place and why.

- Second, they should be *publicly available*. The records only serve the function of accountability to the extent that they are made available to relevant people to scrutinize.

Letters and memos

Private correspondence between people can be used for research purposes. This can take the form of memos sent between people at work or even personal letters exchanged between people. The more private the correspondence, of course, the more difficult it is for the researcher to gain access to the documents. These are really at the other end of the spectrum from the publicly available reports, and pose far more of a challenge for the researcher when it comes to getting hold of such documents and, especially, when it comes to getting permission to use them as research data.

Letters and memos also differ from reports in terms of the extent to which there is any formal obligation on the writer to give a full and accurate portrayal of events. Because they are written to specific people, rather than for a broader public, their contents are likely to rely far more on assumptions about what the other person already knows or what that person feels. They are more likely to 'fill in the bits' rather than paint the whole picture. They can be expected to be from a personal point of view rather than be impartial. When contemplating the use of letters or memos as data for research, then, you need to recognize that they are not very reliable as accounts which depict objective reality, but they are extremely valuable as a source which reveals the writer's own perceptions and views of events.

Diaries

As a source of documentary data, diaries are written by people whose thoughts and behaviour the researcher wishes to study. For research purposes such diaries are important in terms of recording things that have already happened. We are not talking about the kind of diaries which act as a planner, noting commitments in the future that need to be scheduled. For research purposes, the diary is normally a retrospective account of things that have happened.

There are three crucial elements to this kind of diary – three elements which, incidentally, are shared with the literary diary and the statesman's diary.

- *Factual data*: a log of things that happened, decisions made and people involved.
- *Significant incidents*: the identification of things seen as particularly important and a description of the diary-writer's priorities.
- *Personal interpretation*: a personal reflection and interpretation of happenings, plus an account of the personal feelings and emotions surrounding the events described.

Each of these three things has the potential to provide a rich source of data for the researcher. However, the accounts they provide should not be used by the researcher as a statement of objective fact. That would be very naive. As a retrospective account, diaries must always be seen as a *version* of things as seen by the writer, filtered through the writer's past experiences, own identity, own aspirations and own personality.

It is also worth noting that diaries, as a form of documentary data, lend themselves to being analysed in a variety of ways. As a method of data collection they do not prescribe such matters and, as Alaszewski (2005) argues, they can be analysed using approaches as widely different as Content Analysis, Grounded Theory and Discourse Analysis.

Website pages and the Internet

Documents, as a form of data, include material obtained *via* the Internet. In a sense, the medium through which the document is obtained is not the issue. We can read newspapers in their original paper form, or we can read them on microfiche or via a CD-ROM. Equally, we can obtain documents through website pages or email, and this does not, of itself, have a bearing on the use of the output as a document for research. Websites, though, can be treated as documents in their own right. Home Pages, etc. can be treated as a form of document, and their content analysed in terms of the text and images they contain. In effect, they can be treated like *online documents*.

Access to documentary sources

Probably the greatest attraction of using documentary sources is their accessibility. To get hold of the material the researcher needs only to visit the library or go online via a home computer. The Internet provides the researcher with access to a host of government sites that provide a wide range of information on social and economic factors. In the UK a list of government websites can be found at <http://www.open.gov.uk>, and in the USA there are sites like <http://www.access.gpo.gov> and <http://www.fedworld.gov> that offer entry points to search for official data and government publications. This means that vast amounts of information are conveniently available without much cost, without much delay, without prior appointment, without the need for authorization and without any likelihood of ethical problems. Documents, in other words, pose considerably fewer problems than people as a source of data for social researchers.

There are times, however, when the use of documents does not completely side-step the kind of problems that face researchers using other sources. While access to documents in the public domain is certainly straightforward, researchers can sometimes need to use materials whose availability is deliberately restricted. When this is the case, access becomes a crucial part of the research method – more than something that can be taken for granted. When documents are researchers need to enter negotiations with those who hold the data in order to persuade them to allow the researcher the privilege of access to the material. Documents such as police files and medical records, and certain kinds of company reports and memos, might rightly be considered sensitive and confidential by those who 'own' them, and they are only likely to grant access when they are convinced that the researcher will honour the confidentiality of the material and use it in a way that will not harm the interests of anyone concerned.

Access to information on the Internet can be controlled by the actions of certain strategic 'gatekeepers' who can influence what information is made available and who is allowed access to that information. Some information, as we have seen in relation to academic articles and market research data, will only be accessible on condition of payment of money. Separate from this, Internet researchers need to be sensitive to the role of 'moderators' and 'webmasters' in filtering the information. Some sites, but by no means all, are controlled by people whose role it is to monitor the content of the site and the conduct of those who use it. Moderators (mailing lists, bulletin boards, newsgroups, chat rooms) and webmasters (email servers) acting in this capacity are

Access to documents for research

Type of document	Examples	Access via	Typical use
Public domain	Books, journals, official statistics, some company records	Libraries, Internet, Office for National Statistics	Academic research and consultancy
Restricted access	Medical records, police files, internal memos, personal papers/diaries, some tax accounts	Negotiations with gate-keepers, sponsors	Consultancy and academic research
Secret	Cabinet minutes, illegal trade, second set of books for VAT or Inland Revenue, corporate plans	Insider knowledge, participation, deception	Investigative journalism, fraud detection, undercover work

effectively 'gatekeepers'. They have the power to deny access to the site and might need to be persuaded of the relevance and worthiness of a proposed piece of research before they will grant access.

In the case of documents considered to be *secret*, of course, the holders will seek to deny any access to outsiders. Companies may have secret strategic plans regarded as too sensitive for even a *bona fide* researcher. The government wishes to keep many documents secret 'in the national interest'. Records of illegal activities, whether a drug smuggler's diary or a second set of books for VAT returns, are extremely unlikely to be opened to the researcher. Access will not be willingly given. To get access to such secret documents requires the approach of investigative journalism or participant observation with a degree of deception and covert infiltration being used.

The validity of documentary sources

For the purposes of research, documentary sources should never be accepted at face value. Their validity is something that needs to be established rather than being taken for granted and, as Platt (1981) and Scott (1990) have argued, documents need to be evaluated in relation to four basic criteria.

Authenticity

Is it the genuine article? Is it the real thing? Can we be satisfied that the document is what it purports to be – not a fake or a forgery?

Credibility

Is it accurate? Is it free from bias and errors? This will depend on factors like:

- What *purpose* was the document written for?
- *Who produced the document*? What was the status of the author and did he or she have a particular belief or persuasion that would colour the version of things?
- If it reports on events, *was it a first hand report* directly witnessed by the author? How long after the event was the document written?
- *When was the document produced*? In what social context and climate?

Representativeness

Is the document typical of its type? Does it represent a typical instance of the thing it portrays? Is the document complete? Has it been edited? Is the extract treated 'in context'?

Meaning

Is the meaning of the words clear and unambiguous? Are there hidden meanings? Does the document contain argot and subtle codes? Are there meanings which involve 'what's left unsaid' or 'reading between the lines'?

Evaluation of articles, journals and books

Academic journals and commercial publishers generally have their material refereed by experts in the field before the work is published, so the researcher has some assurance about the quality of their content. However, this offers no absolute guarantee. And how does the reader find out which journals are refereed and which publishers are reputable? Some rules of thumb might help here. For journals:

- How long has the journal existed? Generally, a journal which has existed for a long time will be OK. Less confidence can be held about new journals. However, this does not mean old equals good, new equals bad: that would be far too simplistic.
- Does the title involve a national title (e.g. *British Medical Journal, American Journal of Sociology*)? Again, there is nothing cast iron about this, but it offers some clue as to the standing of the journal.
- Is the journal published by, or on behalf of, a professional association or some authority?
- Does the journal contain a list of its editorial board and editorial advisers, and do these people strike you as 'of high standing' in the field?
- Is there a clear statement that articles are refereed?

For books and their publishers the following questions might help with the evaluation of the sources.

- Have you heard of the publisher before? If so, this might be reassuring.
- Is the publisher a university press (e.g. Cambridge University Press)? If so, again this offers some confidence about the academic quality of the work being published.
- Is the book in a second or subsequent edition? If so, there has been sufficient demand for the book to warrant new editions, and this would suggest that it has something worthwhile to say. The same applies to a lesser extent where a book has been reprinted several times. Look for the details, usually contained at the start of the book between the title and contents pages.
- If it is a library book, how frequently has it been out on loan recently? The chances are that a book that is frequently on loan has been recommended, and that is why it is in demand.

Evaluation of Internet documents and web pages

The evaluation of the documents downloaded from the Internet centres around one issue more than others. Because there are few restrictions on what is placed on the Internet, any documents to be used for research need to be considered very carefully in terms of their authorship, their credibility and their authenticity. The documents need to be subjected to the researcher's own quality audit along the lines of those recommended in relation to books and journals – but with even more vigour and rigour.

When it comes to the evaluation of the web pages a similar point applies. For research purposes judgements need to be made about the *credibility* of the site where the pages are located. Judgements about this can be made on the basis of four criteria.

- The *authoritativeness* of the site. A university or government site might add some credibility to the source, whereas a private web page might need to be viewed with caution.
- The *trustworthiness* of the site. Does the site convey a sense of serious and legitimate purpose? Does it contain suitable disclaimers and explicit statements about its purpose?
- How *up-to-date* the site is. Attention should be given to how regularly the pages are updated. Is the date of last updating visible and, crucially, is it recent?
- The *popularity* of the site. The extent of interest in a website and the size of its audience can suggest something about the site's recognition and popularity. These can be gauged by the number of times people have logged on to that site – the number of 'hits' on the site.

Evaluation of official statistics

Certain types of official statistics will, to all intents and purposes, provide an objective picture of reality. Unfortunately, the same cannot be said for certain other types of official statistics. When politicians debate the accuracy of unemployment figures or the significance of particular national economic figures, there is clearly room for some doubt and controversy about the objectivity, the accuracy, the completeness and the relevance of some official statistics. This should alert us to the point that official statistics cannot always be taken as 'objective facts'.

To say this is not to reject the use of all official statistics as a source of data for social research. But what it *does* mean is that before treating a set of official statistics as accurate and objective, the researcher should consider the following factors.

- *The extent to which the event or thing being measured is clear-cut and straightforward.* Basically, the more clear-cut the event, the more confidence we can have in the data. The official statistics on things like births, deaths, marriages and divorce are likely to be virtually complete. Whether or not someone is born or dies, whether a marriage or divorce occurs, does not require much in the way of interpretation by the registrars involved. The events themselves happen or don't happen, with little scope for 'creative accounting' or biased interpretation. All right, a very small number of births and deaths might go unrecorded and slip through the net of the tight official procedures for collecting such data. But the numbers will be sufficiently low not to present any serious challenge to the idea that these official statistics are a full and accurate record. Things like unemployment, homelessness and ill health, though, are far less clear-cut. There are a number of ways of defining these things, and this opens up the possibility of disputes about whether the statistics depict real levels of unemployment, etc., or whether they offer a picture biased by the nature of the definition that has been used.

- *Whether there are vested interests in the statistics that are produced.* When those who produce the statistics stand to gain or lose on the basis of what the figures reveal, the astute researcher should treat them with some caution. Trade figures, hospital waiting lists, sales figures: all have consequences for people who want or need the statistics to reveal a particular trend. And official statistics are not immune to the point. Governments can have a vested interest in a variety of statistics, from trade to inflation, from unemployment to health.
- *The extent to which the statistics are the outcome of a series of decisions and judgements made by people.* The more the statistics rely on decisions and choices by those who produce them, the more the eventual official statistics become open to being challenged. The more the statistics are the end-product of a series of choices made by people – choices that involve judgement and discretion – the more the official statistics can be regarded as a 'social construction' rather than a detached, impartial picture of the real world.

Crime statistics provide a good illustration of the *construction* of official statistics. Crime statistics are based on those crimes that people decide to report to the police. A large proportion of crime, however, never gets reported. Petty crimes may go unreported. Theft is frequently not reported, particularly when people see no chance of recovering their property and when the property is not insured. (If a claim is to be made through insurance, a 'crime number' is needed from the police, and this motivates people to report the crime.) Many crimes are not discovered and so obviously do not get reported (e.g. embezzlement). There are the 'crimes with no victims', where, unless someone is caught by the police, no record of the offence will ever appear (e.g. recreational drug use). In the case of some crimes, there may be an unwillingness of the victim to complain because of the accruing stigma (e.g. rape) or fear of retribution.

Even when a crime is reported to the police, there is a level of discretion open to them about how they interpret things and whether to formalize the matter. A lot of 'crime' is sorted out informally, without ever entering the system as a recorded crime. Even when it is in the system, the nature of the offence is open to some degree of interpretation. From the police officer receiving the report onwards, there is some scope for leeway and interpretation about (a) whether to prosecute, (b) what offence gets noted, (c) whether a caution is given, (d) whether the matter proceeds to court and (e) whether the prosecution is successful or not. At each stage people are taking decisions, using discretion and making judgements. Overall, these can have a marked impact on the end-product: the official statistics. It means that there will be a huge difference (in the case of crime) between the real level of crime in society and the figures that get published by the government as 'the crime rate'. It is estimated that recorded crime may be as little as one-fifth of 'actual' crime.

Evaluation of records of meetings

Records, whether publicly available or on restricted access, purport to depict things that have happened in a full and accurate manner. However, there is ample evidence that such records tend to be partial – in both senses of the word. They will tend to be selective in terms of what they report, emphasizing some things and ignoring others, and thus recording only part of the overall event. They will also tend to reflect a particular interpretation of what happened, recording events from a particular angle. We should remember that when such records are produced as part of public accountability, there will be a tendency to be cautious about what is recorded. Things might have been said 'off the record' or following 'Don't minute this but . . .'. The records, in other words, may be subtly edited to exclude things which might render people vulnerable to criticism when the record is published. *The researcher, therefore, needs to be cautious about accepting such records at face value.* Publicly available records reflect upon matters in a way that is publicly acceptable at a given time and in a given social sphere. They tend to offer a version of reality massaged to meet public expectations.

Content analysis

Content analysis is a method which helps the researcher to analyse the content of documents. Basically, it is a method that can be used with any 'text', whether it be in the form of writing, sounds or pictures, as a way of quantifying the contents of that text. Political scientists might use it to study the transcripts of speeches, educationists to study the content of children's books, and historians to study statesmen's correspondence.

Whatever its specific application, content analysis generally follows a logical and relatively straightforward procedure.

- *Choose an appropriate sample of texts or images.* The criterion for the choice of such a sample should be quite explicit.
- *Break the text down into smaller component units.* The unit for analysis can be each and every word. Alternatively, the analysis can use complete sentences as the unit, whole paragraphs or things like headlines. It can also be based on visual images or the content of pictures.
- *Develop relevant categories for analysing the data.* The researcher needs to have a clear idea of the kinds of categories, issues and ideas that he or she is concerned with and how these might appear in the text. This might take the form of 'key words' associated with the theme. So, for example, a search for sex bias in children's stories might look for instances of boys' names and girls' names – the names being treated as indicative of the nature of the content. The researcher might also wish to code the text in terms of the kinds of names, rather than just how many times such names occur.
- *Code the units in line with the categories.* Meticulous attention to the text is needed to code all the relevant words, sentences, etc. These codes are either written on the text and subsequently referred to, or entered via a computer program specially designed for the purpose.
- *Count the frequency with which these units occur.* The first part of analysis is normally a tally of the times when various units occur
- *Analyse the text in terms of the frequency of the units and their relationship with other units that occur in the text.* Once the units have been coded, a more sophisticated analysis is possible which links the units and attempts to explain when and why they occur in the way they do.

Link up with **Computer Assisted Qualitative Data Analysis, pp. 304–5**

Content analysis has the potential to disclose many 'hidden' aspects of what is being communicated through the written text. The idea is that, quite independent of what the writer had consciously intended, the text carries some clues about a deeper rooted and possibly unintentional message that is actually being communicated. You do not have to base the analysis on what the author *thought* they were saying when the text contains more tangible evidence about its message (Gerbner *et al.*, 1969; Krippendorf, 2004).

Content analysis	
. . . reveals	**. . . by measuring**
1 What the text establishes as relevant	What is contained (e.g. particular relevant words, ideas)
2 The priorities portrayed through the text	How frequently it occurs; in what order it occurs
3 The values conveyed in the text	Positive and negative views on things
4 How ideas are related	Proximity of ideas within the text, logical association

The main strength of content analysis is that it provides a means for quantifying the contents of a text, and it does so by using a method that is clear and, in principle, repeatable by other researchers. Its main limitation is that it has an in-built tendency to dislocate the units and their meaning from the context in which they were made, and even the intentions of the writer. And it is difficult for content analysis to deal with the meaning of the text in terms of its *implied* meanings, how the meaning draws on what has just been said, what follows or even what is left unsaid. In many ways, it is a rather crude instrument for dealing with the subtle and intricate ways in which a text conveys meaning.

In practice, therefore, content analysis is at its best when dealing with aspects of communication which tend to be more straightforward, obvious and simple. The more the text relies on subtle and intricate meanings conveyed by the writer or inferred by the reader, the less valuable content analysis becomes in revealing the meaning of the text.

Image-based research

The documents referred to so far have been text-based. There are, however, alternative kinds of documentary data available to social researchers, ones that are based on *visual* images. Central to the idea of image-based research, visual images can be used as data in their own right – distinct from text, numbers or sounds as a potential source of research information. Just like other documents, visual images can prove to be valuable for the purposes of the research in terms of:

- the factual information they contain;
- how they represent things (the symbolism and hidden meanings communicated through the document or image).

Link up with **The analysis of image-based data, pp. 305–7**

Types of image

For practical reasons there has been a tendency to concentrate on two-dimensional 'still' images, such as photographs, as the source of image-based data. Photographs are relatively inexpensive. They also lend themselves to analysis and reproduction alongside more conventional text-based research, e.g. in printed journals or academic dissertations. Potentially, though, there are a wide variety of visual images that could be used. There have been adventurous attempts on occasion to explore the possibilities of moving images and even three-dimensional objects (Banks, 2001; Emmison and Smith, 2000).

Potential sources of image-based documentary data		
Still	Movie	Object
photographs	video recording	cultural artefacts
advertisements	archive film	clothing and fashion items
drawings		built environment and places
graffiti		body signs/language

The use of 'created' images

The researcher can generate images specifically for the purposes of the investigation – so-called *created* images. The visual images, in this sense, provide primary source data. These images can be valuable as a means of recording things. Researchers can make records of events, people, cultures and so on by photographing, filming or drawing them. Such visual records provide an alternative to tape recordings (*sound*), an alternative to the use of written documents such as field notes, diaries or minutes (*text*) and an alternative to the use of quantitative data such as figures from questionnaires or statistics based on systematic observation (*numbers*).

When embarking on the use of created images the researcher ought to bear in mind certain practical issues. The first concerns *equipment*. Cameras for photographs and camcorders for videos come in a range of technical specifications and prices. They can produce output in film or digital format. The researcher needs to decide what equipment will best suit the purposes of the research and what equipment is actually available. This may well call for some sort of compromise decision that balances the quality and format of the output against the resources that exist. In arriving at the decision the researcher will need to be aware that more sophisticated equipment might call for technical skills and expertise and that any additional technical wizardry attached to more expensive equipment might be wasted without the necessary talent to make use of it. Weighed against this, cheap equipment that produces poor quality images might prove to be a poor saving of resources. Forethought needs to be given to the environments in which the images will be collected. Will the lighting be adequate to avoid flash photography that might be intrusive or distracting? Will better quality film and equipment overcome such a problem? Will a zoom lens be necessary to capture enough detail?

Quite apart from the technical considerations involved with image-based research, when researchers set out to capture data by 'creating' the images first hand they are confronted as well by a range of social and cultural factors that can have a marked impact on their ability to record things 'as they are'. Even when things might seem quite straightforward, there can be problems lurking just beneath the surface. For example, filming *objects* such as buildings, transport facilities and artefacts would appear to be fairly unproblematic as a means of data collection. There are circumstances, however, where filming and photography are not allowed. Some countries might regard it as a security threat depending on the location. There are issues of privacy to be considered, and in galleries and museums there are often restrictions on photography and filming of the artefacts. Forethought needs to be given to the legal and cultural context within which data collection is to take place in order to minimize the risk that the filming or photography of specific objects will be regarded as an offence or as offensive.

When the image-based research involves *people* there is all the more need for sensitivity to the social and cultural context. As Prosser and Schwartz (1998: 119) point out, researchers need to appreciate that 'making pictures can be a threatening act (amply demonstrated by the metaphors photography invokes: we "load", "aim" and "shoot"). The act of being "captured" on film can be *perceived* as threatening even if the researcher's intention is benign, and this likelihood has two important repercussions for the process of data collection:

- It can *limit access* to research sites. If people feel threatened, if they feel that there is an invasion of privacy, they might well refuse to co-operate with the research.
- It can cause people to *become self-conscious* and to act in a way that they would not do normally.

There is, in effect, an element of reflexivity involved with the collection of 'created' images. Prosser (1998: 104–5) writes of this in terms of 'procedural reactivity' and 'personal reactivity'. Procedural reactivity refers to the way the act of taking the photographs makes the researcher more obviously visible when collecting data for the record, and the way that this can alter the natural state of affairs by inhibiting, embarrassing or in some other way altering the behaviour and activities of the person(s) being photographed. Personal reactivity refers to the way the photographer/researcher can have an effect on the situation simply on the basis of their own identity and personal characteristics, and their own judgements in terms of the nature of the photograph that is taken. An example might be a photographer's presence when recording images at the birth of a child and the way the sex and age of the photographer might have a bearing on the types of photograph that are taken and the reaction of the mother, the father and nursing staff to being photographed during this intimate moment.

Bearing the issue of reflexivity in mind, researchers need to be conscious of the way their actions will be perceived. Consideration needs to be given to the impact of things like:

- *The equipment.* Flash photography will be more evident than daylight photography, and a discreet small digital camera will be less visible than bulky, professional camcorder equipment.
- *The situation.* Certain events involve film records more normally than others. Ceremonial events, for instance, might allow the use of created images by the researcher in a way that would not be the case in more personal, intimate circumstances.
- *The people involved.* People who live 'in the public eye', those with high-profile jobs and people like media celebrities, will probably be fairly comfortable in the knowledge that they are being filmed or photographed because it is a routine part of their working lives. They might, however, reserve the right to privacy on occasions when they are 'off duty', regarding this as their personal and private life.
- *Personalities.* Extroverts and publicity seekers will be likely to adore the attention of the camera in a way that more introverted and camera-shy people will not.

The factors come into play, of course, only when people are aware that they are being filmed. This need not always be the case. The researcher might choose to undertake covert research, in which the process of filming is kept secret from those who are being studied. There are particular ethical issues that arise in this case and, to gain approval from any relevant authorizing body (e.g. an ethics committee), a strong case will need to be made for *not* seeking informed consent from those being studied. This pertains, of course, to a range of social research methods, but the fullness of the data captured on film can make people all the more defensive and reticent to co-operate – more than would be the case if the research relied on things like interviews or questionnaire data.

Link up with **Research Ethics, pp. 141–51**

The use of 'found' images

The social researcher can make use of images that already exist – so-called *found* images. These are images that have been produced by other people for reasons not directly connected with the researcher's investigation.

The kind of images used depends largely on the subject discipline of the researcher. Media studies and marketing often use advertisements and newspaper photographs. Anthropologists, historians and sociologists will use images of groups and cultural events portrayed using film, photographs, paintings, graffiti or artefacts. Such items contain a visual record that can be used to provide factual information about groups or events, or the images can be interpreted to provide some better understanding of the ideas and lifestyles that generated the images.

As a source of data, 'found' images sidestep a number of problems associated with the data gathering process for 'created' images. Technical issues about equipment and practical issues of access to locations, for instance, no longer arise, since the image(s) already exists. Immediately, this suggests that the use of found images is an attractive proposition for the social researcher because it requires less skill to produce and may well prove less expensive if it saves fieldwork, travel and production costs. Equally attractively, it overcomes the ethical concerns of getting informed consent in those cases where the image involves living people. Added to this, the Internet has vastly increased the availability of images for social researchers. Images can be downloaded from across the globe to arrive almost instantaneously with the researcher. No fieldwork and no travel are required.

The ease with which found images can be obtained should not seduce the researcher into opting for their use without recognizing that there are also some specific issues that arise in relation to the use of found images that need to be weighed against the ease and cost factors.

Authenticity

As with other documentary data, the social researcher who uses visual images will want to feel certain about the authenticity of the image. This is particularly the case with 'found' images that are to be used as a source of factual information. The researcher needs to be wary about whether the image has been tampered with, changed or edited from the original. Computer software, of course, makes this increasingly simple to do. Photographic images, in particular, are relatively easy to alter and the researcher should not take it as a matter of trust that the image is genuine. As Loizos (2000: 95) warns, 'One fallacy is implied by the phrase 'the camera cannot lie'. Humans, the agents who wield cameras, can and do lie: . . . they can distort the evidential recording capacity of visual data just as readily as they can distort written words.'

Copyright

Ownership of an image is an important issue, particularly if the image is to be reproduced and made publicly available through the process of research. If the image already exists, the chances are that it 'belongs' to some person, company or institution, in which case it is necessary to obtain permission to use the image. At one extreme this might be a fairly informal thing. If, for example, the image to be used is a personal photograph from a family album, the necessary permission could involve little more than getting approval (preferably in writing) from the owner for the use of the image for research purposes. At the other extreme, images based on advertisements or works of art, and drawn from news media, entertainment magazines or the Internet, are the kind of thing that will probably require a very formal request to the copyright holder for permission to reproduce the image. If the copyright holder agrees to this, it might be conditional on the payment of a fee. The fee can be prohibitively large and it is important to make it clear when requesting permission that the image is to be used for the purposes of small-scale, private research from which there will be no monetary gain. Fees might be waived or reduced under these circumstances, though this will depend on the nature of the image and the policies of the particular copyright holder. If the image to be used has an obscure origin and the copyright holder cannot be traced there is a standard solution to the problem, which consists of making a clear statement at the start of any report or dissertation along the lines that 'Efforts have been made to obtain permission from copyright holders of the (photographic images) used. Where the copyright owners have not been traced the author invites further information from anyone concerned and will seek to remedy the situation.' This does presume, of course, that rigorous efforts have indeed been made and the statement should not be used as a way to avoid the work of tracing copyright holders.

> **Key point: copyright and created images**
>
> Where the image has been created by the researcher, there is generally not too much of a problem. The image is usually owned by the researcher. However, this may not always be the case. In some cases ownership of the image might be claimed on behalf of the person or event portrayed. However, as Banks (2001: 168) notes, this issue is 'relevant largely to representations of celebrities, those deemed likely to have a financial interest in the use of their representations'.

Caution

Despite claims that contemporary society has more of a 'visual culture' than in the past, and despite some signs of a growing interest in 'visual research' (Flick, 2002), the use of image-based data remains relatively uncommon in the social sciences. Part of the reason for this is that film, video and three-dimensional images do not readily fit the medium within which research data and analyses are normally presented. They may not fit in dissertations, journals or computer documents that favour a two-dimensional, text-based format. Partly, this might be because of the cost of using full-colour glossy photographic data, or the space that photographic data might consume when there are tight editorial restrictions on the number of pages available. What is clear, however, is that image-based research remains somewhat marginalized and, as yet, struggles to achieve a parity of status in the social sciences with research whose data take the form of numbers or words. The project researcher undertaking small-scale research might do well to bear this in mind.

Advantages of documentary research

- *Access to data*. Vast amounts of information are held in documents. Depending on the nature of the documents, most researchers will find access to the sources relatively easy and inexpensive.
- *Cost-effective*. Documentary research provides a cost-effective method of getting data, particularly large-scale data such as those provided by official statistics.
- *Permanence of data*. Documents generally provide a source of data which is permanent and available in a form that can be checked by others. The data are open to public scrutiny.

Disadvantages of documentary research

- *Credibility of the source*. The researcher needs to be discerning about the information they use. Researchers need to evaluate the authority of the source and the procedures used to produce the original data in order to gauge the credibility of the documents. This is not always easy. Internet documents, in particular, need special scrutiny. Information found on the Internet can be up-to-date and good quality stuff. However, just as easily, it can be out-of-date, poor quality material because there is little control over what is placed on the Internet. From the academic researcher's perspective, the worry is that 'the Internet is characterized by uncontrolled and unmonitored publishing with little peer review' (Cline and Haynes, 2001: 679).

* *Secondary data.* When researchers use documents as a source of data, they generally rely on something which has been produced for other purposes and not for the specific aims of the investigation.
* *Social constructions.* Documents can owe more to the interpretations of those who produce them than to an objective picture of reality.

Checklist for the use of documents (text and visual images)

When undertaking documentary research you should feel confident about answering 'yes' to the following questions: ☑

1 Am I satisfied that the documents/images are genuine in terms of what they purport to be (not drafts, forgeries, misleading second versions, etc.)? ☐

2 Have I considered the credibility of the documents or images in terms of:
   - their source (published book, journal article, official statistics)? ☐
   - their author or creator (status, role, in a position to know)? ☐
   - their sponsorship (organization, funding, pressure group)? ☐
   - the accessibility of the information they use (public domain, restricted, secret)? ☐

3 Have website sources been evaluated in terms of their accuracy and how recently they have been updated (where applicable)? ☐

4 Am I satisfied that I have taken account of possible bias in the document or image arising from:
   - its purpose (description, theory, persuasion)? ☐
   - how representative it is (typical, extreme)? ☐
   - the editing and selection of extracts used in it? ☐
   - its interpretation of facts or theories? ☐
   - sensitivity to the information or image it contains? ☐

5 Have I provided full details of the sources of the texts or images used? ☐

6 Has the research avoided contravening copyright laws? ☐

© M. Denscombe, *The Good Research Guide*. Open University Press.

Part III

Analysis

The process of analysis involves the search for things that lie behind the surface content of the data – core elements that explain what the thing is and how it works. The researcher's task is to probe the data in a way that helps to identify the crucial components that can be used to explain the nature of the thing being studied, with the aim of arriving at some general principles and can be applied elsewhere to other situations.

There are many kinds of analysis that the social researcher can use to do this. In practice, though, the options tend to gravitate around the notions of 'quantitative' and 'qualitative' research. The terms 'quantitative research' and 'qualitative research' are widely used and understood within the realms of social research as signposts to the kind of assumptions being used by the researchers and the nature of the research that is being undertaken. As we probe deeper into the distinction between 'quantitative research' and 'qualitative research', however, it becomes apparent that in the real world of social research things do not fall neatly into the two categories. There are three reasons for this.

1 *In practice, the approaches are not mutually exclusive.* Social researchers rarely, if ever, rely on one approach to the exclusion of the other. Good research tends to use parts of both approaches, and the difference lies in *the extent* to which the research is based in one camp or the other.
2 *In theory, the distinction is too simplistic.* The assumptions associated with the two approaches are frequently shared, frequently overlap and basically do not fall either side of a clear dividing line.
3 Strictly speaking, the distinction between 'quantitative' and 'qualitative' *relates to the treatment of data*, rather than the research methods as such. As Strauss (1987: 2) argues, 'the genuinely useful distinction is in how data are treated analytically'. This is dealt with in Chapters 13 and 14.

We must recognize, then, that a distinction between quantitative and qualitative research is far from 'watertight'.

Bearing this in mind, what is conveyed through the use of labels such as 'quantitative research' and 'qualitative research'? The terms 'quantitative' and 'qualitative' have come to denote contrasting positions in relation to a number of dimensions of social research. Each term implies a commitment to a particular set of assumptions about the nature of the social world being investigated and the appropriate way to investigate it, a position which is in opposition to that linked with the other term. As these polar opposites are listed, though, it is important to bear in mind that the distinctions are based on something of an over-simplification and a caricature, not a depiction of the real world of social research, with people in two entirely separate camps.

Words or numbers

- Quantitative research tends to be associated with numbers as the unit of analysis.
- Qualitative research tends to be associated with words or images as the unit of analysis.

The most elementary distinction between the two approaches lies in the use of words or numbers as the basic unit for analysis. On the one hand, there is 'quantitative research', whose aim is to measure phenomena so that they can be transformed into numbers. Once the phenomena have been quantified, they lend themselves to analysis through statistical procedures – procedures which are very powerful but utterly dependent on receiving numerical data as the input. The obsession of quantitative approaches, then, is with generating data that are numerical, with transforming what is observed, reported or recorded into quantifiable units. On the other hand, qualitative research relies on transforming information from observations, reports and recordings into data in the form of the written word, not numbers. The sources of information, it should be noted, need not differ between quantitative and qualitative approaches. A questionnaire, for example, can be used to produce either quantitative *data* (numbers) or qualitative *data* (words).

Analysis or description

- Quantitative research tends to be associated with analysis.
- Qualitative research tends to be associated with description.

The potential of numbers to be analysed using statistical procedures places quantitative data in a strong position when it comes to analysis. Numbers are particularly well suited to measurable comparisons and correlations whereas qualitative data are better suited to descriptions. Whether dealing with meanings or with patterns of behaviour, qualitative researchers can use detailed and intricate descriptions of events or people. Such 'thick description' (Geertz, 1973), as it is known, is necessary in order to convey the complexity of the situation.

Large-scale or small-scale

• Quantitative research tends to be associated with large-scale studies.
• Qualitative research tends to be associated with small-scale studies.

Statistics tend to operate more safely with larger numbers. It is not surprising, then, that quantitative research tends to favour larger-scale research with larger numbers and greater quantities. The sheer amounts involved, once they have been transformed into numerical data, do not slow down the analysis to any discernible degree. A statistical procedure can be undertaken by a computer on a sample of 2,000 pretty much as quickly as it can on a sample of 20. The results, though, will be more reliable when conducted on 2,000 than on 20. The larger the numbers involved, the more the results are likely to be generalizable and reliable statistically speaking. Size matters.

The same might be said for qualitative research, but, in this case, the adage is more likely to be 'small is beautiful'. There is nothing inherently opposed to large-scale qualitative research, but there *is* a strong tendency for qualitative research to be relatively focused in terms of the scope of the study and to involve relatively few people or situations. Much of this reflects the preference for depth of study and the associated 'thick description' which only becomes possible in relation to limited numbers. It equally reflects the fact that words do not lend themselves to the kind of analysis that can utilize the power of computers, at least nowhere near as much as numbers do. So, for the qualitative researcher, there *is* a vast difference in the time it takes to analyse results from larger amounts of data compared with smaller amounts. Together, these factors account for the association of qualitative research with small-scale studies.

Holistic or specific focus

• Quantitative research tends to be associated with a specific focus.
• Qualitative research tends to be associated with holistic perspective.

The approach of quantitative research is to focus on specific factors and to study them in relation to specific other factors. To do this, it is necessary to isolate variables – to separate them from their natural location intertwined with a host of others – in order to study their working and their effect. Qualitative research, on the other hand, rather than isolating variables and focusing on specific factors, generally exhibits a preference for seeing things 'in context' and for stressing how things are related and interdependent. In line with Lincoln and Guba's 'naturalistic' approach, qualitative research tends to operate on the assumption that social 'realities are wholes that cannot be understood in isolation from their contexts, nor can they be fragmented for separate study of their parts' (Lincoln and Guba, 1985: 39).

Researcher involvement or detachment

- Quantitative research tends to be associated with researcher detachment.
- Qualitative research tends to be associated with researcher involvement.

The whole point of quantitative research is to produce numerical data that are 'objective' in the sense that they exist independently of the researcher and are not the result of undue influence on the part of the researcher himself or herself. Ideally, the numerical data are seen as the product of research instruments which have been tested for validity and reliability to ensure that the data accurately reflect the event itself, not the researcher's preferences. Qualitative research, by contrast, tends to place great emphasis on the role of the researcher in the construction of the data. There is typically little use of standardized research instruments in qualitative research. Rather, it is recognized that the researcher is the crucial 'measurement device', and that the researcher's self (their social background, values, identity and beliefs) will have a significant bearing on the nature of the data collected and the interpretations of that data.

Emergent or predetermined research design

- Quantitative research tends to be associated with a predetermined research design.
- Qualitative research tends to be associated with an emergent research design.

One of the key features of quantitative research is the precision with which research designs are established at the outset of the study. Hypotheses establish exactly the nature of the research question(s), and there is a definite sample or experimental procedure to be undertaken. In marked contrast to this, qualitative research is frequently premised on the idea that the theory and the methods will emerge during the course of the research, and will not be specified at the beginning. Theories can be developed and tested as part of an ongoing process – what Glaser and Strauss (1967) call 'grounded theory'. The sample to be investigated will depend on following up leads, which means that the researcher cannot know at the beginning of the research project exactly who will be involved nor how many people or events will be investigated.

The process of data analysis

The analysis of research data tends to follow a process involving five stages. The stages can be seen in relation to both quantitative and qualitative data, as the text box on the next page shows. However, it also shows that there are differences between quantitative and qualitative data analysis, with quantitative approaches tending to shape their data more consciously and more explicitly in the earlier stages of the process compared with qualitative approaches. More details on the specific approaches to data analysis are provided in Chapters 13 and 14.

The five main stages of data analysis

	Quantitative data	Qualitative data
1 Data preparation	Coding (which normally takes place before data collection) Categorizing the data Checking the data	Transcribing the text Cataloguing the text or visual data Preparation of data and loading to software (if applicable)
2 Initial exploration of the data	Look for obvious trends or correlations	Look for obvious recurrent themes or issues Add notes to the data Write memos to capture ideas
3 Analysis of the data	Use of statistical test, e.g. descriptive statistics, factor analysis, cluster analysis Link to research questions or hypotheses	Code the data Group the codes into categories or themes Comparison of categories and themes Quest for concepts (or fewer, more abstract categories) that encapsulate the categories
4 Representation and display of the data	Tables Figures Written interpretation of the statistical findings	Written interpretation of the findings Illustration of points by quotes and pictures Use of visual models, figures and tables
5 Validation of the data	External benchmarks Internal consistency Comparison with alternative explanations	Data and method triangulation Member validation Comparison with alternative explanations

Adapted from Creswell, J.W. and Plano Clarke, V.L. (2007) *Designing and Conducting Mixed Methods Research*. Thousand Oaks, CA: Sage, p. 129, Table 7.1.

13

Quantitative data

Numbers • Types of quantitative data • Preparing quantitative data for analysis • Describing the frequencies and their distribution • Looking for connections: tests for association and difference • Representing the data • Checklist for the presentation of quantitative data • Validation of the data • Advantages of quantitative analysis • Disadvantages of quantitative analysis • Checklist for the use of basic statistics

This chapter focuses on basic aspects of the analysis and presentation of quantitative data. There is no attempt in the context of this book to cover more advanced statistical procedures that use quantitative data for testing hypotheses or forecasting outcomes. Such 'inferential' statistics are valuable, but they require a level of familiarity with statistics that project researchers might not have the time or inclination to acquire. For those who want to study the statistical analysis of quantitative data in more depth there are many textbooks and online resources that are readily available, and reference should be made to such sources. The majority of project researchers, however, will prefer to restrict their analysis to the use of basic descriptive statistics – comfortable in the knowledge that these can provide a straightforward, yet rigorous, way of organizing the data, presenting the results and providing some basic analysis of the data. The premise of this chapter, then, is that, properly used, simple '*descriptive*' statistics can offer the project researcher a succinct and precise way of:

- organizing the data;
- summarizing the findings;
- displaying the evidence;
- describing the profile of findings (how the data are distributed);
- exploring connections between parts of the data (correlations and associations).

> **Key point**
>
> **Quantitative data can be used very effectively without the need for complex statistical analysis.**

Numbers

Quantitative data take the form of numbers. They are associated primarily with strategies of research such as surveys and experiments, and with research methods such as questionnaires and observation. These are not, however, the only sources of quantitative data. For example, the use of content analysis with texts (such as interview transcripts) can also produce numerical data. The kind of research method used, then, is *not* the crucial thing when it comes to defining quantitative data. It is the nature of the data that the method produces that is the key issue. It is important to bear this point in mind and to recognize that quantitative data can be produced by a variety of research methods, as the text box below shows.

Sources of quantitative data

Numbers	*Research method*
• Answers to closed-ended questions	Questionnaires
• Content analysis of transcripts	Interviews
• Measurements from experiments • Observation schedule used with events	Observation
• Official statistics (health, education, trade, etc) • Business data (performance, employment, etc.) • Content analysis of things like company reports	Documents

---

Types of quantitative data

Numbers can represent different types of things, and social researchers who want to use quantitative data need to be absolutely clear about the type of numerical data they are using. This makes a major difference to what can be done with the data, statistically speaking, and the kind of conclusions that can be drawn from the analysis. There are certain statistical techniques that work with some kinds of data that will not work with others. In this respect, numerical data can be considered under six headings. The first four concern the distinction established by Stevens (1946) between four types of measurement. These are called nominal, ordinal, interval and ratio. In addition to this, researchers should also be aware of the difference between 'discrete' and 'continuous' data. The underlying point is that *researchers wanting to use quantitative data need to understand what kind of data they are working with and appreciate the possibilities and limitations associated with that particular kind of numerical data.*

Nominal data

Nominal data come from counting things and placing them into a category. They are the lowest level of quantitative data, in the sense that they allow little by way of statistical manipulation compared with the other types. Typically, there is a head count of members of a particular category, such as male/female or White/South Asian/African Caribbean. These categories are based simply on names; there is no underlying order to the names.

Ordinal data

Like nominal data, ordinal data are based on counts of things assigned to specific categories, but, in this case, the categories stand in some clear, ordered, ranked relationship. The categories are 'in order'. This means that the data in each category can be compared with data in the other categories as being higher or lower than, more or less than, etc., those in the other categories.

The most obvious example of ordinal data comes from the use of questionnaires in which respondents are asked to respond on a five-point scale such as:

Strongly agree	Agree	Neutral	Disagree	Strongly disagree
1	2	3	4	5

The responses coded as 2 (agree) can legitimately be seen as more positive than those coded as 3, 4 or 5 (neutral, disagree, strongly disagree), but less positive than those coded 1 (strongly agree). This scale is known as the Likert scale. It is worth stressing that *rank order is all that can be inferred*. With ordinal data we do not know the *cause* of the order, or by how much they differ.

Interval data

Interval data are like ordinal data, but the categories are ranked on a scale. This means that the 'distance' between the categories is a known factor and can be pulled into the analysis. The researcher can not only deal with the data in terms of 'more than' or 'less than', but also say how much more or how much less. The ranking of the categories is *proportionate*, and this allows for direct contrast and comparison.

Calendar years provide a suitable example of such data. Data collected for the years 1966, 1976, 1986, 1996 and 2006 not only differ in terms of being earlier or later than one another, they are also earlier or later by a known time-span interval. This allows the researcher to use addition and subtraction (but not multiplication or division) to contrast the difference between various periods: the difference between 1976 and 1986 can be directly compared with the difference between 1996 and 2006, and so on.

Ratio data

Ratio data are like interval data, except that the categories exist on a scale which has a 'true zero' or an absolute reference point. When the categories concern things like incomes, distances and weights, they give rise to ratio data because the scales have a zero point. Calendar years, in the previous example, do not exist on such a scale, because the year 0 does not denote the beginning of all time and history. The important thing about the scale having a true zero is that the researcher can compare and contrast the data for each category in terms of ratios, using multiplication and division, rather than being restricted to the use of addition and subtraction as is the case with interval data. Ratio data are the highest level of data in terms of how amenable they are to mathematical manipulation.

Discrete data

Certain data are based on phenomena which naturally come in whole units. Numbers of children per family, in reality, have to be whole numbers. We might aggregate the numbers to arrive at an average figure of 1.9 or whatever, but we do not suppose that there exists anywhere 0.9 of a child belonging to a family. In this example, our measurement of children per family can be exact for each and every household, with no need for approximations or results accurate to the nearest fraction. The *discrete data* come in chunks: 1, 2, 3, 4, and so on.

Continuous data

Contrasted with this there are certain kinds of data which, for practical purposes, are inevitably measured 'to the nearest unit' simply because they do not come in neat, discrete chunks. Such things are measured to the nearest small unit because, as a variable, they are *continuous*. People's height, age and weight are obvious examples here. In principle, there is no end to the precision with which we might try to measure these items. We could measure height in millimetres, weight in grams, age in seconds. For practical purposes, however, such precision would be counter-productive, because it would throw up vast arrays of data which would not lend themselves to analysis. When variables are continuous, the researcher, in effect, needs to categorize the data. The unit of data is not exact height, exact weight, exact age; rather, it is 'height falling within a range of 2 cm', 'weight to the nearest 0.5 kilograms', or 'age at last birthday'.

The significance of continuous data lies with the implicit categories which are formed by the researcher to cope with difficulties of measuring points/units on a sliding scale. The researcher needs to be absolutely clear about the boundaries to such categories and exactly where the mid-point of the category resides. The accuracy of statistics based on continuous data depends on knowing the boundaries and mid-point to the categories of the data.

Preparing quantitative data for analysis

Coding the data

The raw data with which the social researcher works sometimes occur 'naturally' in the form of numbers. This is convenient. However, on many occasions the researcher starts off with material in the form of words or pictures and needs to transform the material from this format into the only format suitable for quantitative analysis: numbers. This involves a process of 'coding' the data. Coding, in essence, entails the attribution of a number to a piece of data, or group of data, with the express aim of allowing such data to be analysed in quantitative terms. Such coding is usually done at an early stage in the research process and, in fact, the general advice as far as quantitative analysis is concerned is to do the coding prior to the collection of the data.

Link up with **Questionnaires, Chapter 9**

If this sounds a bit abstract, it might be useful to illustrate the process briefly in relation to the use of questionnaires. Suppose that the researcher is interested in people's occupations, and intends to conduct a survey of 1,000 people. The questionnaire might contain a question asking the respondent to state his or her occupation. This would result in a mass of data, all in the form of words, covering a huge range of possibilities. In this format the data are difficult to handle and very difficult to analyse. Imagine the researcher's problem when faced with a list of 1,000 separate jobs. To make the task of analysis possible, the researcher needs to identify a smaller number of *categories* of jobs, and then to assign each job listed to one of the categories. Each category will have a numerical code, and so the process of analysis involves coding each of the words by giving it a numerical value which accords with the category of job to which it fits.

Where the researcher knows in advance that they want to generate quantitative data, it makes good sense to sort out the categories and their respective numbers and build these into the design of the research. Things like a person's occupation can be categorized in advance using existing official classifications. Instead of people being asked to state what their job is, they can be asked to identify which category of occupations best fits their own. The result of doing it this way is that, if there are, say, ten categories of occupation used, the researcher will obtain results in the form of numbers in each of the ten categories, rather than the list of 1,000 words. The data, in this format, are ready for analysis.

Grouping the data

The first stage in the analysis of quantitative data is to organize the raw data in a way that makes them more easily understood. As Figure 5 shows, it is rather difficult to make sense of raw data when the number of items goes above ten.

Days absent from work through illness during the previous year, 30 employees					
1	12	0	9	4	7
5	3	6	15	10	8
4	36	3	13	3	3
3	6	3	6	0	0
10	5	8	0	10	2

(Source: Human Resources Dept, Healthy Life Insurance Co.)

FIGURE 5 Raw data example

Initially, it is some help to construct an *array of the raw data*, i.e. to arrange the data in order. As Figure 6 shows, this immediately helps in terms of getting some grasp of what the data hold.

Days absent from work through illness during the previous year, 30 employees					
0	2	3	5	8	10
0	3	3	6	8	12
0	3	4	6	9	13
0	3	4	6	10	15
1	3	5	7	10	36

(Source: Human Resources Dept, Healthy Life Insurance Co.)

FIGURE 6 Array of raw data example

A further stage in organizing the data is to make a *tally of the frequencies* (see Figure 7). This gives a clearer picture of which frequencies were the most common and is far better in terms of being able to 'read' the data. It immediately suggests certain things about the data and invites questions about why certain frequencies are more common than others. Is this sheer fluke, or is there some underlying cause?

Days absent from work through illness during the previous year, 30 employees					
Days	*Frequency*	*Days*	*Frequency*	*Days*	*Frequency*
0	4	5	2	10	3
1	1	6	3	12	1
2	1	7	1	13	1
3	6	8	2	15	1
4	2	9	1	36	1

(Source: Human Resources Dept, Healthy Life Insurance Co.)

FIGURE 7 Tally of frequencies example

Where there are a large number of frequencies, the researcher can organize the data by grouping the frequencies (see Figure 8). Such *grouped frequency distributions* are a very valuable and commonly used strategy for the organization of raw data.

Days absent from work through illness during the previous year, 30 employees	
Group	*Frequency*
0–2 days	6
3–5 days	10
6–8 days	6
9–11 days	4
12–14 days	2
15+ days	2

(Source: Human Resources Dept, Healthy Life Insurance Co.)

FIGURE 8 Grouped frequency distribution example

 Caution: the effect of grouping the data

It is worth bearing in mind that as soon as researchers create groups they are imposing on the data in a pretty strong way. The data in the format of a grouped frequency distribution may be easier to understand, but they have moved away from a natural or raw state and begin to bear the hallmarks of the creative shaping of data by the researcher.

Describing the frequencies and their distribution

When describing the distribution of a set of data there are two basic questions that might be asked.

- What is the mid-point or the average?
- How wide is the spread, and how even is the spread?

Whether or not the researcher chooses to use statistics, it seems that these are very reasonable and common-sense things to consider. They are elementary. The use of statistics, though, adds something to the way these are considered by providing some universal benchmarks for dealing with each and some precision to the way in which researchers deal with the questions.

What is the mid-point or average?

Statisticians will point out that there are *three types of average*, which are collectively known as 'measures of central tendency'. These are the *mean*, the *median* and the *mode*. When describing data, then, social researchers need to be aware of the difference between the three and decide which is most appropriate for their specific purposes.

The mean (the arithmetic average)

The mean is what most people have in mind when, in common parlance, they think about 'the average'. It is a measure of central tendency in the sense that it describes what would result if there were a totally *equal distribution of values* – if the total amount or frequencies were spread evenly.

$$1 \quad 4 \quad 7 \quad 11 \quad 12 \quad 17 \quad 17 \quad 47$$

To calculate the mean of the values above:

1 Add together the total of all the values for a variable or category (= 116)
2 Divide this total by the number of cases (÷ 8)
3 Mean = 14.5

For social researchers, the mean has certain strengths and certain limitations when it comes to describing the data.

- *The mean can be used only with real (cardinal) numbers*. This gives it precision and opens it up to further mathematical processing. Weighed against this strength, calculations of the mean are not appropriate for some kinds of social data. Clearly it makes no sense to think of this kind of average when the researcher is dealing in nominal data; how can you average two sexes, four ethnic groups or ten occupations? The mean only works with real numbers.

• *The mean is affected by extreme values ('outliers')*. Because the mean includes *all* values it is prone to being affected by the odd one or two values that might be vastly different from the rest. Extreme or unusual values get included in the overall mean, and can shift the figure for the mean towards any such 'outliers'. Two things will minimize the impact of such outliers. First, a *large data set* will shroud the influence of the odd one or two outliers. An outlier will have less of a distorting impact on a large sample than it will on a small sample, because the extent of its deviation from the rest will get subdivided more and more as the size of the sample gets bigger. Second, and linked to this, calculations of the mean are safest when there are relatively few outliers, and the outliers that do exist have a tendency to balance up and cancel each other out.

• *Use of the mean may lead to strange descriptions*. When we conclude, for example, that the average size of households in Britain has fallen from 2.91 persons in 1979 to 2.3 persons in 2000, we clearly do not mean this as a *literal* description of the situation. What does 0.3 of a person look like? It is a *statistical* description.

The median (the middle point)

The idea of 'average' can sometimes carry with it the idea of 'middle of the range', and this is the sense in which the median operates. The median is the mid-point of a range.

Calculation of the median is really very straightforward. Values in the data are placed in either ascending or descending rank order and the point which lies in the middle of the range is the median. With even numbers of values, it is the mid-point of the two central values. So, in the following set of data, the *median* is 11.5, half-way between the two middle values.

$$1 \quad 4 \quad 7 \quad 11 \downarrow 12 \quad 17 \quad 17 \quad 47$$

There are some crucial advantages and limitations connected with the use of the median as a measure of central tendency.

• *It can be used with ordinal data* as well as interval and ratio data. This opens up the scope of uses to many areas which are not suitable for the arithmetic mean.

• Because it is an ordinal operation, *the median is not affected by extreme values*, the 'outliers'. Looking at the values above, it should be clear that the value of 47, an obvious outlier, does not affect the calculation of the median. It would, though, affect the calculation of the mean. As far as the median is concerned, that value could lie anywhere between 18 and infinity because its sole significance is that it exists as a value in the range which is greater than 17. Now this, of course, can cut both ways. While the median is unaffected by outliers, it is equally insensitive to the implications of any such extreme values. It effectively eliminates such data from the picture.

- *The median works well with a low number of values*. In fact, in contrast to the mean, it is better suited to low numbers of values.
- We have the advantage of knowing that *exactly half the values are above the median* and half the values are below the median. It offers a quick and easy-to-grasp measure of the central point of the data.
- The main disadvantage of the median is that it does not allow for further mathematical processing.

The mode (the most common)

As the name suggests, when social researchers use the mode as a measure of central tendency they have in mind the most fashionable or popular figure. But this does not imply that they are looking for the best liked value in the data. It is the value which is *most common* that is the mode.

Identification of the modal value simply consists of seeing which value among a set occurs most frequently: this is the mode. In the set below, *the mode is 17*.

$$1 \quad 1 \quad 4 \quad 4 \quad 7 \quad 11 \quad 12 \quad 17 \quad 17 \quad 17 \quad 47$$

As with the mean and the median, there are certain strengths and weaknesses pertaining to the use of the mode, and these need to be considered.

- *The mode can be used with nominal data*, as well as ordinal, interval and ratio data. It has the widest possible scope for application, then, in relation to social data. As a measure of central tendency it makes sense, for example, to talk about the most commonly watched soap opera on TV, whereas we cannot sensibly talk about the mean or median soap opera.
- Like the median, it is *unaffected by outliers* or extreme values. It focuses only on the most common value and ignores all others.
- It shares with the median the limitation that the mode *does not allow any further mathematical processing* to be undertaken on it. It is a standalone end-product.
- One other limitation: there *might not be one most popular value*, or some values might share top spot, so that there might be two or more modes.

How wide is the spread of data? How even is the spread of data?

If researchers wish to describe a set of frequencies it will help if they can provide a measure of central tendency. The *profile* of the data, however, can only be described effectively when there is also some idea of the way the data are spread out from that central point – how they are dispersed.

> **Key point**
> Statistical measures of dispersion or spread are a logical complement to measures of central tendency in any description of the data.

The range

This is the most simple way of describing the spread of data. It is none the less effective, and a valuable method of giving an instant image of the dispersion of the data. The range of the data is calculated by subtracting the minimum value from the maximum value. In the set of values below, the *range* is 44 (i.e. 47 minus 3).

3   4   7   11   12   17   17   47

Although a statement of the range has value as an instant picture of how wide the data are spread, it does have a rather serious limitation as a statistic. It is governed by the extreme values in any set and may consequently give a biased picture of the spread of the values between the extremes. In the example above, the range of 44 is obviously determined by the outlier value of 47. Visually, it is evident that seven of the eight values lie within a range of just 14. So, although reference to the range of values is quick and easy, it needs to be used cautiously and with attention paid to any extreme values and the way these might give a misleading impression of the spread.

Fractiles

Fractiles are based on the idea of dividing the range of the data into fractions. Each fraction contains the same number of data cases. When *quartiles* are used, the data are divided into four sections. *Deciles* operate on the same principle but, as the name suggests, they divide the range into tenths. Where *percentiles* are used, the data are divided into 100 equal parts.

There are two uses of fractiles for social researchers. First, they can be used for the selection of cases to analyse. Researchers can use them as a way of eliminating extreme highs and lows from the data they wish to examine. For example, by focusing on those cases that come in the second and third quartiles researchers know that they are dealing with exactly half of all the cases and, more than that, they are dealing with the half that are 'in the middle'. This middle part of the range is known as the 'inter-quartile range'. With incomes, for instance, use of the inter-quartile range overcomes the possibility of some very high incomes distorting the overall picture, since these would occur in the top quartile. Likewise, by not using the bottom quartile the researchers would eliminate very low incomes from their analysis.

A second use of fractiles is for comparison. They allow comparisons to be made between those cases that occur at one end of the range and those that occur elsewhere in the range. The top quarter can be compared with the bottom quarter, or the highest 10 per cent with the lowest 10 per cent. The most prominent use of this is in comparisons of income and wealth. The top decile (the 10 per cent of all earners who earn more than the other 90 per cent of earners) can have their pay compared with the 10 per cent of all earners who earn the least. The comparison can be in terms of how much is earned. Here the researchers can calculate the mean earnings of the top decile and compare this with the mean earnings of the bottom decile. Or the proportion of all income going to those in the top decile can be compared with the proportion going to those in the lowest decile. Used in such a way, *fractiles are a valuable tool for the social scientist in describing the spread in a frequency distribution.*

Standard deviation

An alternative method of dealing with the spread of data comes in the form of the *standard deviation*. Instead of treating the spread in terms of the overall range of the values, the standard deviation measures the spread of data relative to the arithmetic mean of the data. It is not an absolute measure of the difference between the highest value and the lowest value, as is the case with the use of ranges. More subtly, *the standard deviation uses all the values (not just top and bottom) to calculate how far in general the values tend to be spread out around the mean.*

There are variations in the formulae used for calculating the standard deviation, and there are certain complications that set in when it is used with grouped frequencies. However, these should not detain us, because computer software will generally take care of the mathematics involved. The basic point is this: the greater the dispersion, the larger the standard deviation.

There are a number of factors associated with the use of the standard deviation as a measure of dispersion.

- The standard deviation lends itself to further mathematical analysis in a way that a straightforward description of the spread does not.
- Following from this, the standard deviation assumes huge importance in social research, because it is the basis of so many other statistical procedures.
- Because it takes the arithmetic mean as the basis of its calculations, only those kinds of data that lend themselves to this measure of central tendency can be used. That is, the standard deviation can be used only with cardinal

numbers (interval and ratio data). It is meaningless to use it with nominal or even, strictly speaking, with ordinal data.

Looking for connections: tests for association and difference

One of the main things we might wish to do once we have collected our quantitative data is to check whether there is any *association*, or link, between two or more sets of data. Does one category of data match another, or does one category vary along with another? Alternatively, we might wish to check whether there is any *difference* between two sets of data where we might have expected there to be a similarity. Either way, we want to move beyond describing and presenting the data (descriptive statistics) to a position where we are *looking for connections*.

Looking for connections, at one level, can be a very straightforward process. In essence, it need only involve looking at the data in the tables or the charts to see what links are evident. However, appearances can be deceptive. They may not tell the whole truth. They may not tell the truth at all! Looking at the data for connections may be a good starting point but, from the point of view of good research, it remains just that – a starting point. Suppose there is an *apparent* connection between two variables. Should this lead the researcher to conclude that the association is real and prompt him or her to conduct further research on the basis that a link had been discovered between the two variables? The answer has to be 'No, at least not yet.'

For research purposes, the mere appearance of a connection is not enough. Good researchers want to know:

- whether the findings were a fluke;
- how strong the connection is between the two variables;
- whether one causes the other, or whether the two are mutually interdependent.

These seem reasonable questions to ask of the data. Although we may be able to 'see' a link in a table or chart, we really need something more positive to support what appears on the surface to be a link between the variables. We need some reassurance that the findings were not a one-off fluke. We need something to give us confidence that what we have found is a genuine association of the two. And this is where *statistical tests of significance* prove to be of enormous benefit. Such statistical tests provide an estimate of the probability that any association we find between two or more variables is the product of sheer chance rather than a genuine connection between such variables –

connections that will be found on other occasions. They provide a benchmark for researchers, indicating whether to proceed on the assumption that the apparent connection is real or whether to treat the data as unreliable evidence on the point.

Statistical tests of significance start from the assumption that, despite what might appear in the data, there is no real association between the variables. The frame of mind is that of the sceptic: 'Go on. Convince me that the apparent relationship should be taken seriously. Convince me it is not a fluke, a one-off chance happening!' In the trade this takes the form of what is called the *null hypothesis*. Using the null hypothesis, researchers do not set out to prove the existence of an apparent relationship between variables. Instead, they start from the premise that there is no such relationship – a position that, as scientists, they will hold unless they can be convinced that what was found did not arise by chance.

Statistical tests of significance arrive at a figure that is an estimate of the likelihood that any perceived association is due to chance. The figure is a *probability*, based on statistical theory and procedures, that what *appears* to be contained in the data is actually the outcome of chance. It appears at the end of the computation of statistics in the form '$p < 0.12$' or whatever figure pertains.

If the probability is estimated to be greater than 1 in 20 that the results are a one-off, the sceptically minded researcher will consider that the null hypothesis stands. The researcher will not be convinced that any connection in the data is to be taken seriously. If, on the other hand, it is estimated that there is a probability of less than 1 in 20 that the results arose by chance, the apparent connection is deemed to be *statistically significant*. Within the conventions of statistics, it is held that where the probability is less than 1 in 20 any association in the data may be treated as likely to be genuine and real.

Social researchers generally look for a probability of less than 1 in 20 ($p < 0.05$) that the results arose by chance.

 Caution: the meaning of 'significance'

Statistical significance does not necessarily imply social significance. The researcher needs to be wary of mixing the two senses of 'significance'. Statistical significance only relates to the amount of confidence we have that the findings we obtained were not the product of pure chance. It does *not* automatically imply that the findings are 'important'. That is something to be shown elsewhere by other means.

Statistical tests for association and difference

How do I find out if two variables are associated to a significant level?

Probably the most flexible and certainly the most commonly used statistical test for this is the *chi-square test*. The chi-square test works with nominal data as well as ordinal, interval and ratio data – which does much to explain its popularity. The columns and rows can use nominal data based on things like sex, ethnicity and occupation, factors which feature prominently in data collected by social researchers. (See Figure 9.)

It works on the supposition that if there were no relationship between the variables then the units would be distributed in the cells of the contingency table in equal proportion. This means that if there were three times as many women as men in a sample, we would start from the assumption that women would account for 75 per cent of the amounts or frequencies we are measuring – for instance, absences from work. If there is no connection between sex and absenteeism from work, we might expect the larger proportion of women in the sample to account for a larger proportion of absences – in the strict ratio of 3:1. This 'expected' distribution (based on the null hypothesis) is, in other words, a theoretical distribution based on a starting premise that the two variables concerned do not affect each other. In reality, it is extremely unlikely that the research findings will match this theoretical distribution. Almost certainly there will be a difference between what might be expected and what is actually found in practice. And this difference, the difference between what was 'observed' and what was 'expected', is the key to the chi-square test. The chi-square test uses the extent of difference (in the cells of a contingency table) between what was observed and what might have been expected in order to calculate whether we can have confidence that the observed relationship

Days absent from work through illness during the previous year, by sex of employee

			Sex		
			Male	Female	Total
Days lost	0–5 days	Count	8	7	15
		Expected count	7.0	8.0	15.0
	6 or more days	Count	6	9	15
		Expected count	7.0	8.0	15.0
Total		Count	14	16	30
		Expected count	14.0	16.0	30.0

	Value	d.f.	(2-sided)
Pearson chi-square	0.536*	1	0.464

* 0 cells (0.0%) have expected count less than 5. The minimum expected count is 7.00.

FIGURE 9 Chi-square and contingency table examples

was actually due to something other than pure chance – whether it was real or a fluke.

The main restriction on the use of the chi-square test is that there needs to be a sufficiently large data set and/or a sufficiently even distribution among the various categories in order to get a minimum of five in each cell. Where cells in the contingency table have fewer than five in them it threatens the accuracy of the statistic. There are ways around this should it become a problem. There is a statistical fix which can be used (e.g. Yates correction factor), and most computer programs will put this into operation automatically. Alternatively, the categories can be combined and reduced in number to ensure that each cell has enough data in it.

There is a danger with the use of the chi-square test that the results are heavily affected by the categories which are used. Where categories are combined (for example, to ensure a minimum of five in each cell) or where categories are based on *grouped* frequencies, the researcher needs to be very aware that:

* the 'boundaries' for the categories are creations of the researcher;
* use of different combinations or boundaries will affect the chi-square statistic.

The flexibility in terms of categories in the columns and rows, then, turns out to be both a strength and a potential weakness of the test.

How do I see if two groups or categories are different to a significant level?

Project researchers often wish to compare two sets of data to see if there is a significant difference between them. For example, a teacher might wish to compare two sets of test scores obtained from students: one set obtained at the start of the school year, the other set obtained from the same students on the same test at the end of the school year. Alternatively, she might wish to compare the results obtained from students in one class with those from another. In small-scale research the need to compare two such groups or categories in these ways is very common.

The most appropriate statistical test for this purpose is the *t*-test. The *t*-test provides the researcher with a statistical test of significance. It uses the means of the two sets of data and their standard deviations to arrive at a figure which tells the researcher the specific likelihood that any differences between the two sets of data are due to chance.

Researchers using the *t*-test take the null hypothesis as their starting point. They presume that there is no real difference until they can be persuaded otherwise by a statistical test which tells them that there is a very strong likelihood that any variation found between the two sets of data were the result of something other than pure chance. As with the chi-share test, researchers normally treat differences as 'real' (not a fluke) when they find that there is a probability of less than 1 in 20, usually expressed as '$p < 0.05$', that any difference between the two sets of data were due to chance.

The *t*-test

We have two sets of marks obtained from two classes who have both taken the same test at about the same time. Is there a significant difference between the scores obtained by students in class A and the scores obtained by those in class B? The *independent groups* t-*test* can be used to answer this.

class A (%)	class B (%)
70	55
60	45
45	70
80	75
55	50
65	55
65	40
50	60
80	75
55	50
65	55
65	40
50	60
25	70
80	55
45	
75	
70	
55	
50	

The *t*-test has two notable strengths which are of particular benefit for small-scale research. The *t*-test works well with small sample sizes (less than 30) – an obvious advantage with small-scale research – and the groups do not have to be exactly the same size. A data set of 20 items can be compared with a data set of 15, for example.

There are other statistical tests which compare the results from two sets of data that will work with ordinal data rather than interval or ratio data. For example, the *Mann–Whitney U test* is a well-known test that works by using the rank-ordering of cases in each group. This is why it can work with ordinal data such as examination *grades* (A, B+, B, etc.) if actual percentage scores are not available. The Mann–Whitney U test works by producing one overall ranking which is made from both groups being investigated. The positions of members of each group on this combined ranking are then used as the basis for calculating whether there is a statistically significant difference between the two groups.

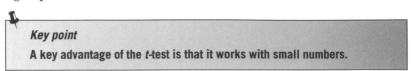

> **Key point**
> A key advantage of the *t*-test is that it works with small numbers.

How do I see if three or more groups or categories are significantly related?

This question is likely to be moving beyond the scope of interest for project researchers. It suggests a fairly large data set with more than two variables potentially connected and worthy of statistical test. It calls for a basic *factor analysis*, such as one-way *ANOVA* (analysis of variance). This test analyses the variation within and between groups or categories of data using a comparison of means.

How do I assess the strength of a relationship between two variables?

This question is not concerned with the *likelihood* of any apparent connection between two variables being real; it is concerned with how *closely* two variables are connected. The relevant statistics here are *correlations*.

Correlations between two variables can be visualized using a *scatter plot*. These need ratio, interval or ordinal data, and cannot be used with nominal data. They also require reasonably large data sets to work best. (See Figure 10.)

The two most commonly used correlation statistics are Spearman's rank correlation coefficient (which works with ordinal data) and Pearson's product moment correlation coefficient (which works with interval and ratio data).

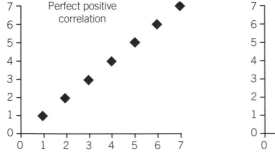 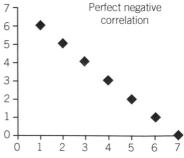

FIGURE 10 Correlations and scatter plot examples

These statistical tests are used to arrive at a *correlation coefficient* based on the data. The correlation coefficients range as follows:

+1	0	−1
perfect positive correlation (one goes up, other goes up)	no relationship	perfect negative correlation (one goes up, other goes down)

In reality, correlations are unlikely to be perfect. Researchers generally regard any correlation coefficient between 0.3 and 0.7 (plus or minus) as demonstrating some reasonable correlation between two variables. 0.3 is reasonably weak, 0.7 is reasonably strong.

It is important to appreciate that correlation is different from cause. The connection between two variables that might be demonstrated using a correlation test says nothing about which variable is the dependent and which is the independent one. It says nothing about which is the cause and which is the effect. It only establishes that there is a connection, with a specified closeness of fit between the variables.

Researchers wishing to investigate connections in terms of cause and effect need to use *regression analysis*.

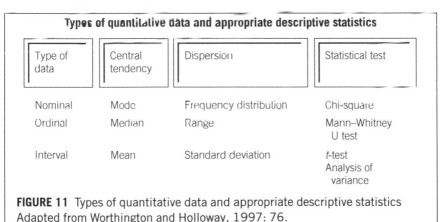

Types of quantitative data and appropriate descriptive statistics

Type of data	Central tendency	Dispersion	Statistical test
Nominal	Mode	Frequency distribution	Chi-square
Ordinal	Median	Range	Mann–Whitney U test
Interval	Mean	Standard deviation	t-test Analysis of variance

FIGURE 11 Types of quantitative data and appropriate descriptive statistics Adapted from Worthington and Holloway, 1997: 76.

Representing the data

With descriptive data, the process of transforming a mass of raw data into tables and charts is vital as part of *making sense of the data*. And it is, indeed, a process of *making* sense. The transformation is done by researchers on the data. It is a process of artfully moulding, extracting and refining the raw data, so that the meaning and significance can be grasped.

Computer software provides a major help on this score. Statistical packages allow the researcher to code and recode data, to group and regroup data and to undertake statistical analyses. And there are packages which help with the presentation of tables and charts based on the data. However, the problem is that the project researcher can actually become overwhelmed by the help on offer through such packages. The power of such software can produce a rather daunting range of possibilities for analysing and presenting the data.

> **Key point**
>
> Word-processing and spreadsheet packages generally contain a table-making and a chart-making facility. So 'drawing' the tables and charts is not a problem. The task facing the researcher is to use these facilities to present the data in a way which is clear, precise and informative.

What follows is not an attempt to cover this vast range of possibilities. This would take a separate book. There are, though, certain 'basics' that can help the project researcher to keep an eye on the target without getting side-tracked by the plethora of statistical analyses that are available at the press of a button, or the bewildering variety of templates for presenting results through tables and charts.

Essentials for the presentation of tables and charts

The point of producing a table or chart is to convey information in a succinct manner and use visual impact to best effect. Its success or otherwise hinges on how well it achieves these things. The skill of producing good tables and charts rests on the ability to:

- *present enough information* without 'drowning' the reader with information overload;
- help the reader to interpret the table or chart through *visual clues and appropriate presentation*;
- use an *appropriate type of table or chart* for the purpose at hand.

There are certain pieces of information which must always be included. If these are absent, then the table or chart ceases to have much value as far as the reader is concerned (see Figure 14 as an illustration). The table or chart must always have

- a *title*;
- *information about the units being represented* in the columns of the table or on the axes of the chart (sometimes this is placed by the axes, sometimes by the bars or lines, sometimes in a *legend*);
- the *source* of the data, if they were originally produced elsewhere.

Added to this, in most cases – though not all:

- the horizontal axis is the '*x* axis' and is used for the independent variable;
- the vertical axis is the '*y* axis' and is used for the dependent variable.

There are some exceptions to the rule about the *x* axis being the horizontal axis, and these are mentioned below. When constructing a chart or table, though, it is important for the researcher to have a clear view about which variable is seen to be the 'cause' and which is the 'effect'. The variable which is treated as the 'cause' is the independent variable (normally on the horizontal axis) and the variable which is being affected is the dependent variable (normally on the vertical axis). Dates (for example, 1977, 1987, 1997, 2007) are usually on the horizontal axis and are treated as an independent variable.

Key point

As far as tables and charts are concerned, simplicity is a virtue.

If the researcher pays attention to these points, the remaining dangers to the success of the table or chart generally come from trying to be too ambitious and putting in too much detail. Simplicity is a virtue that is hard to overstress in relation to the production of tables and charts. If too much data are supplied in a table, it becomes almost impossible for the reader to decipher the meaning of the data. If too many frequencies are presented in a chart, it becomes difficult to grasp the key points. Too many patterns, too many words, too many figures, and the impact of the table or chart is lost. Having said this, of course, there need to be sufficient data in the table or chart to make it worthwhile and 'say something' of interest, and essential details need to be incorporated for the sake of precision. This means that *the researcher is often obliged to compromise between the amount of information that can be conveyed and the visual impact of the table or chart.*

Tables

One of the main virtues of tables is their flexibility. They can be used with just about all types of numerical data. Computer software offers a variety of templates for tables, which aid the presentation of data in a visually attractive fashion.

The degree of complexity of the table depends on two things: the audience being addressed and the restrictions imposed by the format of the document in which the table appears. For the purposes of most project researchers it is likely that tables will remain fairly simple in structure. If the table *does* need to involve a considerable number of rows, the researcher should be prepared to insert horizontal and vertical 'breaks' or blank lines to ease reading and to avoid the eye slipping to the wrong line of data (see Figure 12).

Days absent from work through illness during the previous year, 30 employees								
Days	*Frequency*		*Days*	*Frequency*		*Days*	*Frequency*	
0	4		5	2		10	3	
1	1		6	3		12	1	
2	1		7	1		13	1	
3	6		8	2		15	1	
4	2		9	1		36	1	

(Source: Human Resources Dept, Healthy Life Insurance Co.)

FIGURE 12 Table example

One particularly common use of tables is to present a comparison of sets of nominal data. Such tables are known as *contingency tables* (see Figure 13). They allow a visual comparison of the data and also act as the basis for statistical tests of association, such as the *chi-squared test*.

Days absent from work through illness during the previous year, 30 employees		
Days lost	*Male* ($n = 14$)	*Female* ($n = 16$)
0–5 days 6 or more days	21 74	18 82
(Source: Human Resources Dept, Healthy Life Insurance Co.)		

FIGURE 13 Contingency table example

Bar charts

Bar charts are an effective way of presenting frequencies, and they are very common in reports of small-scale research. *They can be used with nominal data and with discrete data.* The principle behind them is that the bars should be of equal width, with the height of the bars representing the frequency or the amount for each separate category. Conventionally, there is a space between each bar. Their strength is that they are visually striking and simple to read – provided, that is, that not too many categories are used. The fewer the categories (bars) the more striking the impact. Beyond ten categories bar charts tend to become too crowded and confusing to read. Figure 14 shows a simple bar chart.

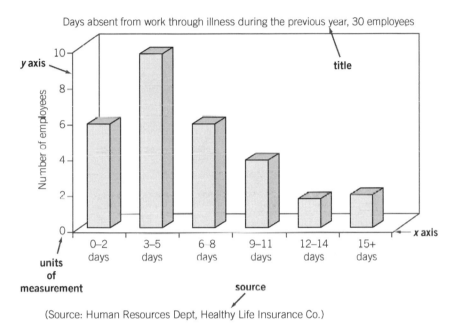

(Source: Human Resources Dept, Healthy Life Insurance Co.)

FIGURE 14 Simple bar chart example

There are many variations on the standard bar chart. The *pictogram* embellishes the basic idea by using symbols or images instead of the standard bar. It does not tell you anything more, but it catches the eye more readily.

Bar charts are sometimes turned on their sides to make it easier to label the categories (see Figure 15). In such *horizontal bar charts*, the vertical axis becomes the *x* axis – as an exception to the convention.

Sometimes each bar incorporates the component elements of the total for a category. This is known as a *stacked bar chart* (see Figure 16). Interestingly, stacked bar charts can be used as an alternative to pie charts (see below) because they show clearly the relative proportions of the factors that make up the total. They have an advantage, too. A number of stacked bars can be incorporated into the same chart, allowing a more direct visual contrast than could be achieved by placing a similar number of pie charts together.

Days absent from work through illness during the previous year, 30 employees

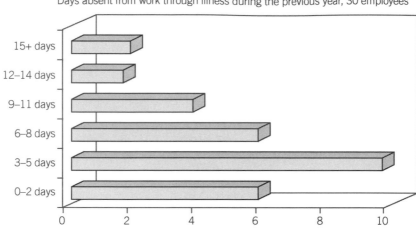

(Source: Human Resources Dept, Healthy Life Insurance Co.)

FIGURE 15 Horizontal bar chart example

Days absent from work through illness during the previous year, 30 employees

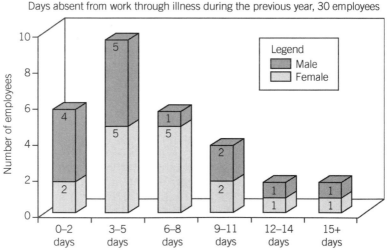

(Source: Human Resources Dept, Healthy Life Insurance Co.)

FIGURE 16 Stacked bar chart example

Histogram

A histogram, like a bar chart, is a valuable aid to presenting data on frequencies or amounts (see Figure 17). Like a bar chart, the bars are normally of equal width and where they *are* of equal width, the height of the bar is used to depict variations in the frequencies or amounts. What distinguishes a histogram from a bar chart is that the *histogram is used for continuous data*, whereas a bar chart is used for discrete data or nominal data. In contrast to the bar chart:

- there are no gaps between the bars;
- the data 'flow' along the *x* axis, rather than being distinct and separate items.

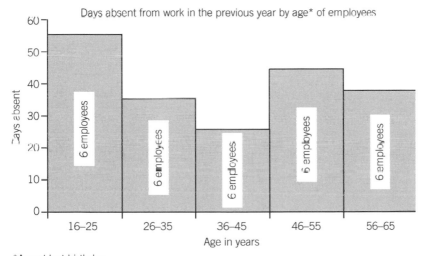

Days absent from work in the previous year by age* of employees

*Age at last birthday
(Source: Human Resources Dept, Healthy Life Insurance Co.)

FIGURE 17 Histogram example

Scatter plot

A scatter plot is used to display the *extent of a relationship* between two variables (see Figure 18). The data are represented by unconnected points on a grid, and the clustering or spread of such points is the basis for detecting a close co-variation between two variables, or a not so close co-variation. The more closely the points come together, the closer the relationship between the variables on the *x* axis and the *y* axis. The more spread out the points are, the less closely the variables are connected. The extent of the relationship is made nicely visible; indeed the scatter plot is particularly good at showing patterns and deviations. There is a drawback, however. It does need a reasonable amount of data to reveal such a pattern.

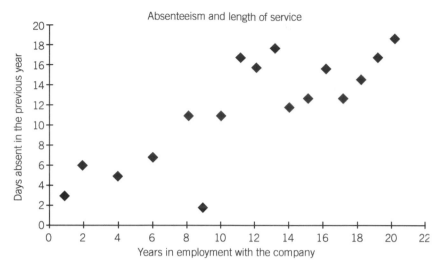

(Source: Human Resources Dept, Healthy Life Insurance Co.)

FIGURE 18 Scatter plot example

Line graph

A line graph is used for depicting development or progression in a sequence of data (see Figure 19). It is good for showing *trends in data*. The most common

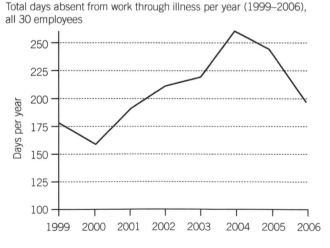

(Source: Human Resources Dept, Healthy Life Insurance Co.)

FIGURE 19 Line graph example

use of the line graph is with dates. A time sequence is plotted left to right on the *x* axis. The line varies in height according to the frequency or the amount of the units. Line graphs work better with large data sets and big variations. A bar chart can be used to do the same thing, and sometimes bars and lines are combined within the same chart.

Pie charts

Pie charts, as their name suggests, present data as segments of the whole pie (see Figure 20). Pie charts are visually powerful. They convey simply and straightforwardly the *proportions* of each category which go to make up the total. In most cases, the segments are presented in terms of percentages.

To enhance their impact, pie charts that wish to draw attention to one particular component have that segment extracted from the rest of the pie. On other occasions, all segments are pulled away from the core in what is known as an *exploded pie chart*.

Weighed against their visual strength, pie charts can only be used with one data set. Their impact is also dependent on not having too many segments. As a rule of thumb, a pie chart should have no more than seven segments and have no segment which accounts for less than 2 per cent of the total.

Proportion of employees absent from work through illness during the previous year, by total days absent, 30 employees

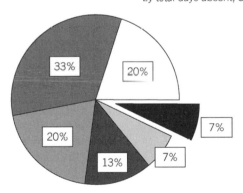
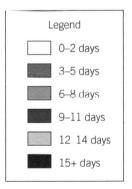

(Source: Human Resources Dept, Healthy Life Insurance Co.)

FIGURE 20 Pie chart example

As a form of chart they tend to take up quite a lot of space on a page. The labels need to be kept horizontal, and this spreads the chart out across the page. As good practice, incidentally, the proportions should be shown as a figure, where possible *within the segments*.

Caution

The presentation of quantitative data in graphs and charts can be used to mislead and give the wrong impression. Playing around with the scales on the *x* axis and the *y* axis can artificially exaggerate or under-play the appearance of differences in the data. Care needs to be taken to avoid distorting the data in this way.

Tables and charts: which ones to choose

The researcher needs to make certain strategic decisions in relation to the choice of which way to represent the quantitative data. It is not a matter of some charts being better than others as much as some charts being better suited to specific purposes than others. Early on, researchers need to decide whether the chart they have in mind is concerned with presenting information:

- On amounts or frequencies   (in which case tables, bar charts or histograms are appropriate)
- Showing the extent of a relationship   (in which case scatter plots or contingency tables are appropriate)
- Covering a span of time   (in which case line graphs are appropriate)
- About proportions of a total   (in which case pie charts or stacked bar charts are appropriate)

Checklist for the presentation of quantitative data

When presenting quantitative data you should feel confident about answering 'yes' to the following questions: ☑

1 Is the choice of table or chart appropriate for the specific purpose of the data?   ☐

2 Does the table or chart contain enough information to 'say something' significant?   ☐

3 Does the table or chart avoid 'information overload'?   ☐

4 Is the table or chart clear and thoughtfully designed?   ☐

5 Is there a title effectively indicating what the information is about?   ☐

6 Have the columns and rows (tables) or the axes (charts) been labelled?   ☐

7 Has information been supplied on the units being represented in the columns of the table or on the axes of the chart?   ☐

8 Has the source of the data been indicated if they are taken from elsewhere?   ☐

9 Is the independent variable on the horizontal axis (x axis) (unless a horizontal bar chart or a pie chart)?   ☐

10 Has a legend been incorporated where appropriate?   ☐

11 Does the contrast in shading adequately distinguish the separate bars/segments?   ☐

© M. Denscombe, *The Good Research Guide*. Open University Press.

Validation of the data

The analysis of quantitative data should include efforts to ensure that, as far as possible:

- the data have been recorded accurately and precisely;
- the data are appropriate for the purposes of the investigation (we must feel assured that we are measuring the right thing);
- the explanations derived from the analysis are correct.

The first step towards validation of the data involves checking the data to make sure that they contain no errors arising from mistakes with data entry. This can be quite a laborious process, but it is vital (unless the data files are constructed automatically). Where the data files have been entered via a manual process, with people typing in data from one source to another, there is the prospect of errors. It is the duty of the researcher to inspect the data files and check them against the sources. With small-scale research this might well involve the whole dataset; with larger research it can involve checking a sample. For example, a questionnaire survey involving 100 completed questionnaires with 15 questions on each would require 1500 keystrokes to enter the data manually. Even an error rate of 0.5% would mean that 7 or 8 responses would be wrong. The researcher should take measures to eliminate such errors from the final 'cleansed' data file.

To address the three points above there are also a number of checks that can be undertaken which are designed to provide assurances about the validity of the data. If the data are to be regarded as valid then the researcher needs to know that:

- *The research instrument does not vary in the results it produces on different occasions when it is used.* In principle this can be checked by using the research instrument on a later occasion and then comparing the results. The 'test-retest' approach should produce results that are very similar, thus boosting the researcher's confidence that the instrument is reliable. Alternatively, there are ways of splitting the dataset in half and comparing one half with the other in terms of the findings they contain. Again, a good level of consistency using this 'split-half' approach serves to validate the data.
- *Respondents provide the same kind of answers to similar questions and generally answer in a consistent fashion.* There are two main ways in which quantitative researchers can address this issue. First, they can look for consistency within the data in terms of respondents with similar profiles giving similar answers. Overall, the researcher is looking for consistent patterns of responses. Second, researchers can use 'check questions' that are deliberately placed within a questionnaire to see whether people's responses are the same to a very similar question.

- *Different researchers would arrive at similar conclusions when looking at the same data.* When researchers are recording data based on observations there is the possibility that individuals might arrive at different conclusions about 'what happened' and thus record different data. To confirm that this is not the case, it is possible to check on *inter-observer consistency* by comparing the results recorded by two or more researchers.
- *The findings will apply to other people and other contexts.* The validity of the data can be assessed in terms of how far the findings from the research can be generalized. This requires comparison with other similar settings to see whether the results would apply equally well in different circumstances.
- *The analysis is 'correct'.* It might be better to say 'works' rather than 'correct', but the underlying point is much the same. The researcher needs to validate the research by checking that the analysis is better than the available alternatives. To do this, they need to consider whether competing theories might provide a better job of explaining the data than the one offered by the researcher. Serious consideration needs to be given to alternative explanations of the research results.

Advantages of quantitative analysis

- *Scientific.* Quantitative data lend themselves to various forms of statistical techniques based on the principles of mathematics and probability. Such statistics provide the analyses with an aura of scientific respectability. The analyses *appear* to be based on objective laws rather than the values of the researcher.
- *Confidence.* Statistical tests of significance give researchers additional credibility in terms of the interpretations they make and the confidence they have in their findings.
- *Measurement.* The analysis of quantitative data provides a solid foundation for description and analysis. Interpretations and findings are based on measured quantities rather than impressions, and these are, at least in principle, quantities that can be checked by others for authenticity.
- *Analysis.* Large volumes of quantitative data can be analysed relatively quickly, provided adequate preparation and planning has occurred in advance. Once the procedures are 'up and running', researchers can interrogate their results relatively quickly.
- *Presentation.* Tables and charts provide a succinct and effective way of organizing quantitative data and communicating the findings to others. Widely available computer software aids the design of tables and charts, and takes most of the hard labour out of statistical analysis.

Disadvantages of quantitative analysis

- *Quality of data*. The quantitative data are only as good as the methods used to collect them and the questions that are asked. As with computers, it is a matter of 'garbage in, garbage out'.
- *Technicist*. There is a danger of researchers becoming obsessed with the techniques of analysis at the expense of the broader issues underlying the research. Particularly with the power of computers at researchers' fingertips, attention can sway from the real purpose of the research towards an overbearing concern with the technical aspects of analysis.
- *Data overload*. Large volumes of data can be a strength of quantitative analysis but, without care, it can start to overload the researcher. Too many cases, too many variables, too many factors to consider – the analysis can be driven towards too much complexity. The researcher can get swamped.
- *False promise*. Decisions made during the analysis of quantitative data can have far-reaching effects on the kinds of findings that emerge. In fact, the analysis of quantitative data, in some respects, is no more neutral or objective than the analysis of qualitative data. For example, the manipulation of categories and the boundaries of grouped frequencies can be used to achieve a data fix, to show significance where other combinations of the data do not. *Quantitative analysis is not as scientifically objective as it might seem on the surface.*

Checklist for the use of basic statistics

When using basic statistics in the research you should feel confident about answering 'yes' to the following questions: ☑

1 Am I clear about which type(s) of data I am using (nominal, ordinal, interval, ratio)?

2 Is the statistical procedure appropriate for the type of data I have collected (i.e. nominal, ordinal, interval, ratio)?   ☐

3 If the analysis is describing frequencies, has any statistical test used with the data been confirmed as appropriate?   ☐

4 If the analysis is looking for connections, has any statistical test used with the data been confirmed as appropriate?   ☐

5 Have research questions been couched in the form of a null hypothesis?   ☐

6 Is the dataset sufficiently large to warrant statistical analysis?   ☐

7 Have any statistical tests of significance achieved a satisfactorily low probability ($p < 0.05$) to justify conclusions based on the data?   ☐

© M. Denscombe, *The Good Research Guide*. Open University Press.

14

Qualitative data

Words and visual images • The principles of qualitative data analysis • The process of qualitative data analysis • Preparing qualitative data for analysis • Familiarity with the data • Interpreting the data: codes, categories and concepts • Key decisions in the analysis of qualitative data • Verifying the data • Representing the data • Computer assisted qualitative data analysis • The analysis of image-based data • Discourse analysis • Advantages of qualitative analysis • Disadvantages of qualitative analysis • Checklist for the analysis of qualitative data

Words and visual images

Qualitative data take the form of words (spoken or written) and visual images (observed or creatively produced). They are associated primarily with strategies of research such as ethnography, phenomenology and grounded theory, and with research methods such as interviews, documents and observation. Qualitative data, however, can be produced by other means. For example, the use of open-ended questions as part of a survey questionnaire can produce answers in the form of text – written words that can be treated as qualitative data. The kind of research method used, then, does *not* provide the defining characteristic of qualitative data. It is the nature of the data produced that is the crucial issue. It is important to bear this point in mind and to recognize that qualitative data can be produced by a variety of research methods, as the text box opposite shows.

Sources of qualitative data		
Words and visual images		**Research method**
• Interview talk • Narratives (for life histories)	}	Interviews
• Diaries, minutes of meetings • Scripts (e.g. for political speeches or media programmes)	}	Documents
• Interactions between people (including naturally occurring actions, responses, language) • Events (e.g. ceremonies, rituals, performances) • Pictures (e.g. photographs, artwork, video recording)	}	Observation
• Answers to open-ended questions		Questionnaires

The principles of qualitative data analysis

The analysis of qualitative data is based upon four guiding principles. The first of these is that the analysis of the data and the conclusions drawn from the research should be firmly rooted in the data. In direct contrast to armchair theorizing and abstract reasoning, there is a commitment to 'grounding' all analyses and conclusions directly in the evidence that has been collected.

The second principle, linked with the first, is that *the researcher's explanation of the data should emerge from a careful and meticulous reading of the data*. This does not imply that the data can 'speak for themselves' or that their meaning is self-evident; this would be an extremely naive approach to take. Indeed, it is important to emphasize that the meaning of qualitative data always involves a process of interpretation in which the researcher produces meaning out of the 'raw' data. What it proposes, instead, is that researchers should derive their explanations of the phenomenon in question by looking closely at the empirical data that have been collected.

The third principle is that the researcher should *avoid introducing unwarranted preconceptions* into the data analysis. These might be personal prejudices or biases arising from knowledge of previous theories and research in the particular area of investigation. Either kind of preconception tends to be regarded as a hindrance to good analysis to the extent that it blinkers the researcher's vision of the data. This does not mean the researcher should (or could) approach the subject matter without any reference to, or knowledge of, previous research on the topic, but it does mean that the analysis of the qualitative data should not be based on concepts imported directly from existing theories or previous research.

The fourth principle is that the analysis of data should involve an *iterative process*. The development of theory, hypotheses, concepts or generalizations should be based on a process that constantly moves back and forth comparing the empirical data with the codes, categories and concepts that are being used.

These principles are broadly based on the use of *inductive* logic. This reflects the fact that most qualitative researchers prefer to move from the data to the theory and from the particular to the general. But this is not a hard and fast rule and there are occasions when qualitative data might be used in a different way. For the most part, however, the analysis of qualitative data is based on a logic of discovering things from the data, of generating theories on the basis of what the data contains, and of moving from the particular features of the data towards more generalized conclusions or theories.

The process of qualitative data analysis

A great deal has been written on the procedures that ought to be used when analyzing qualitative data. The guidance varies in just how systematic the authors think that the procedures should be and, as might be expected, there are some areas of disagreement or difference of emphasis. Broadly speaking, though, most experts in the field would recognize five stages involved in the analysis of qualitative data. In logical order these are:

- preparation of the data;
- familiarity with the data;
- interpreting the data (developing codes, categories and concepts);
- verifying the data;
- representing the data.

In practice, the stages between the initial data collection and the completed analysis do not actually take place as a nice logical sequence with each stage being completed before moving on to the next. There are times when the researcher needs to go back and forth between stages – particularly in relation to coding, interpreting and verifying the data. This is not because he/she has forgotten to do something at an earlier stage and is trying to remedy the situation by returning to the earlier stage to put things right. It is, instead, because the process of analysing qualitative data tends to be *iterative* with stages being revisited as part of what Creswell (1998: 142) and Dey (1993: 53) have described as a 'data analysis spiral'.

The iterative nature of the process does not imply that the stages can be used in any order. Nor does it imply that the stages lack some discrete function in the journey from raw data to completed analysis. It is just that the qualitative researcher will often move back and forth between stages as part of the normal process of data analysis.

Preparing qualitative data for analysis

Qualitative data can come in a variety of formats: fieldwork notes, interview transcripts, texts, photographs, etc. Whatever the format, the data need to be prepared and organized before they can be analysed. It is important to appreciate that qualitative data, in 'raw' condition, is likely to be difficult to interrogate in any systematic and meaningful fashion. In all probability it will prove difficult for the researcher to compare aspects of the data or find recurrent themes. Before the data can be used for research purposes, therefore, they need to be collected, processed and filed in a way that makes them amenable to analysis. The nature of this preparation, as might be expected, will vary depending on the kind of format in which the 'raw' data arrives but there are four pieces of practical advice which can be applied in most circumstances.

First and foremost, *back-up copies should be made of all original materials*. Because qualitative data tend to be irreplaceable, it is good practice to make a duplicate of any recordings, to make copies of computer files and to photocopy any visual images or documents such as field notes or transcripts. This can prove to be something of a chore. It is time-consuming and can be expensive. But any loss or damage to the material can be catastrophic for the research. The original should be stored safely – preferably in a location quite separate from the back-up copies, which now become the 'working copies' that the researcher uses for analysis.

Second, as far as possible, *all materials should be collated and organized in a compatible format*. This could mean using the same software/document templates for all text files or, in the case of hardcopy materials, using the same size pages/record cards. This not only helps with the storage of the materials, it also makes life very much easier when it comes to sifting through the materials and searching for particular items of data.

Third, where possible *the data should be collated in a way that allows researchers' notes and comments to be added alongside* at a later stage. So, for example, when recorded interviews are transcribed, the page template should include a wide margin to the right-hand side of the page so that the researcher can add notes next to the relevant text. Experienced researchers think ahead on this score.

Field notes, for instance, will be kept in a notebook which is specially prepared to have a blank column on the right of each page for later comments.

Fourth, it is very important that *each piece of 'raw data' material should be identified with a unique serial number* for reference purposes. The format of this does not matter particularly, as long as it enables each separate item to be identified exactly in terms of where it should be located. The importance of this is twofold. First, when analysing the data it is vital that the researcher is able to return to points in the data which are of particular interest. Without an adequate reference system, it will be virtually impossible for the researcher to navigate back and forth through the data, or to record which bits of data are significant. Second, on a very practical note, when you are searching through the volumes of data files, it is all too easy to muddle the order or lose the place where the piece of raw data was originally located. A sound reference code is needed to relocate such material.

This indexing of the raw data offers an early opportunity to retain the confidentiality and anonymity of data if required. This can be illustrated in the instance of labelling an audio recording with details of when and where it was recorded. Rather than label the tenth page of the transcript of an interview that took place with Ms Hallam at Dovedale High School as [Hallam: Dovedale: p.10], the teacher and school could be identified via a separate coding list. Ms Hallam might be allocated T07 (the seventh teacher interviewed, perhaps), Dovedale High School might be allocated the code 13 (as school number 13), so that the actual code to appear on the raw data sheets would be anonymized as [T07:13: p.10].

Familiarity with the data

Having organized and prepared the data in a suitable fashion, the next task for the researcher is to become thoroughly familiar with the data. This means reading and re-reading text data, or looking and re-looking at image data. It entails getting a feel for the data and becoming immersed in the minute details of what was said, what was done, what was observed and what is portrayed through the data. There is no set number of readings of the data that can act as a target for establishing familiarity but there are, perhaps, three levels of initial reading that provide a necessary platform for the coding and categorization of the data that follows during the next stage of the analysis.

To start with, the researcher can take a fairly superficial look at the text or images. Because some time might have elapsed since the data were collected, and because there is likely to be a considerable amount of data to work on, the aim should be to refresh the researcher's memory about the content of the data and to remind him/her about the broad scope of the material that is available.

Returning to the data for further inspection, the researcher should begin to cross-reference the material with field notes so that they are better able to understand the data *in context*. Reading the data in conjunction with field notes can help the researcher to recall any relevant background factors that, at the time, were considered as significant for understanding the data. With interview transcripts, for example, more in-depth consideration can be given to the circumstances surrounding the interview and to events that might have influenced what was said during the interview.

Subsequent re-readings of the data should involve the researcher in 'reading between the lines' to see if there are *implied meanings* contained in the data that are significant in terms of the topic of research. The researcher should also begin to look for things that were not in evidence that might be expected to exist. Silences and spaces have considerable importance for the analysis of qualitative data.

The rationale behind this stage in qualitative data analysis is that, having become thoroughly familiar with the data, the researcher is in a position to identify appropriate codes that can be applied to them. It would, of course, be counter-productive to embark on coding until the researcher has a sound grasp of the data. However, it would be wrong to suggest that this stage of familiarization somehow comes to an end at a point when the coding begins. There are two reasons for this. First, familiarity will continue to grow throughout the whole period of data analysis as a direct result of the iterative nature of the process. As the researcher proceeds to refine codes and develop new ones they will regularly return to the data, all the time becoming more familiar with the content. Second, it is likely that new data will be collected after the process of analysis has started. With emergent research designs, popular with qualitative researchers, data collection continues alongside data analysis, with new data being collected in direct response to the lines of enquiry established by the analysis of earlier data. Familiarization with this new data will need to take place at the same time as the analysis of data proceeds.

Quantification of qualitative data: content analysis

If the researcher prefers to use a quantitative approach to the analysis of the text or visual images he/she can use *content analysis*.

Link up with **Content analysis, pp. 236–8**

Interpreting the data: codes, categories and concepts

Having prepared the 'raw' data and become thoroughly familiar with the data the conditions are right for starting the more formal process of interpretation. There are some authoritative accounts of how this should be done that provide extensive detail and advice (e.g Bryman, 2007; Creswell, 1998; Dey, 1993; Marshall and Rossman, 1999; Miles and Huberman, 1994; Prosser, 1998; Strauss and Corbin, 1998; Silverman, 2006). A project researcher who is embarking on the analysis of qualitative data might be advised to refer to such sources for detailed guidance. In essence, though, the process of interpreting the data involves a series of four tasks:

• *Code the data.* Codes are tags or labels that are attached to the 'raw' data. They can take the form of names, initials or numbers; it does not matter as long as the code is succinct and is used systematically to link bits of the data to an idea that relates to the analysis.
• *Categorize these codes.* The next task is to identify ways in which the codes can be grouped into categories. The categories act as an umbrella term under which a number of individual codes can be placed. The terms 'taxonomy' and 'typology' are sometimes applied to this stage in the analysis, reflecting the general idea of classifying the various components of the data under key headings.
• *Identify themes and relationships among the codes and categories.* A further stage in the analysis comes as the researcher begins to identify relationships between the codes or categories of data, or becomes aware of patterns and themes within the data. The task for the researcher is to 'make the link'.
• *Develop concepts and arrive at some generalized statements.* The final stage of the analysis requires the researcher to develop some generalized conclusions based on the relationships, patterns and themes that have been identified in the data. These might take the form of concepts or hypotheses. Occasionally, the researcher might be ambitious enough to suggest a theory based on the empirical research. More prosaically, they could consist of a narrative explanation of the findings.

These tasks, as has been noted, form part of an iterative process. They are steps in the 'data analysis spiral' which means that each task is likely to be revisited on more than one occasion as the codes, categories and concepts get developed and refined. The iterative nature of the process also means that, ideally, the researcher should *return to the field to check out emerging explanations.* In practice, it is not always feasible to do this but it should remain an aspiration that, where possible, gets built into the planning and design of the qualitative research.

Key decisions in the analysis of qualitative data

To arrive at generalized conclusions, whatever form they take, the researcher needs to interpret the data and make significant decisions that shape the final outcome of the process of analysis. To move through the four tasks outlined above researchers need to:

- *Prioritize certain parts of the data.* Decisions need to be made about which parts of the data are more important than others. Attention has to be focused on these parts, with other parts of the data being relegated to the sidelines somewhat. The importance of such parts of the data, it should be stressed, is determined solely by their significance for the emerging analysis.
- *Reduce the number of codes, categories and themes.* At the beginning there are likely to be a large number of codes, categories and themes – too many to be useful for any meaningful analysis. Part of the analysis, then, is to identify where there is sufficient congruence between them to allow some to be merged, and others to be brought together within a broader category. Each of the codes brought together within the category will have some feature that is shared with the others and, of course, this feature will be particularly relevant for the emerging analysis.
- *Develop a hierarchy of codes, categories and themes.* Making sense of the data will involve differentiating among codes (categories and themes) in terms of higher level and lower level codes. The higher level codes will be broader and more inclusive. Crucially, though, the task for the researcher is to develop hierarchical pyramids of codes by subsuming some (lower level) codes under other broader codes (higher level). The categories will necessarily operate at a higher level of generality which will allow them to cover a number of lower-level, more specific codes.
- *Move towards key concepts* (see Frequently Asked Questions, 'What is a concept?' p. 332). The analysis needs to use the higher level codes (categories and themes) for the identification of key concepts that are related to the data. These concepts provide the basis of the researcher's analysis of the data and are the foundations for any generalized conclusions that the researcher might draw.
- *Compare the new generalized conclusions with alternative theories or explanations.* The researcher should review their analysis in the light of other explanations of similar data. Competing theories should be considered, and the analysis should be evaluated in relation to the alternatives. Particular attention should be paid to any instances within the researcher's own data that might appear to contradict the conclusions.

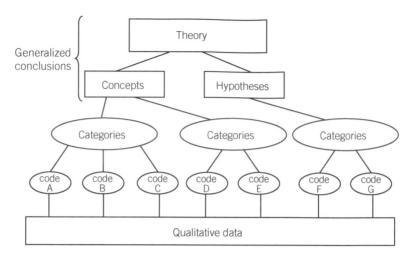

FIGURE 21 The analysis of qualitative data

How to code the data

The use of codes in connection with the interpretation of data is quite distinct from the process of putting a *reference* code on the various pieces of data so that the parts can be identified and stored in an organized manner. During the interpretation of the data the researcher engages in *analytic* coding.

Whatever the form of the data – interview transcripts, field notes, documents, photographs or video recordings – the first thing the researcher needs to do is decide on the *units* that will be used for coding the data. This process is sometimes known as 'unitizing' the data. With text data the units could be as small as individual words, they could be lines in the text, complete sentences or they could be paragraphs. Whichever, a decision needs to be made on what chunks of the data are to have codes attached to them.

Next, a decision needs to be made about the kind of thing that will be coded. Obviously, this will be guided to a considerable extent by the nature of the research problem but, to give an indication of the coding decision involved at this point, the researcher could base his/her coding on things like:

- a kind of event;
- a type of action;
- a shade of opinion;
- an instance of the use of a particular word or expression;
- an implied meaning or sentiment.

Finally, a decision needs to be made on the choice of initial codes that might usefully be applied to the data. The researcher can use respondent categories for this purpose; that is, base the initial codes on something that springs from the contents of the data. Or, the initial codes can be based on personal/professional hunches about what will prove useful for the analysis. The choice is not crucial at the initial phase of analysis because the codes are subject to a continual process of refinement during the research, so if the initial codes are 'incorrect', later versions will be refined and improved.

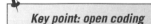

Link up with the **example of coding in the chapter on Interviews, pp. 197–8**

> *Key point: open coding*
>
> The initial stages of coding align quite closely with what the Grounded Theory approach calls '*open coding*': 'The aim of open coding is to discover, name and categorize phenomena; also to develop categories in terms of their properties and dimensions.' (Strauss and Corbin, 1990: 181)
>
> Link up with **Grounded theory, Chapter 6**

The use of memos

As the analysis progresses, new things will emerge as relevant or new interpretations might spring to mind. As new insights come to the researcher the ideas need to be noted. Brief thoughts can be appended to the data but more detailed insights are easier kept as *memos*. These memos are of practical value as a means for logging new thoughts and exploring new possibilities in relation to the analysis of the data. Such memos, in addition, are valuable in the way they provide a documented record of the analytic thinking of the researcher as they refine the codes and categories. In this sense memos are a note pad on which the researcher records how and why decisions were taken in relation to the emerging analysis of the data. They provide a *permanent and tangible record* of the researcher's decision-making which, in principle at least, other researchers could inspect. In effect, they render the process of analysis explicit and accountable, and can form part of the 'audit trail' (see below). It is not surprising, therefore, that the use of memos is generally recommended as good practice in relation to the analysis of qualitative data.

Verifying the data

The verification of qualitative research is vital. The researcher must have some way of demonstrating that their findings are 'true' otherwise there are no good grounds for anyone to believe them. In the absence of verification, the research would lack credibility and, as Silverman (2000, 2006) has stressed, *credibility is essential for all research* whether it be qualitative or quantitative in nature.

The credibility of research is something that *needs to be demonstrated* as part and parcel of the research process itself. It should not be taken for granted. Researchers should not assume that people are naive and will take their findings at face value. Nor should they count on people to trust the researcher's word on the quality of the findings as an act of faith. For the research to achieve credibility it needs to demonstrate in some way or other that the findings are based on practices that are acknowledged to be the bases of good research. Conventionally, the bases for judging the quality of research have been:

- *Validity*. This refers to the accuracy and precision of the data. It also concerns appropriateness of the data in terms of the research question being investigated. The basic question is 'Are the data the right kind for investigating the topic and have they been measured correctly?'
- *Reliability*. This refers to whether a research instrument is neutral in its effect and consistent across multiple occasions of its use. This is frequently translated as the question 'Would the research instrument produce the same results on different occasions (all other things being equal)?
- *Generalizability* (external validity). This refers to the prospect of applying the findings from research to other examples of the phenomenon. It concerns the ability of research findings to explain, or occur in, similar phenomena at a general or universal level rather than being something that is unique to the particular case(s) used for the research.
- *Objectivity*. This refers to the absence of bias in the research. It denotes research that is impartial and neutral in terms of the researcher's influence on its outcome, and it denotes processes of data collection and analysis that are fair and even-handed.

The credibility of qualitative research is not easily judged using these criteria. It is not feasible, for instance, to check the quality of research and its findings by replicating the research in the same way that scientists might repeat an experiment. The first reason for this is that it is virtually impossible to replicate a social setting. Time inevitably changes things and the prospects of assembling equivalent people in similar settings in a social environment that has not changed are, to say the least, slim. The second reason is that the researcher tends to be intimately involved in the collection and analysis of qualitative data, so closely involved that the prospects of some other researcher being able to produce identical data and arrive at identical conclusions are equally slim.

Recognizing such difficulties, some qualitative researchers have suggested abandoning any commitment to these conventional ways of judging the quality of research. The majority, though, have been rather more reticent to abandon the conventional criteria used by the positivistic research. They make the point that, although the nature of qualitative research means that it will never be possible to be verified in the same way as quantitative research, there is still a need to address the need for verification (e.g. Bryman and Burgess, 1994; Kirk and Miller, 1986; Miles and Huberman, 1994; Seale *et al.*, 1999; Silverman, 2006). Such qualitative researchers have adopted a more pragmatic or 'subtle' realist perspective 'that does not give up on scientific aims as conventionally conceived, but also draws on the insights of postscientific conceptions of social research' (Seale *et al.*, 1999: x). The discussion and guidance that follow are rooted in this point of view.

Validity *(or 'credibility')*

The issue here is the extent to which qualitative researchers can demonstrate that their data are accurate and appropriate. Lincoln and Guba (1985) make the point that it is not possible for qualitative researchers to prove in any absolute way that they have 'got it right'. (As a consequence, they prefer to use the term 'credibility' in relation to this aspect of the verification of research.) There are, though, steps to be taken that can help with the task of persuading readers of the research that the data are *reasonably likely* to be accurate and appropriate. These steps provide no guarantee, because none are available. They offer, instead, reassurances that the qualitative data have been produced and checked in accord with good practice. It is on this basis that judgements can be made about the credibility of the data.

To address the matters of accuracy and appropriateness of data qualitative researchers can use:

- *Triangulation.* Avoiding any naive use of triangulation, the researcher can use contrasting data sources to bolster confidence that the data are 'on the right lines'.

Link up with **Triangulation, pp 134–9**

- *Respondent validation.* The researcher can return to the participants with the data and findings as a means of checking the validity of the findings. This allows a check on factual accuracy and allows the researcher's understandings to be confirmed (or amended) by those whose opinions, views or experiences are being studied. There are, though, some limitations to respondent validation, notably in the sense that the analysis of the data might take the explanation beyond something that would be immediately recognizable to the respondent.

- *Grounded data*. One of the key benefits of qualitative research is that the findings will have been grounded extensively in fieldwork and empirical data. Qualitative research tends to involve relatively long times spent 'on location' conducting the fieldwork, and it builds on a detailed scrutiny of the text or visual images involved. This provides a solid foundation for the conclusions based on the data and adds to the credibility of the research.

Reliability *(or 'dependability')*

With qualitative research the researcher's 'self' tends to be very closely bound up with the research instrument – sometimes an integral part of it. As a participant observer or interviewer, for example, the researcher becomes almost an integral part of the data collecting technique. As a result, the question of reliability translates from 'Would the research instrument produce the same results when used by different researchers (all other things being equal)?' to 'If someone else did the research would he or she have got the same results and arrived at the same conclusions?' In an absolute sense there is probably no way of knowing this for certain (as indicated above). Yet there are ways of dealing with this issue in qualitative research – ways that accord broadly with what Lincoln and Guba (1985) call 'dependability'. Principally, these revolve around the demonstration that their research reflects procedures and decisions that other researchers can 'see' and evaluate in terms of how far they constitute *reputable procedures and reasonable decisions*. This acts as a proxy for being able to replicate research. Only if such information is supplied is it possible to reach conclusions about how far another researcher would have come up with comparable findings. As a check on reliability this calls for an explicit account of the methods, analysis and decision making and 'the provision of a fully reflexive account of procedures and methods, showing the readers in as much detail as possible the lines of enquiry that led to particular conclusions' (Seale *et al.*, 1999: 157). In effect, the research process must be open for audit.

Audit trail

An audit trail should be constructed and mapped out for the reader – allowing them to follow the path and key decisions taken by the researcher from conception of the research through to the findings and conclusions derived from the research. But, as Lincoln and Guba (1985: 319) stress, 'An inquiry audit cannot be conducted without a residue of records stemming from the inquiry, just as a fiscal audit cannot be conducted without a residue of records from the business transactions involved'. This is why it is good practice to keep a fairly detailed record of the process of the research decisions. The principle behind the audit trail is that research procedures and decision making could be checked by other researchers who would be in a position to confirm the existence of the data and evaluate the decisions made in relation to the data collection and analysis.

Generalizability *(or 'transferability')*

Qualitative research tends to be based on the intensive study of a relatively small number of cases. Inevitably, this raises questions about how representative those cases are and how likely it is that what was found in the few cases will be found elsewhere in similar cases. The thorny issue is often raised through the question; 'How can you generalize on the basis of such a small number?' Statistically speaking, this is a reasonable question. It is one that is difficult to dodge.

Some qualitative researchers try to side-step the issue by asserting that it is not their business to make such generalizations. They argue that the findings from things like case studies are worthwhile in their own right simply as a depiction of the specific, possibly unique, situation. This, however, is a minority position. The majority of qualitative researchers accept that the issue is relevant but argue that it needs to be approached in a different way when being used in relation to qualitative research. They point out that generalizability is based on the statistical probability of some aspect of the data recurring elsewhere, and it is a probability that relies on a large sample that is representative of the wider population. Research based on small numbers and qualitative data needs an alternative way of addressing the issue. This alternative way is what Lincoln and Guba (1985) have called 'transferability'. This is an imaginative process in which the reader of the research uses information about the particular instance that has been studied to arrive at a judgement about how far it would apply to other comparable instances. The question becomes 'To what extent *could* the findings be transferred to other instances?' rather than 'To what extent *are* the findings likely to exist in other instances?'

Information for comparisons

The researcher needs to supply information enabling others to infer the *relevance and applicability of the findings* (to other people, settings, case studies, organizations, etc.). In other words, to gauge how far the findings are transferable, the reader needs to be presented with relevant details on which to base a comparison. If, for example, the research is on the eating habits of young people and it is based on interviews with 55 students in one school, the findings might not be generalizable to the population of students in all schools. However, armed with appropriate information about the age/sex/ethnicity of the students and the social context of the school it becomes possible to think about how the findings might apply to similar students in similar schools. Armed with the appropriate information the reader can consider the transferability of the findings.

Detailed description of the phenomenon (text or visual image)

One of the strengths of qualitative research is the way it can provide rich and detailed descriptions of the phenomenon it is investigating. These are often referred to as 'thick descriptions' (Geertz, 1973). Such descriptions are 'thick' in the sense that they are multi-layered, providing the reader with insights at a number of levels about a variety of topics. They enable a depth of understanding about the situation or events being described, something that is particularly valuable in terms of the transferability of findings.

Objectivity *(or confirmability)*

This issue of objectivity concerns the extent to which qualitative research can produce findings that are free from the influence of the researcher(s) who conducted the enquiry. At a fundamental level, it needs to be recognized straight away that no research is ever free from the influence of those who conduct it. Qualitative data, whether text or images, are always the product of a process of interpretation. The data do not exist 'out there' waiting to be discovered (as might be assumed if a positivistic approach were adopted) but are produced by the way they are interpreted and used by researchers. This has consequences for the prospects of objectivity. First it raises questions about the involvement of the researcher's 'self' in the interpretation of the data and, second, it raises questions about the prospects of keeping an open mind and being willing to consider alternative and competing explanations of the data.

The researcher's 'self'

The researcher's identity, values and beliefs cannot be entirely eliminated from the process of analysing qualitative data. There are, though, two ways in which qualitative researchers can deal with this involvement of the self. On the one hand, they can deal with it by saying:

> The researcher's identity, values and beliefs play a role in the production and analysis of qualitative data and therefore researchers should be on their guard to distance themselves from their normal, everyday beliefs and to suspend judgements on social issues for the duration of their research.

At this end of the scale, researchers know that their self is intertwined with their research activity, but proceed on the basis that they can exercise sufficient control over their normal attitudes to allow them to operate in a detached manner, so that their investigation is not clouded by personal prejudices. In this case, the researcher needs to suspend personal values and beliefs for the purposes of the production and analysis of the data.

On the other hand, qualitative researchers could take the position that:

The researcher's identity, values and beliefs play a role in the production and analysis of qualitative data and therefore researchers should come clean about the way their research agenda has been shaped by personal experiences and social backgrounds.

At the extreme, this approach can take the form of celebrating the extent to which the self is intertwined with the research process. There are those who argue that their self gives them a privileged insight into social issues, so that the researcher's self should not be regarded as a limitation to the research but as a crucial resource. Some feminist researchers and some researchers in the field of 'race' make the case that their identity, values and beliefs actually *enable* the research and should be exploited to the full to get at areas that will remain barred to researchers with a different self. So some feminists argue that only a woman can truly grasp the significance of factors concerned with the subordination of women in society. Some black researchers would make a similar point in relation to 'race' inequality.

Between the two positions outlined above lie a variety of shades of opinion about the degree to which the researcher's self can and should be acknowledged as affecting the production and analysis of qualitative data. However, there is a general consensus on the key point: *the role of the self in qualitative research is important*. To ignore the role of the researcher's self in qualitative research, then, would be ill-advised. As a matter of good practice, it is better to confront the issue of objectivity and the self by providing the following.

A reflexive account of researcher's self

The analysis of qualitative data calls for a reflexive account by the researcher concerning the researcher's self and its impact on the research. There is a growing acceptance among those involved in qualitative data analysis that some *biographical details about the researcher warrant inclusion as part of the analysis*, thus allowing the writer to explore the ways in which he or she feels personal experiences and values might influence matters. The reader of the research, by the same token, is given valuable information on which to base a judgement about how reasonable the writer's claims are with regard to the detachment or involvement of self-identity, values and beliefs.

An open mind

Qualitative researchers, like all researchers, need to approach the analysis of the data with an open mind. If they do not, they can be accused of lacking objectivity. In practice, a way of demonstrating such openness is for the researcher to take seriously the possibility of having 'got it wrong'. This is actually a fundamental point in relation to the production of knowledge. It is linked to the argument that good research is concerned not with the verification of findings but with their 'falsification'. For the project researcher there are perhaps two aspects of this which can be addressed quite practically. Qualitative researchers should:

• *Avoid neglecting data that do not fit the analysis.* Qualitative researchers such as Seale *et al.* (1999) and Silverman (2006) have argued that good research should not ignore those instances within the data that might appear to disconfirm the researcher's analysis. There might be only a few such 'outliers'. There might be just the occasional bit of data that does not fit nicely or that contradicts the general trend. These should not be ignored, but should be actively investigated to see if there is an explanation for them that can be accommodated within the emerging analysis, of whether there is some genuine significance in them. Looking for, and accounting for, negative instances or deviant cases that contradict the emerging analysis is important.
• *Check rival explanations.* Alternative possible explanations need to be explored. The researcher needs to demonstrate that he or she has not simply plumped for the first explanation that fits, rather than seeing if rival theories work or whether there are hidden problems with the proposed explanation.

Representing the data

An explanation of statistical techniques and data manipulation always accompanies the use of quantitative data in research yet, all too often, an account of the comparable processes is missing or very scant when it comes to reports that have used qualitative data. The process that leads from the data to the researcher's conclusions gets ignored, with the reader of the research report being given little or no indication of how the data were actually analysed. The quality of qualitative research is increasingly coming under the microscope in this respect (Seale *et al.*, 1999, 2004; Silverman, 2006) and, quite rightly, those who use qualitative data are now expected to include in their accounts of research a description of the processes they used to move from the raw data to their findings.

Qualitative researchers, however, face a special challenge when it comes to depicting the process involved in the analysis of their data (Woods, 2006). Partly, this is because the process itself can be quite complicated. As Marshall and Rossman (1999: 150) put it:

[Qualitative] data analysis is the process of bringing order, structure, and interpretation to the mass of collected data. It is a messy, ambiguous, time-consuming, creative, and fascinating process. It does not proceed in a linear fashion: it is not neat.

As well as this, the data themselves are not as amenable to being presented in a concise fashion as quantitative data. Quantitative data can be represented using statistics and tables. These provide a succinct and well-established means enabling researchers to encapsulate the findings from large volumes of data and provide the reader with explicit information about the techniques used for data analysis. The challenge for qualitative researchers, on the other hand, is to depict their data within the confines of a relatively few pages when dealing with:

- a fairly complicated and messy process of data analysis;
- a relatively large volume of data based on words or images.

To deal with this challenge, qualitative researchers need to come to terms very quickly with the fact that it is not feasible for them to present all of their data. They need to be selective in what they present and acknowledge that they have to act as an editor – identifying key parts of the data/analysis and prioritizing certain parts over others.

Next, and linked with the editorial role, it needs to be recognized that the data chosen for inclusion within a report does not constitute evidence that proves a point. It is more likely to be introduced as an illustration of a point that is being made. Because the reader of the report does not normally have access to all the data, they have no way of knowing whether the selection was a fair reflection of the data or not. Further discussion of this point can be found in relation to the use of extracts from interview transcripts.

Link up with **the use of interview extracts in Chapter 10, pp. 199–200**

Finally, the representation of qualitative data/analysis involves an element of 'rhetoric'. That is, the credibility of the research owes something to the skill of the researcher in managing to produce a persuasive account of the research that 'touches the right buttons' and conveys a sense of authority and authenticity. There are some different styles of writing that qualitative researchers can employ to achieve this (van Maanen, 1995; Woods, 2006). Without delving into the rhetorical devices themselves, the point to note is that the credibility of qualitative research, although it still depends on providing relevant factual details relating to the research procedures, also relies on the literary skills of the researcher to write a convincing account. This applies more to qualitative research than it does to quantitative research.

Computer assisted qualitative data analysis

The use of computers for the analysis of qualitative data is generally referred to by the acronym CAQDAS which stands for 'Computer assisted qualitative data analysis'. There are a number of computer software packages that have been developed specifically for the analysis of qualitative data. Some of these are more popular than others and some are more expensive than others. An Internet search using the acronym CAQDAS will locate some excellent sites that review the range of software. In the UK, the University of Surrey has a well-established and particularly valuable CAQDAS site. See also Lewins and Silver's (2007) guidance on the selection of appropriate software to meet the specific needs of the researcher, and Gibbs' (2002) introduction to the use of *NVivo* for qualitative data analysis. Word processing packages also have potential for the analysis of qualitative data. Their text management facilities with integral coding fields ensure that many, if not most, project researchers will have some computer software available to help with their analysis.

The main advantages of using such software to aid the analysis of qualitative data stem from the superb abilities of computers to manage the data. Computers offer a major advance in terms of:

- *Storage of data*. Interview transcripts, field notes and documents can be kept in text files. Copies are quick and easy to make.
- *Coding of data*. The data can be easily coded – in the sense of both *indexing* the data (serial codes) and *categorizing* chunks of the data as a preliminary part of the analysis.
- *Retrieval of data*. The search facilities of the software make it easy to locate data once it has been coded and to pluck it out for further scrutiny.

Weighed against these benefits there are three limitations. First, there are dangers of overestimating the extent to which computer programs can actually *do* the analysis. As Tesch (1993: 25–6) warns, 'The computer does not make conceptual decisions, such as which words or themes are important to focus on, or which analytic step to take next.'

Second, the use of computers for the analysis of qualitative data might exacerbate the tendency to focus on the literal or superficial content of the text and further decontextualize the chunks of data that are analysed. Computer programs cannot analyse the temporal sequence in the data. They cannot understand the implied meanings which depend on events in the background. To be fair, the computer programs in this respect are only extending and exaggerating a potential hazard facing any procedure which seeks to analyse the data through a systematic chunking and coding. The point is that dedicated software packages do this more quickly and more extensively, and hence are potentially more dangerous.

Third, there is the danger of *data overload*. The point is that the processing power of the computer offers the researcher the enticing prospect of using ever more complex codes and connections. Yet this can actually turn out to be counterproductive as far as research is concerned as the researcher becomes overwhelmed by the amount of data and, inevitably, more distanced from the data. The more there is, the more difficult it becomes to familiarize yourself with the data.

Fourth, the use of computer software, no matter how straightforward, involves some start-up time. For the first-time user there is the time taken in getting to know the package and understand its potential. There is also the time taken for inputting the data. Depending on the volume of data that are to be analysed, and the time-frame for project, the start-up time might prove to be a deterrent to the use of computer-assisted analysis of the qualitative data.

The analysis of image-based data

The kind of analysis used for image-based data depends on the purposes for which the data were collected. Broadly, images are used for either, or both, of two reasons:

- for the factual information they contain;
- for the cultural significance and symbolic meaning that lies behind their content.

There are a variety of strands to the analysis of visual images. Without becoming embroiled in the detail of the differences it is perhaps possible to identify three elements to the analysis of image-based data.

- the image itself: contents, genre, styles;
- the producer: intentions and context (by whom, when, under what circumstances, why, the intention of the creator);
- the viewer: interpretation and context.

The image itself can be valuable as a source of *factual information*. There is a case to be made that images provide a relatively reliable source of data – preferable, at least, argues Collier (2001: 59), to the 'deceptive world of words'. Objectively frozen in time, the image contains evidence of things with a clarity that words could never hope to match. Photographs from archives, film from distant fieldwork settings, snapshots from a family album, each contains a firm record of events that can be subsequently analysed by the researcher. 'Such images are produced to serve as records of reality, as documentary evidence of the people, places, things, actions and events they depict. Their analysis is a matter of extracting just that kind of information from them' (van Leeuwen and Jewitt, 2001: 4).

Link up with **Image-based research, pp. 238–44**

To help get to grips with the information contained in large collections of images researchers can use *content analysis*, and it is quite possible to produce quantitative data as part of the analysis of images (see Bell, 2000 for a detailed account of this). In practice, however, image-based research has largely favoured a qualitative approach. The key reason for this is that social researchers in recent years have become reluctant to take the content of images entirely 'at face value'. Rather than accepting images as neutral depictions of reality (along with the positivistic connotations this has), most social researchers in the twenty-first century would acknowledge, as Rose (2001) argues, that images do not contain 'one right meaning'. What they depict is open to interpretation and it would be rather naive to presume that the contents of visual images are self-explanatory. Without entirely abandoning the use of images in terms of their ostensive content (the 'facts' they portray), researchers have become more inclined to treat the contents as something that needs to be interpreted. The image is not created 'literally' but is interpreted. The meaning of the image is the thing of value for the researcher, the meaning as given within a particular culture, within a given time, within a social context within which it was produced.

Another way of interpreting an image is as a *cultural artefact*. As a cultural artefact, the focus moves away from just the content of the image and what this can tell the researcher, to incorporate, also, questions about the context in which the image was produced. What purpose did/does it serve? Why was it produced? As a source of evidence, the value of the image is in what lies behind the surface appearance. To give an illustration, a photograph might appear to show a family on a seaside beach. At one level the researcher could use the image to get factual information about the style of beachwear worn at the time the photograph was taken. Provided the photograph was authentic, the image acts as a source of factual data. However, that same image might be interpreted as a cultural artefact by asking questions about how and why it was produced. Who took the photograph? Why was it taken? What importance is attached to it that might explain why it has been kept over a long period of time? What equipment was used to take the photograph? Such lines of enquiry could help researchers to understand the significance of family holidays, the role of photo albums and the nature of leisure activity in their cultural context. The meaning of the photograph, that is, goes beyond the superficial content depicting two adults and two children at the seaside.

Many advertisements now 'play', quite consciously, with the relationship between the three aspects. They 'invite' the viewer to:

- look at the content at face value;
- acknowledge the producer's message (to buy);
- relate the image and message to themselves, their own wants and needs.

Another approach to the analysis of images interprets them in terms of what they denote. It probes the image as a *symbolic representation* whose interest lies not as much in the 'facts' contained in the image as in the significance attached to the contents by those who view it. Images, used in this way, provide a source for uncovering ideologies and cultural codes. Drawing on the field of 'semiotics', the researcher first considers the various aspects of the content to see what they denote. Taken at face value, what do they 'say'? Next the researcher considers the connotations of the key elements in the image. What associations spring to mind when looking at those elements? Then, in the final stage of analysis, semiotics moves towards drawing contrasts and similarities with other signs in a way that helps us to understand the symbolism of the image. (See Penn, 2000 for further information on the semiotic analysis of still images.)

It is important to note that reading the message is not entirely an individual, personal thing in which each viewer interprets things differently. While there is certainly some scope for variation, semiotics and cultural studies operate on the premise that there is a degree of consensus among viewers about the meaning of an image. People who come from a similar cultural background, who are members of the same society or who have been brought up within a particular ideological tradition (e.g. democracy, Christianity) might be expected to make sense of images in roughly the same way. As members of social groups they will have been *socialized* into ways of seeing what is meant by visual images – learning from others since their early years how to make sense of visual clues contained in things like signs, advertisements, portraits and music videos. We learn not to treat images simply in terms of their 'literal' contents. Road signs that point upwards are not interpreted to mean 'go upwards'.

 Caution

When using images for research purposes there is always the danger that they might be 'taken out of context'. Events prior and subsequent to the moment captured by the image might have a crucial bearing on the meaning that can be attributed to it.

Discourse Analysis

Discourse Analysis is an approach to the analysis of qualitative data that focuses on the implicit meaning of the text or image rather than its explicit content. It is based on the premise that words and pictures are used not simply to depict reality; they are used instead as a way of creating and sustaining reality. Discourse Analysis involves a 'deconstruction' of the data in order to expose the ways in which text or visual images do the work of creating or sustaining particular aspects of social life. This approach is familiar within the fields of social psychology, sociology and linguistics and is used in relation to a wide range of social research areas including, for example, cultural studies, marketing (especially advertising), education and feminist studies.

Discourse Analysis stems from the philosophical influence of people like Wittgenstein (1968) and Austin (1962) who argued that language should be recognized as something more subtle and more creative than a straightforward transmitter of factual information. Rather than acting as a representation of reality, they argued, language should be treated as an active creator of reality in its own right. One of the main tenets of Discourse Analysis, indeed, is that the words that appear in a text are not determined by the thing they are used to represent. Words are chosen. And they are chosen with the purpose of having some effect on those who read them. The aim of Discourse Analysis then, is to 'unpack' the text or image in order to reveal:

- what people are trying to do through the talk, text or image;
- what background assumptions are needed in order for this to be achieved.

There have been a number of developments of this line of thought, notable among which have been the works of postmodernists such as Foucault and Derrida. Underlying the many strands, Discourse Analysis generally approaches the analysis of talk, text and images on the basis that they should never be taken 'at face value' but, instead, should be investigated to reveal the hidden messages that they contain and the kind of thinking that needs to be going on in the background – implicit and unspoken – in order for them to work. This involves the researcher in a 'deconstruction' of the data. The data are analysed by taking them apart to reveal how they:

- create meaning;
- contain hidden messages;
- reflect, generate and reinforce cultural messages;
- involve the reader as an active, not passive, interpreter of the message's content.

In line with other approaches to qualitative data analysis, Discourse Analysis likes to keep *close to the data*. The approach is premised on the idea that background assumptions ('discourses') are displayed and transmitted through talk, text or images. The task of the researcher is to interrogate the data with the aim of showing just how the discourse can be evidenced through the particular data being studied. Discourse Analysis, in this sense, does not differ from the kind of qualitative data analysis outlined elsewhere in this chapter to the extent that it relies on

* a close scrutiny of the text/image; and,
* a firm grounding of conclusions within the data.

It does differ, however, in the extent to which the researcher approaches the analysis of the data *'without presuppositions'*. On this point there is a distinct contrast with, for example, the Grounded Theory approach. In principle, grounded theory follows a line of inductive reasoning in which there is an expectation that the data themselves should provide the source for any interpretation made by the researcher. There are, it should be said, variations within the grounded theory camp concerning the degree to which the data *alone* contain the necessary ingredients for analysis. However, it is still fair to say that the Grounded Theory approach sees the data as the primary and principal generator of the concepts and theories emerging from the research.

Link up with **Grounded theory, Chapter 6**

Discourse Analysis, by contrast, tends to rely on concepts and theories generated in separation from the specific instance of talk, text or images that is being analysed. This is almost inevitable because Discourse Analysis, in its attempt to reveal the cultural assumptions that need to come into play in order to understand the data, looks at what is *absent* from the text or image as well as what is contained. It looks at what is *implied* as much as what is explicit. The question arises: 'How would you know what was missing if you did not have some idea of what should be expected to "fill the gaps" and "speak the unspoken"?' The researcher who undertakes Discourse Analysis, therefore, needs to use *prior assumptions* to analyse the data to a degree that grounded theorists would not find comfortable. They must use existing knowledge about society, culture, politics, etc. and analyse the data with certain necessary preconceptions about the meanings contained in the data.

'Critical Discourse Analysis' tends to add a political bite to the approach. It explores the ways the hidden, background meanings that are used to make sense of a text or image serves the interests of some groups more than others. In fact, this approach explores how power in society is achieved through discourse and how this is evident in particular instances of text or images. In doing so, it relies quite heavily on the use of political, economic and social ideologies as its frame of reference for understanding the meanings embodied in the data.

'Conversation Analysis', like other variants of Discourse Analysis, focuses attention on how things get done through language use. In this instance, researchers look at naturally-occurring talk and the way that routine aspects of everyday life get accomplished through language. There have been studies of things like taking turns in everyday conversation, greeting people, starting a school lesson – apparently mundane and minute parts of social life, but ones that advocates of *ethnomethodology* stress are the fundamental building blocks of social interaction – without which there would be no such thing as social life. The structure and sequencing of the talk is crucial from this perspective.

Conversation Analysts are inclined to underplay the extent to which they draw on presuppositions. However, their analysis must still rely on cultural insights. Indeed, the researcher's background knowledge can be argued to be absolutely essential to the sensible interpretation of routine conversation. For any reasonable interpretation, it is vital that the researcher has appropriate background knowledge, shared with those doing the talking. Otherwise, they would literally have no way of knowing what was going on.

It should be clear through the discussion so far that there are a range of approaches subsumed under the generic heading of Discourse Analysis. It is important to appreciate that these can focus on quite different subject matters and that they can use forms of analysis that do not always map neatly on to one another (Wooffitt, 2005). However, as Potter and Wetherell (1994) note, they share a particular strength in terms of dealing with the subtlety of qualitative data. Whether dealing with everyday talk, interview transcripts or advertising posters they avoid taking things at face value and allow the nuances of the data to be explored in a way that approaches such as content analysis cannot. They are, in this respect, quite the opposite of content analysis in which the analysis of data focuses purely on the explicit content of the data – the words and pictures being taken at face value.

Link up with **Content analysis, pp. 236–8**

A disadvantage of using Discourse Analysis, on the other hand, is that it does not lend itself to the kind of audit trail that might be needed to satisfy conventional evaluations of the research. It is not easy to verify its methods and findings. This is because the approach places particularly heavy reliance on the insights and intuition of the researcher for interpreting the data. Some Discourse Analysts eschew the idea that their research can, or should, be subject to any process of verification. They argue, in effect, that the findings stand as just 'the researcher's interpretation' – no better and no worse than anybody else's. No more scientific; no more credible. This is a controversial stance, and it is one that could prove unwise for a project researcher to adopt. But, unless the researcher is prepared to risk taking this 'postmodernist' position, they need to be aware of the difficulties of verification inherent in the approach. With this in mind, what practical guidance can be given in relation to Discourse Analysis?

1 *Be clear about which aspects of discourse are being studied.* The researcher needs to specify whether the particular talk, text or image is being used in relation to:

- the shared background meanings and cultural assumptions necessary to make sense of the data themselves (micro);
- the wider ideology and cultural relations that are created and reinforced through the data (macro).

2 *Be clear about which aspects of deconstruction are best applied.* There is no hard and fast process involved in Discourse Analysis, but the researcher who embarks on deconstructing the data needs to have a clear vision of the things he/she is looking for and the way these link with the micro and macro aspects of discourse. A number of relevant questions to be asked include:

- Is there evidence of a wider ideology being communicated via the talk, text and images?
- Do the data reflect particular social, political or historical conditions in which they were produced?
- In what way does the talk, text or image stem from other sources ('intertexuality')?
- How is power or influence being exerted through the talk, text or image?
- Whose version of reality is being portrayed through this talk, text or image?
- How are people, processes and objects categorized and defined through the talk, text or image?
- Are there people, processes or objects that are notably absent or excluded?
- Are there contradictions within the talk, text or image? How are these coped with?
- What things are missing from the talk, text or image?
- Are there views that appear to be suppressed?
- Are there things that are not said that might have been expected to be stated?
- What rhetorical or linguistic devices are being used to argue the point?
- What version of things is being portrayed as normal/abnormal, legitimate/illegitimate, moral/immoral, natural/unnatural, etc.?
- Would alternative interpretations of the talk, text or image be possible or likely depending on the particular audience?

Advantages of qualitative analysis

- *The data and the analysis are 'grounded'.* A particular strength associated with qualitative research is that the descriptions and theories such research generates are 'grounded in reality'. This is not to suggest that they depict reality in some simplistic sense, as though social reality were 'out there' waiting to be 'discovered'. But it does suggest that the data and the analysis have their roots in the conditions of social existence. There is little scope for 'armchair theorizing' or 'ideas plucked out of thin air'.
- *There is a richness and detail to the data.* The in-depth study of relatively focused areas, the tendency towards small-scale research and the generation of 'thick descriptions' mean that qualitative research scores well in terms of the way it deals with complex social situations. It is better able to deal with the intricacies of a situation and do justice to the subtleties of social life.
- *There is tolerance of ambiguity and contradictions.* To the extent that social existence involves uncertainty, accounts of that existence ought to be able to tolerate ambiguities and contradictions, and qualitative research is better able to do this than quantitative research (Maykut and Morehouse, 1994: 34). This is not a reflection of a weak analysis. It is a reflection of the social reality being investigated.

> **Key point**
>
> What is important about well-collected qualitative data? One major feature is that they focus on naturally occurring, ordinary events in natural settings, so that we have a strong handle on what 'real life' is like. (Miles and Huberman, 1994: 10)

- *There is the prospect of alternative explanations.* Qualitative analysis, because it draws on the interpretive skills of the researcher, opens up the possibility of more than one explanation being valid. Rather than a presumption that there must be, in theory at least, one correct explanation, it allows for the possibility that different researchers might reach different conclusions, despite using broadly the same methods.

Disadvantages of qualitative analysis

- *The data might be less representative.* The flip-side of qualitative research's attention to thick description and the grounded approach is that it becomes more difficult to establish how far the findings from the detailed, in-depth study of a small number of instances may be generalized to other similar instances. Provided sufficient detail is given about the circumstances of the research, however, it *is* still possible to gauge how far the findings relate to other instances, but such generalizability is still more open to doubt than it is with well conducted quantitative research.

*   *Interpretation is bound up with the 'self' of the researcher.* Qualitative research recognizes more openly than does quantitative research that the researcher's own identity, background and beliefs have a role in the creation of data and the analysis of data. The research is 'self-aware'. This means that the findings are necessarily more cautious and tentative, because it operates on the basic assumption that the findings are a creation of the researcher rather than a discovery of fact. Although it may be argued that quantitative research is guilty of trying to gloss over the point – which equally well applies – the greater exposure of the intrusion of the 'self' in qualitative research inevitably means more cautious approaches to the findings.

*   *There is a possibility of decontextualizing the meaning.* In the process of coding and categorizing the field notes, texts or transcripts there is a possibility that the words (or images for that matter) get taken literally *out of context*. The context is an integral part of the qualitative data, and the context refers to both events surrounding the production of the data, and events and words that precede and follow the actual extracted pieces of data that are used to form the units for analysis. There is a very real danger for the researcher that in coding and categorizing of the data the meaning of the data is lost or transformed by wrenching it from its location (a) within a sequence of data (e.g. interview talk), or (b) within surrounding circumstances which have a bearing on the meaning of the unit as it was originally conceived at the time of data collection.

*   *There is the danger of oversimplifying the explanation.* In the quest to identify themes in the data and to develop generalizations the researcher can feel pressured to underplay, possibly disregard, data that 'doesn't fit'. Inconsistencies, ambiguities and alternative explanations can be frustrating in the way they inhibit a nice clear generalization – but they are an inherent feature of social life. Social phenomena are complex, and the analysis of qualitative data needs to acknowledge this and avoid attempts to oversimplify matters.

*   *The analysis takes longer.* The volume of data that a researcher collects will depend on the time and resources available for the research project. When it comes to the analysis of that data, however, it is almost guaranteed that it will seem like a daunting task. This is true for quantitative research as much as it is for qualitative research. But, as Bryman and Burgess (1994: 216) point out, when it comes to the analysis of seemingly vast amounts of quantitative data 'the availability of standard statistical procedures and computer programs for handling them is generally perceived as rendering such data non-problematic'. The analysis of the data can be achieved relatively quickly and the decision making behind the analysis can be explained fairly

succinctly. When researchers use qualitative data, however, the situation is rather different. Primarily, this is because qualitative data are generally *unstructured* when they are first collected in their 'raw' state (e.g. interviews, field notes, photographs). Computer programs can assist with the management of this data and they can even help with its analysis, but nowhere near to the extent that they can with quantitative data. In the case of qualitative data, the techniques used for the analysis are more time-consuming and the decisions made by the researcher are less easily described to the reader of the research. The result is that qualitative data takes considerably longer to analyse.

Checklist for the analysis of qualitative data

When analysing qualitative data you should feel confident about answering 'yes' to the following question: ☑

1. Has the research identified themes and relationships in the units of data? ☐

2. Have the emerging categories and explanations been checked out by returning to the field? ☐

3. Have sufficient details been incorporated to allow an 'audit' of key decisions in the process of the research? ☐

4. Have relevant details been supplied to permit readers to think about the transferability of the findings? ☐

5. Does the analysis avoid decontextualizing the meaning of the data? ☐

6. Does the explanation avoid oversimplifying issues? ☐

7. Have the findings been checked for external reliability with other comparable studies? ☐

8. Has the topic been approached with an 'open mind'? ☐

9. Have alternative explanations been considered? ☐

10. Does the research report include some reflexive account of the researcher's *self* and its possible impact? ☐

© M. Denscombe, *The Good Research Guide*. Open University Press.

15

Writing up the research

Producing accounts of the research • Different audiences for research •
Vital information to be included when writing up the research •
Conventions for writing up the research • The Harvard referencing system •
Style and presentation when writing up the research • The structure of
research reports • Writing up qualitative research • The research methods
chapter or section • Checklist for writing up the research

'Writing up' is a integral part of the research process. It is not something tagged on at the end. Nor is it a simple, straightforward task. Far from it, writing up is skilful. It involves a blend of interpretation, craft and convention aimed at producing a formal record of the research that can be evaluated by others. Writing up, in essence, calls on researchers to exercise skill and judgement as they:

- produce an *account* of the research;
- tailor reports to meet the requirements of *different audiences*;
- adopt an appropriate *style of writing* and take account of *certain technical conventions*.

Producing accounts of the research

When researchers write up their work they cannot produce a literal description of what took place. It is almost impossible to envisage a literal account of the research process, because:

- There are always limitations to the space available to provide the account of what happened, which means the researcher needs to provide an *edited version* of the totality. Decisions need to be made about what details are included and which are considered less important and can be missed out of the account.
- The editorial decisions taken by the researcher are likely to be shaped by the researcher's need to present the methods in their best possible light. Quite rationally, the researcher will wish to put a positive spin on events and to bring out the best in the process. Without resorting to deceit or untruths, the account of research will almost certainly entail some upbeat *positive filtering*. The point, after all, is to justify the procedures as 'good' research.
- Although research notes will be used to anchor the description of what happened during the course of the research, the writing up is inevitably *a retrospective vision*. Situations and data are likely to have a different meaning when viewed from the end of the research process from that at the time they occurred. They will be *interpreted with the wisdom of hindsight*.
- The impact of social norms and personal values on the way we interpret events pretty well guarantees that, to a greater or lesser extent, any account of research should be regarded as a *version of the truth* rather than a literal depiction of what happened. Within the social sciences, the idea of a purely objective position is controversial, and a researcher would be naive to presume that his or her account can stand, without careful consideration, as an 'objective' description of what really occurred.

The end product, therefore, no matter how scrupulous it attempts to be, must always be recognized for what it is – an *account* of the research.

Different audiences for research

Differing audiences have differing expectations when it comes to reading the research, and the researcher needs to decide how to pitch the account of the research to meet the expectations of the group whose views are considered most important. The easy illustration of this comes in the form of research reports produced for an academic qualification as part of an examined course – an undergraduate project, a masters dissertation, a doctoral thesis. The researcher should need little reminding that the work will be assessed by supervisors and examiners who will be focusing on detail, rigour, precision, coherence and originality as top priorities. A different audience might bring different expectations. In the case of commissioned research, the audience is likely to be more concerned with receiving a report which is succinct, easy to digest and strong on practical outcomes. In principle, the research could be just the same; the way it is written up, though, will reflect the needs of the differing audiences.

Vital information to be included when writing up the research

Although reports of research respond to the needs of a target audience and rely on an element of interpretation by the researcher, this does not make them idiosyncratic. Far from being one-offs that reflect just the specific audience and the specific researcher, there are some aspects of writing up research which are, if not universal, at least very widely accepted. There is some general consensus that when writing up research the report should include sections which:

- explain the purpose of the research;
- describe how the research was done;
- present the findings from the research;
- discuss and analyse the findings;
- reach conclusions.

Conventions for writing up the research

There are conventions which cover the writing up of research. These conventions deal with things like *referencing* (the way in which references are made to sources used by the researcher and the way that these are listed in the References section towards the end of the report on the research), the *layout* of the document, the *order* in which material should be presented and the kinds of *essential information* the researcher needs to provide.

Authors are normally provided with specific guidance by the institution or publisher for whom the work is being produced. University regulations will contain details covering style and presentation. Academic journals always include guidance to authors which spell out the journal's own policy as far as the presentation of work is concerned. These should be respected as the principal guidelines.

In addition, there are some general sources of information on such conventions. For the production of dissertations there is, for example, the British Standards specification no. 4821. Although this was withdrawn in 1990, it has not been superseded and is still recommended by the British Library. For the production of academic articles and for referencing techniques, the researcher could turn to the *Publication Manual of the American Psychological Association*. There are also books devoted to guidance for authors on the technical conventions associated with writing up research – for example, K. L. Turabian's *Manual for Writers of Term Papers, Theses and Dissertations* (University of Chicago Press, 6th edn, 1996).

 Caution

There is no single set of rules and guidelines for writing up the research which covers all situations and provides a universally accepted convention.

Constructing a research report

The researcher needs to tailor the research report to meet:

- the expectations of the specific audience for whom the work is being written;
- the conventions which operate at a general level with respect to the production of reports on research in the social sciences.

These will affect:

- the style of presentation;
- the detail and length of the account;
- the amount of technical detail included;
- the terminology used.

The Harvard referencing system

There are conventions for referring to the ideas, arguments and supporting evidence gleaned from others. There are two that are generally recognized: the numerical system and the Harvard system. The numerical system involves placing a number in the text at each point where the author wishes to refer to a specific source. The full references are then given at the end of the book or individual chapters, and these can be incorporated into endnotes. It is the other system, the Harvard system, however, which is more commonplace these days and, for that reason, further details will concentrate on this convention.

In the Harvard system, the sources of ideas, arguments and supporting evidence are indicated by citing the name of the author and the date of publication of the relevant work. This is done at the appropriate point in the text. Full details of the author's name and the publication are subsequently given at the end of the report, so that the reader can identify the exact source and, if necessary, refer to it directly. As used in this book, the Harvard system involves referring to authors in the text in the following ways:

- Baker (2007) argues that postmodernism has a dubious future.
- It has been argued that postmodernism has a dubious future (Baker, 2007).
- The point has been made that 'it is not easy to see what contribution postmodernism will make in the twenty-first century' (Baker, 2007: 131).

In the *References section* towards the end of the research report, the full details of 'Baker, 2007' are given, as they are for all the authors' works cited in the report. For Baker, it might look like this:

Baker, G. (2007) The meaning of postmodernism for research methodology, *British Journal of Health Research*, 25: 249–66.

As far as the References section is concerned, there are seven key components of the Harvard system:

- *Author's name and initial(s)*. Alphabetical order on authors' surnames. Surname followed by forename or initial. If the book is an edited volume, then (ed.) or (eds) should follow the name.
- *Date of publication*. To identify when the work was written and to distinguish different works published by the same author(s).
- *Title*. The title of a book is put in italics, and uses capital letters for the first letter of the main words. Papers and articles are not in italics and have titles in lower case.
- *Journal name* (if applicable). This is put in italics and details are given of the number, volume and page numbers of the specified article. If the source is a contribution to an edited volume then details are given about the book in which it appears (i.e. editor's name, title of edited volume).
- *Publisher*. Vital for locating more obscure sources. This is included for books but not for journals.
- *Place of publication*. Helpful in the location of obscure sources.

- *Edition.* If the work appears in a second or subsequent edition this needs to be specified.

Real examples are to be found in the References section in this book, and can be used to illustrate the principles further.

Style and presentation when writing up the research

The rules of style for writing up research are really like the rules for writing which operate for the English language in general. Inexperienced writers should stick to the rules. Experienced writers might break the rules, but the assumption is that they know they are breaking the rules and are doing so consciously for a particular purpose, to achieve a specific effect. Project researchers, then, are best advised to stick to the rules.

Use the third person

There are occasional circumstances where research might be written up using the first person: 'I distributed 164 questionnaires . . . I received 46 per cent back . . . From the research I found that . . .'. Sometimes this is to be found in qualitative research when researchers are keen to emphasize their personal involvement and the role of their personal identity in the collection and analysis of the data. Or, it might be used in the context of an informal report intended for restricted distribution. It is more conventional, however, to write research reports in the third person: 'Research involved the distribution of 164 questionnaires . . . A response rate of 46 per cent was achieved . . . Findings from the research indicated that . . .'. This is particularly the case for formal reports such as dissertations and theses.

Use the past tense

For the most part, this convention poses little trouble because researchers are reflecting upon events that happened in the past. It might be the recent past, but none the less the writing up refers to things that were done and events that happened.

Ensure good standards of spelling and grammar

Perhaps obvious, this convention is still worth stressing. Word-processing packages can be used as spell-checkers and can help with the writing style. Scrutiny of the text by the researcher is still needed, however, to avoid those text errors which cannot be picked up by the spell-checker; where 'at' has been typed instead of 'an', for example.

Develop logical links from one section to the next

A good report is one that takes the reader on a journey of discovery. The pathways of this journey should be clear, and the reader should never be left in doubt about the direction of the discussion or the crucial points that are being argued. The logic of the discussion should build point on point towards a final conclusion. (See 'The structure of research reports', opposite.)

Use headings and sub-headings to divide the text into clear sections

Judicious use of headings and sub-headings can separate the text into blocks in a way that makes the reader's task of understanding the overall report far easier. They act as signposts. As with signposts, too few and the reader gets lost, too many and the reader gets confused. As with signposts, their success depends on being clear and being in the right place.

 Caution: breaking with convention

If project researchers choose to break these rules, they should be aware that they run the risk of having their report perceived as poorly written. If this is a risk that is deemed worth taking, they need to offer some explanation of *why* the rules have been broken to avoid any such impression. So, for example, if a researcher decides quite consciously to present an account of the research which uses the first person, there should be some acknowledgement that this is not conventional and some justification offered for its use.

Be consistent in the use of the referencing style

Whether the *Harvard* or the *numerical* style is used, there should be consistency throughout the report. Use one or the other, not both.

Use care with the page layout

The visual element of the presentation is important, and the researcher should give some consideration to things like the page layout and the use of graphs, tables and illustrations to enhance the appeal of the report.

Present tables and figures properly

Tables and figures should be presented in a consistent style that provides the reader with the necessary information to decipher the meaning of the data contained in them. As indicated in Chapter 13, there should be:

- a clear and precise title;
- the source of the table or figure (if it is not original material);
- the units of measurement being used (£, cm, tonnes, etc.);
- x axis as the independent variable (where relevant).

The structure of research reports

Research reports tend to be structured according to certain conventions. The order in which they present material, and even the headings used, tend to conform to a familiar pattern – a pattern which is dictated largely by the need to present information in a logical order, with each new section building on information that has been provided earlier. The project researcher would do well to use such a structure for guidance when it comes to writing up.

The familiar structure for research reports, in some contexts, has become formalized into a template for dividing up the material and presenting it in a preordained sequence. Following the lead of scientific journals, there are journals for social research which insist on the report conforming with the use of headings such as 'Abstract', 'Introduction', 'Methods', 'Findings', 'Discussion', 'Conclusions'. If researchers are writing for such journals they must adopt this rigid format. Elsewhere, researchers can exercise a little more freedom in their construction of the research report, being a bit flexible with the order and using headings that are somewhat different. Writing up research for a PhD, for instance, allows some leeway from this structure, as does writing up a commissioned piece of research whose audience is likely to have different priorities. But, even where researchers do not find themselves constrained by explicit, externally imposed formats, there remains the same underlying rationale to the writing up of research, and this should guide the researcher. The conventional structure can and should be adapted to meet the requirements of specific audiences and specific kinds of research, but it equally provides a robust template that all social researchers can use to guide their construction of a research report.

The conventional structure for reporting research divides the material into three parts: the preliminary part, the main text and the end matter. This is as true for a full length book as it is for a PhD, for a brief journal article and for a workplace project.

The preliminary part

Title

The title itself needs to indicate accurately the contents of the work. It also needs to be fairly brief. A good way of combining the two is to have a two-part title. The first part acts as the main title and gives a broad indication of the area of the work. The second part adds more detail. For example, 'Ethnicity and friendship: the contrast between sociometric research and fieldwork observation in primary school classrooms'.

Abstract

An abstract is a synopsis of a piece of research. Its purpose is to provide a brief summary which can be circulated widely to allow other people to see, at a glance, if the research is relevant to their needs and worth tracking down to read in full. An abstract is normally about 250–300 words in length, and is presented on a separate sheet.

Key words

Researchers are often asked to identify up to five 'key words'. These words are 'identifiers' – words that capture the essence of what the report is all about. The key words are needed for cross-referencing during library searches.

List of contents

Depending on the context, this can range from being just a list of chapter headings and their starting page through to being an extensive list, including details of the contents within the major section of the report; for instance, based on headings and sub-headings.

List of tables and figures

This should list the titles of the various tables and figures and their locations.

Preface

This provides the opportunity for the researcher to give a personal statement about the origins of the research and the significance of the research for the researcher as a person. In view of the importance of the 'self' in the research process, the Preface offers a valuable place in the research report to explore, albeit briefly, how the research reflects the personal experiences and biography of the researcher.

Acknowledgements

Under this heading, credit can be given to those who have helped with the research. This can range from people who acted as 'gatekeepers' in relation to fieldwork, through to academic supervisors, through to those who have commented on early drafts of the research report.

List of abbreviations

If the nature of the report demands that many abbreviations are used in the text, these should be listed, usually alphabetically, under this heading, alongside the full version of what they stand for.

The main text

The main text is generally divided into sections. The sections might be chapters as in the case of a larger piece of work or headings as in the case of shorter reports. In either case, they are normally presented in the following order.

Introduction

For the purposes of writing up research there needs to be an introduction. This may, or may not, coincide with a section or chapter titled as an 'Introduction', depending on how much discretion is open to the researcher and how far this is taken. The important thing is to recognize that, at the beginning, the reader needs to be provided with information about:

- the *background* to the work (in relation to significant issues, problems, ideas);
- the *aims* of the research;
- key *definitions* and concepts to be used;
- optionally, in longer pieces, an *overview* of the report (mapping out its contents).

Literature review

This may be presented as an integral part of the 'Introduction' or it may appear as a separate chapter or section. It is, though, essential that in the early stages of the report there is a review of the material that already exists on the topic in question. The current research should build on existing knowledge, not 'reinvent the wheel'. The literature review should demonstrate how the research being reported relates to previous research and, if possible, how it gives rise to particular issues, problems and ideas that the current research addresses.

Methods of investigation

At this point, having analysed the existing state of knowledge on a topic, it is reasonable to describe the methods of investigation. See the section on 'The research methods chapter or section' (pp. 328–9) for guidance on how this should be done.

Findings

This is where the reader gets introduced to the data. Aspects of the findings are singled out and described. The first step is to say, 'This is what was found with respect to this issue . . . This is what was found with respect to another issue . . .'. The aim for the researcher is to be able to present relevant findings before going ahead to analyse those findings and see what implications they might have for the issues, problems or ideas that prompted the research. First things first: let's see what we have found. Then, and only then, as a subsequent stage, will we move on to considering what significance the data might have in the context of the overall aims of the research.

Discussion and analysis

Here, the findings that have been outlined are subjected to scrutiny in terms of what they might mean. They are literally discussed and analysed with reference to the theories and ideas, issues and problems that were noted earlier in the report as providing the context in which the research was conceived. The researcher 'makes sense' of the findings by considering their implications beyond the confines of the current research.

Conclusions and recommendations

Finally, in the main text, the researcher needs to draw together the threads of the research to arrive at some general conclusion and, perhaps, to suggest some way forward. Rather than let the report fizzle out as it reaches the end, this part of the report should be constructive and positive. It can contain some of the following things:

- a retrospective evaluation of the research and its contribution;
- recommendations for improving the situation, guidelines or codes of practice;
- identification of new directions for further research.

The end matter

Appendices

This is the place for material which is too bulky for the main body of the text, or for material which, though directly relevant to the discussion, might entail too much of a sidetrack if placed in the text. Typical items that can be lodged in an appendix are:

- extensive tables of data;
- questionnaires used in a survey;
- extracts from an interview transcript;
- memos or minutes of meetings;
- technical specifications.

Notes

These will mainly occur when the researcher is using a numerical referencing system. They also offer the opportunity for scholarly details to be added which would interrupt the flow of the reading were they to be put directly into the text.

References

See the section on the Harvard system of referencing above.

Index

Provision of an index is usually restricted to large reports and books. It is unlikely that the kind of report produced by a project researcher would require an index.

Writing up qualitative research

For the qualitative researcher, the presentation of research in sections under the headings of 'abstract', 'introduction', 'findings', 'methods', 'discussion' and 'conclusions' might seem inappropriate and not in keeping with the way the research actually evolved. Headings like these might seem to accord with a design and execution of research more in line with experiments and surveys than ethnography or grounded theory, and therefore pose a difficulty for the qualitative researcher when it comes to meeting the conventions associated with writing up research. They would seem to be artificial and inappropriate.

Rather than ditch such headings, however, qualitative researchers might well consider using them as a template for constructing their accounts of the research – a template which gives some structure to the accounts and which is comfortably recognized by those coming from different traditions within the social sciences. While acknowledging that writing up qualitative research involves much more of a retrospective reconstruction of what actually happened than would be the case with more positivist approaches, it still needs to be recognized as just that – a retrospective *account* rather than a literal depiction of the rationale and the events. By latching on to the traditional conventions, the interpretive social researcher is provided with a template for reporting the research. The template, in this case, does not provide a means for faithfully reporting in some structured sequential manner what actually happened in the process of research. It does, however, provide a means for reconstructing and presenting the research in a way that:

- addresses and highlights the key issues;
- is clearly comprehendable to the reader;
- is logically ordered.

The research methods chapter or section

In all accounts of research there needs to be some description and justification of the methods used to collect the data. In larger works, this appears in a separate chapter. In shorter reports and articles, it tends to be curtailed to a section under a 'research methods' heading or to a clearly identifiable paragraph or two. Within the confines of the available space, the researcher needs to explain how the research was conceived, designed and executed. This is vital in order for the reader to make some informed evaluation of the study. Basically, if the reader is not told how and why the data were collected, he or she cannot make any judgement about how good the research is and whether any credibility should be given to its findings or conclusions.

Within the confines of the space available, the methods section should do three things.

Describe how the research was conducted

Precise details need to be given, using specific and accurate numbers and dates.

- *What* method(s) were used (the technical name)?
- *When* did the research take place (month and year, duration of research)?
- *Where* did the research take place (location, situation)?
- *How* was access to the data or subjects obtained?

- *Who* was involved in the research (the population, sample, cases, examples)?
- *How many* were involved in the research (precise numbers)?
- *How* were they selected (sampling technique)?

Justify these procedures

An argument needs to be put forward supporting the choice of method(s) as:

- reasonable in terms of the resources and time available;
- appropriate under the circumstances for collecting the necessary type of data;
- suitable for addressing the issues, problems or questions that underpin the research;
- having rigour, coherence and consistency – a professional standard;
- producing data that are representative, valid and reliable;
- conforming with ethical standards.

Acknowledge any limitations to the methods employed

Good research evaluates the weaknesses as well as the strengths of its methodology. When writing up the research, then, the researcher should acknowledge:

- any inherent limitations of the methodology;
- the scope of what can, and cannot, be concluded on the basis of the research that was undertaken;
- any ways in which resource constraints had a direct influence on the volume or kind of findings produced;
- any reservations about the authenticity, accuracy or honesty of answers;
- any ways in which, in retrospect, alternative methods might have proved to be more useful;
- any unexpected factors which arose during the research that influenced the outcome.

Checklist for writing up the research

When writing up the research you should feel confident about answering 'yes' to the following questions: ☑

1 Is there a suitable structure and logical development to the report? ☐

2 Is the text written in a clear style, free of spelling and grammatical errors? ☐

3 Does the writing style meet the expectations of the main audience for the research? ☐

4 Have the necessary conventions been followed in the writing up of the research? ☐

5 Are the references complete and do they follow a recognized style (e.g. Harvard)? ☐

6 Are the tables, figures, illustrations and diagrams properly labelled? ☐

   Do they enhance the visual attractiveness of the report, as well as supplying necessary information in a succinct manner? ☐

7 Has a detailed and precise description of the research process been provided? ☐

8 Has the choice of method(s) been justified in relation to the type of data required and the practical circumstances surrounding the research? ☐

9 Have the limitations of the research methodology been acknowledged? ☐

© M. Denscombe, *The Good Research Guide*. Open University Press.

Frequently asked questions

What is the difference between research strategies and research methods?

Strategies are broad approaches to research that are concerned with the direction and scale of a research project and its underlying philosophy. Strategies involve the aims and design principles that shape the overall investigation. Research methods are tools used for the collection of empirical data. They are the means by which the researcher collects or produces different kinds of data.

What is analysis?

Analysis means the separation of something into its component parts. To do this, of course, the researcher first needs to identify what those parts might be, and this links with a further meaning of analysis, which is to trace things back to their underlying sources. Analysis, then, involves probing beneath the surface appearance of something to discover the component elements which have come together to produce it. By tracing things back in this fashion, the researcher aims to expose some *general* principles that can be used to explain the nature of the thing being studied and can be applied elsewhere to other situations.

What is a concept?

A concept is a basic idea. It is an idea that is generally abstract and universal rather than concrete and specific. And it is basic in the sense that it cannot be easily explained in terms of other ideas or equated to other ideas. In terms of ideas, then, a concept is a basic building block that captures the *essence* of a thing (e.g. 'love', 'relevance').

When should I use Internet research methods?

The Internet offers some fabulous possibilities for research. It holds the prospect of gathering huge volumes of data, of operating at a global level, of getting information quickly – and doing all this at relatively low cost. These obvious attractions, however, should not seduce the researcher into using the Internet on every possible occasion, irrespective of whether it happens to be the best tool for the job. There are pros and cons to using the Internet, just as there are with other research strategies (see Hine, 2005). In particular, researchers need to consider the benefits for data collection that the new technology offers when weighed against methodological concerns related to things like:

- sample bias;
- interaction effect;
- response rate;
- ethics.

A decision on whether it is appropriate to use '*e*-research' should be based on an awareness of the implications of these factors and upon an evaluation of the respective advantages and disadvantages in relation to the specific topic that is to be investigated.

What is positivism?

Positivism is an approach to social research which seeks to apply the natural science model of research to investigations of the social world. It is based on the assumption that there are patterns and regularities, causes and consequences in the social world, just as there are in the natural world. These patterns and regularities in the social world are seen as having their own existence – they are real. For positivists, the aim of social research is to discover the patterns and regularities of the social world by using the kind of scientific methods used to such good effect in the natural sciences.

What is 'qualitative research'?

Qualitative research is an umbrella term that covers a variety of approaches to social research drawing on disciplines such as sociology, social anthropology and social psychology. What these approaches have in common are:

- the use of text and images as their basic data (rather than numbers);
- an interpretive approach that regards knowledge as socially constructed;
- a concern with meanings and the way people understand things;
- an interest in the activities of social groups (such as rituals, traditions and relationships);
- an interest in patterns of behaviour, cultural norms and types of language use.

However, what actually gives qualitative research its distinct identity is the fact that it has its own special approach to the collection and analysis of data which, as Chapter 14 shows, marks it out as quite different from quantitative research.

What is reflexivity?

Reflexivity concerns the relationship between the researcher and the social world. Contrary to positivism, reflexivity suggests that there is no prospect of the social researcher achieving an entirely objective position from which to study the social world. This is because the concepts the researcher uses to make sense of the world are also a part of that social world. Reflexivity is an awkward thing for social research. It means that what we know about the social world can never be entirely objective. A researcher can never stand outside the social world they are studying in order to gain some vantage point from which to view things from a perspective which is not contaminated by contact with that social world. Inevitably, the sense we make of the social world and the meaning we give to events and situations are shaped by our experience as social beings and the legacy of the values, norms and concepts we have assimilated during our lifetime. And these will differ from person to person, culture to culture.

What is reliability?

Researchers need to feel confident that their measurements are not affected by a research instrument that gives one reading on the first occasion it is used and a different reading on the next occasion when there has been no real change in the item being measured. This is why they are concerned with the 'reliability' of a research instrument. A good level of reliability means that the research instrument produces the same data time after time on each occasion that it is used, and that any variation in the results obtained through using the instrument is due entirely to variations in the thing being measured. None of the variation is due to fluctuations caused by the volatile nature of the research instrument itself. So a research instrument such as a particular experiment or questionnaire is said to be 'reliable' if it is *consistent*, and this is generally deemed to be a good thing as far as research is concerned.

What sample size do I need?

If you are using a random sample as part of a large survey then there is statistical calculation for the precise number needed for the survey. The size of the sample will depend on the level of accuracy that is required, and there are plenty of websites which provide a facility that will do the maths. Try a web search on 'calculate sample size'. For qualitative research and small-scale research, however, the exact sample size is more difficult to estimate. It will reflect the time and resources available, and the number of suitable people who can be identified and contacted for inclusion. As a rule of thumb the sample should be sufficient in size for the purposes of the research and be comparable with the sample size of similar pieces of research. See pages 25–8, 94–7 for further information on this point.

What is a theory?

A theory is a proposition about the relationship between things. In principle, a theory is universal, applying at all times and to all instances of the thing(s) in question. In the social sciences, the notion of 'theory' needs to be treated more cautiously than in the natural sciences, because of the *complexity* of social phenomena and because people react to knowledge about themselves in a way that chemicals and forces do not.

What is validity?

In a broad sense, validity means that the data and the methods are 'right'. In terms of research data, the notion of validity hinges around whether or not the data reflect the truth, reflect reality and cover the crucial matters. In terms of the methods used to obtain data, validity addresses the question, 'Are we measuring suitable indicators of the concept and are we getting accurate results?' *The idea of validity hinges around the extent to which research data and the methods for obtaining the data are deemed accurate, honest and on target.*

REFERENCES

Alaszewski, A. (2005) *Using Diaries for Social Research*. London: Sage.

Austin, J.L. (1962) *How to do Things with Words*. Oxford: Clarendon.

Ball, S. (1990) Self-doubt and soft data: social and technical trajectories in ethnographic fieldwork, *International Journal of Qualitative Studies in Education*, 3: 157–71.

Banks, M. (2001) *Visual Methods in Social Research*. London: Sage.

Becker, H. and Geer, B. (1957) Participant observation and interviewing: a comparison, *Human Organization*, 16(3): 28–35.

Bell, P. (2000) Content analysis of visual images, in T. van Leeuwen and C. Jewitt (eds) *The Handbook of Visual Analysis*. London: Sage.

Berger, P. and Luckmann, T. (1967) *The Social Construction of Reality*. London: Allen Lane.

Bloor, M., Frankland, J., Thomas, M. and Robson, K. (2001) *Focus Groups in Social Research*. London: Sage.

Boutilier, M., Mason, R. and Rootman, U. (1997) Community action and reflective practice in health promotion research, *Health Promotion International*, 12(1): 69–78.

Bruckman, A. (2002) *Ethical Guidelines for Research Online*. <http://www.cc.gatech.edu/~asb/ethics/> (accessed 26 September 2006)

Bryman, A. (1988) *Quality and Quantity in Social Research*. London: Unwin Hyman.

Bryman, A. (1989) *Research Methods and Organization Studies*. London: Routledge.

Bryman, A. (2006) Integrating quantitative and qualitative research: how is it done? *Qualitative Research*, 6(1): 97–113.

Bryman, A. (2007) *Qualitative Research*. London: Sage.

Bryman, A. and Burgess, R.G. (eds) (1994) *Analyzing Qualitative Data*. London: Routledge.

Buchanan, E.A. (ed.) (2004) *Readings in Virtual Research Ethics*. Hershey, PA: Information Science Publishing.

Bulmer, M. (1984) *The Chicago School of Sociology: Institutionalization, Diversity, and the Rise of Sociological Research*. Chicago: University of Chicago Press.

Burgess, R.G. (1984) *In the Field: An Introduction to Field Research*. London: Allen and Unwin.

Campbell, D.T. and Fiske, D.W. (1959) Convergent and discriminant validation by the multitrait-multimethod matrix, *Psychological Bulletin*, 56(2): 81–105.

Cline, R.J.W. and Haynes, K.M. (2001) Consumer health information seeking on the Internet: the state of the art, *Health Education Research*, 16(6): 671–92.

Collier, M. (2001) Approaches to the analysis of visual images, in T. van Leeuwen and J. Jewitt (eds) *Handbook of Visual Analysis*. London: Sage.

Collins, K.M.T., Onwuegbuzie, A.J. and Sutton, I.L. (2006) A model incorporating the rationale and purpose for conducting mixed-methods research in special education and beyond, *Learning Disabilities: A Contemporary Journal*, 4(1): 67–100.

Coomber, R. (1997) Using the Internet for survey research, *Sociological Research Online*, 2(2) <http://www.socresonline.org.uk/socresonline/2/2/2.html>

Couper, M.P. (2000) Web surveys, *Public Opinion Quarterly*, 64(4): 464–95.

Coxon, A.P. (2005) Integrating qualitative and quantitative data: what does the user need? *Forum: Qualitative Social Research (FQS)*, 6(2): article 40, May 2005. <http://www.qualitative-research.net/fqs-texte/2–05/05–2–40-e.htm#lit>

Creswell, J.W. (1998) *Qualitative Inquiry and Research Design: Choosing Among Five Traditions*. Thousand Oaks, CA: Sage.

Creswell, J.W. (2003) *Research Design: Qualitative, Quantitative, and Mixed Methods Approaches*. Thousand Oaks, CA: Sage.

Creswell, J.W. and Plano Clark, V. (2007) *Designing and Conducting Mixed Methods Research*. Thousand Oaks, CA: Sage.

Croll, P. (1986) *Systematic Classroom Observation*. London: Falmer.

Crotty, M. (1996) *Phenomenology and Nursing Research*. Melbourne: Churchill Livingstone.

Delamont, S. (1992) *Fieldwork in Educational Settings*. London: Falmer.

Denscombe, M. (1983) Interviews, accounts and ethnographic research on teachers, in M. Hammersley (ed.) *The Ethnography of Schooling: Methodological Issues*. Driffield: Nafferton Books.

Denscombe, M. (2006) Web-based questionnaires: an assessment of the mode effect on the validity of data, *Social Science Computer Review*, 24(2): 246–54. DOI 10.1177/0894439305284522.

Denzin, N.K. (1970) Strategies of multiple triangulation, in N.K. Denzin (ed.) *The Research Act in Sociology. A Theoretical Introduction to Sociological Method*. New York: McGraw-Hill, pp. 297–313.

Denzin, N.K. (1989) *The Research Act*, 3rd edn. Englewood Cliffs, NJ: Prentice Hall.

Denzin, N.K. (1999) Cybertalk and the method of instances, in S. Jones (ed.) *Doing Internet Research: Critical Issues and Methods for Examining the Net*. Thousand Oaks, CA: Sage.

Devault, M. (1990) Talking and listening from women's standpoint, *Social Problems*, 37(1): 96–116.

Dey, I. (1993) *Qualitative Data Analysis: A User-friendly Guide for Social Scientists*. London: Routledge.

Dillman, D.A. (2007) *Mail and Internet Surveys: The Tailored Design Method*, 2nd edn. New York: Wiley.

Edwards, A. and Talbot, R. (1994) *The Hard-pressed Researcher: A Research Handbook for the Caring Professions*. London: Longman.

Elliott, J. (1991) Action Research for Educational Change. Buckingham: Open University Press.

Emmison, M. and Smith, P. (2000) *Researching the Visual: Images, Objects, Contexts and Interactions in Social and Cultural Inquiry*. London: Sage.

Festinger, L., Reicken, H. and Schachter, S. (1956) *When Prophecy Fails*. Minneapolis: University of Minnesota Press (republished London: Harper & Row, 1964).

Flanders, N.A. (1970) *Analyzing Teacher Behavior*. Reading, MA: Addison-Wesley.

Flick, U. (2002) Qualitative research: state of the art, *Social Science Information*, 41(1): 5–24.

Galton, M., Simon, B. and Croll, P. (1980) *Inside the Primary Classroom*. London: Routledge and Kegan Paul.

Geertz, C. (1973) Thick description: toward an interpretive theory of culture, In C. Geertz (ed.) *The Interpretation of Cultures*. New York: Basic Books.

Gerbner, G., Holsti, O., Krippendorf, K., Paisley, W. and Stone, P. (eds) (1969) *The Analysis of Communication Content.* New York: Wiley.

Gibbs, G. (2002) *Qualitative Data Analysis: Explorations with NVivo.* Maidenhead: Open University Press.

Glaser, B. (1978) *Theoretical Sensitivity.* Mill Valley, CA: Sociology Press.

Glaser, B. (ed.) (1995) *Grounded Theory, 1984–1994.* Mill Valley, CA: Sociology Press.

Glaser, B. (1999) The future of grounded theory, *Qualitative Health Research,* 9(6): 836–45.

Glaser, B. and Strauss, A. (1967) *The Discovery of Grounded Theory.* Chicago: Aldine.

Glaser, J., Dixit, J. and Green, D. (2002) Studying hate crime with the Internet: what makes racists advocate racial violence, *Journal of Social Issues,* 58(1): 177–93.

Gorard, S. and Taylor, C. (2004) *Combining Methods in Educational and Social Research.* Maidenhead: Open University Press.

Goulding, C. (2002) *Grounded Theory: A Practical Guide for Management, Business and Market Researchers.* London: Sage.

Greene, J.C., Caracelli, V.J. and Graham, W.F. (1989) Toward a conceptual framework for mixed-method evaluation designs, *Educational Evaluation and Policy Analysis,* 11(3): 255–74.

Griffin, J. (1962) *Black Like Me.* London: Collins.

Grundy, S. and Kemmis, S. (1988) Educational research in Australia: the state of the art (an overview), in S. Kemmis and R. McTaggart (eds) *The Action Research Reader,* 3rd edn. Geelong, Victoria: Deakin University Press.

Haglund, K. (2004) Conducting life history research with adolescents. *Qualitative Health Research,* 14(9): 1309–19.

Halfpenny, P. (1997) The relation between quantitative and qualitative social research, *Bulletin de Méthodologie Sociologique,* 57: 49–64.

Hammersley, M. (1990) What's wrong with ethnography? The myth of theoretical description, *Sociology,* 24: 597–615.

Hammersley, M. (1992) *What's Wrong with Ethnography?* London: Routledge.

Hammersley, M. (1996) The relationship between qualitative and quantitative research: paradigm loyalty versus methodological eclecticism, in J.E.T. Richardson (ed.) *Handbook of Qualitative Research Methods for Psychology and the Social Sciences.* Leicester: British Psychological Society, pp. 159–74.

Hammersley, M. and Atkinson, P. (1983) *Ethnography: Principles in Practice.* London: Tavistock.

Heidegger, M. (1962) *Being and Time.* Oxford: Basil Blackwell.

Hine, C. (2000) *Virtual Ethnography.* London: Sage.

Hine, C. (ed.) (2005) *Virtual Methods: Issues in Social Research on the Internet.* Oxford: Berg.

Hoinville, G., Jowell, R. and associates (1985) *Survey Research Practice.* Aldershot: Gower.

Howell, N. (1990) *Surviving Fieldwork: A Report of the Advisory Panel on Health and Safety in Fieldwork.* Washington, DC: American Anthropological Association.

Humphreys, L. (1970) *Tearoom Trade.* Chicago: Aldine.

Husserl, E. (1931) *Ideas: General Introduction to Pure Phenomenology.* London: George Allen and Unwin.

Husserl, E. (1970) *Cartesian Meditations: An Introduction to Phenomenology.* The Hague, Martinus Nijhoff.

Johnson, R.B. and Onwuegbuzie, A.J. (2004) Mixed methods research: a research paradigm whose time has come, *Educational Researcher*, 33(7): 14–26.

Kirk, J. and Miller, M. (1986) *Reliability and Validity in Qualitative Research*. Beverly Hills, CA: Sage.

Kozinets, R.V. (1998) On netnography: initial reflections on consumer research investigations of cyberculture, *Advances in Consumer Research*, 25: 366–71.

Kozinets, R.V. (2002) The field behind the screen: using netnography for marketing research in online communities, *Journal of Marketing Research*, 39: 61–72.

Krippendorf, K. (2004) *Content Analysis: An Introduction to its Methodology*, 2nd edn. Thousand Oaks, CA: Sage.

Kugelmann, R. (1999) Complaining about chronic pain, *Social Science and Medicine*, 49(12): 16–63.

Layder, D. (1993) *New Strategies in Social Research*. Cambridge: Polity Press.

Layder, D. (1998) *Sociological Practice: Linking Theory and Social Research*. London: Sage.

Lee, R. (1995) *Dangerous Fieldwork*. Thousand Oaks, CA: Sage.

Lewin, K. (1946) Action research and minority problems, *Journal of Social Issues*, 2: 34–46.

Lewins, A. and Silver, C. (2007) *Using Qualitative Software: A Step-by-Step Guide*. London: Sage.

Lincoln, Y. and Guba, E. (1985) *Naturalistic Enquiry*. Newbury Park, CA: Sage

Locke, K. (2001) *Grounded Theory in Management Research*. London: Sage.

Loizos, P. (2000) Video, film and photographs as research documents, in M.W. Bauer and G. Gaskell (eds) *Qualitative Researching with Text, Image and Sound*. London: Sage.

McCabe, S.E. (2004) Comparison of web and mail surveys in collecting illicit drug use data: a randomized experiment, *Journal of Drug Education*, 34(1): 61–73.

McFee, G. (1992) Triangulation in research: two confusions, *Educational Research*, 34(3): 215–19.

Malinowski, B. (1922) *Argonauts of the Western Pacific*. London: Routledge and Kegan Paul.

Mann, C. and Stewart, F. (2000) *Internet Communication and Qualitative Research: A Handbook for Researching Online*. London: Sage.

Marshall, C. and Rossman, G.B. (1999) *Designing Qualitative Research*, 3rd edn. Thousand Oaks, CA: Sage.

Maykut, P. and Morehouse, R. (1994) *Beginning Qualitative Research: A Philosophical and Practical Guide*. London: Falmer.

Mayo, E. ([1933] 2003) *The Human Problems of an Industrial Civilization*. London: Routledge.

Mead, M. (1943) *Coming of Age in Samoa: A Study of Adolescence and Sex in Primitive Societies*. Harmondsworth: Penguin.

Mead, M. ([1930] 1963) *Growing Up in New Guinea*. Harmondsworth: Penguin.

Miles, M. and Huberman, A. (1994) *Qualitative Data Analysis*. Thousand Oaks, CA: Sage.

Milgram, S. (1974) *Obedience to Authority*. New York: Harper and Row.

Morgan, D.L. (2006) Focus group, in V. Jupp (ed.) *The Sage Dictionary of Social Research Methods*. London: Sage, pp. 121–3.

Morley, J. (1998) The private theater: a phenomenogical investigation of daydreaming, *Journal of Phenomenological Psychology*, 29(1): 116–35.

Moustakas, C. (1992) Firebrand – the experience of being different, *The Human Psychologist*, 20(2/3): 175–88.

Oakley, A. (1981) Interviewing women: a contradiction in terms, in H. Roberts (ed.) *Doing Feminist Research*. London: Routledge and Kegan Paul.

O'Connell Davidson, J. (1995) The anatomy of 'free choice' prostitution, *Gender, Work and Organization*, 2: 1–10.

O'Dochartaigh, N. (2002) *The Internet Research Handbook*. London: Sage.

Penn, G. (2000) Semiotic analysis of still images, in M.W. Bauer and G. Gaskell (eds) *Qualitative Researching with Text, Image, Sound*. London: Sage.

Platt, J. (1981) Evidence and proof in documentary research, *The Sociological Review*, 21(1): 31–66.

Plummer, K. (2001) *Documents of Life 2: An Invitation to a Critical Humanism*, 2nd edn. London: Sage.

Polsky, N. (1967) *Hustlers, Beats and Others*. Harmondsworth: Penguin.

Porter, S. (1993) Critical realist ethnography: the case of racism and professionalism in a medical setting, *Sociology*, 27: 591–601.

Potter, J. and Wetherell, M. (1994) Analysing discourse, in A. Bryman and R.G. Burgess (eds) *Analysing Qualitative Data*. London: Routledge.

Prosser, J. (1998) The status of image-based research, in J. Prosser (ed.) *Image-based Research: A Sourcebook for Qualitative Researchers*. London: Falmer.

Prosser, J. and Schwartz, D. (1998) Photographs within the sociological research process, in J. Prosser (ed.) *Image-based Research: A Sourcebook for Qualitative Researchers*. London: Falmer.

Ragin, C. (1994) *Constructing Social Research*. Thousand Oaks, CA: Pine Forge Press.

Ragin, C. and Becker, H. (1992) *What Is a Case? Exploring the Foundations of Social Enquiry*. New York: Cambridge University Press.

Reichardt, C.S. and Rallis, S.F. (1994) Qualitative and quantitative inquiries are not incompatible: a call for a new partnership, in C.S. Reichardt and S.F. Rallis (ed.) *The Qualitative-Quantitative Debate: New Perspectives*. San Francisco, CA: Jossey-Bass, pp. 85–92.

Reimer, J. (1979) *Hard Hats: The Work World of Construction Workers*. Beverly Hills, CA: Sage.

Rocco, T.S., Bliss, L.A., Gallagher, S. and Perez-Prado, A. (2003) Taking the next step: mixed methods research in organizational systems. *Information Technology, Learning and Performance Journal*, 21(1): 19–29.

Roethlisberger, F.J. and Dickson, W.J. ([1939] 2003) *Management and the Worker*. London: Routledge.

Rose, G. (2001) *Visual Methodologies*. London: Sage.

Sartre, J.-P. (1956) *Being and Nothingness: An Essay on Phenomenological Ontology*. New York: Philosophical Library.

Schön, D. (1983) *The Reflective Practitioner: How Professionals Think in Action*. New York: Basic Books.

Schutz, A. (1962) *Collected Papers, Volume 1*. The Hague: Martinus Nijhoff.

Schutz, A. (1967) *The Phenomenology of the Social World*. Evanston, IL: Northwestern University Press.

Scott, J. (1990) *A Matter of Record*. Cambridge: Polity Press.

Seale, C., Gobo, G. and Gubrium, J. (1999) *The Quality of Qualitative Research*. London: Sage.

Seale, C., Gobo, G., Gubrium, J. and Silverman, D. (eds) (2004) *Qualitative Research Practice*. London: Sage.

Seymour, J.E. (1999) Revisiting medicalization of 'natural' death, *Social Science and Medicine*, 49(5): 691.

Silverman, D. (1985) *Qualitative Methodology and Sociology*. Aldershot: Gower.

Silverman, D. (2000) *Doing Qualitative Research: A Practical Handbook*. London: Sage.

Silverman, D. (2006) *Interpreting Qualitative Data: Methods for Analyzing Talk, Text and Interaction*, 3rd edn. Thousand Oaks, CA: Sage.

Simon, A. and Boyer, G. (1970) *Mirrors of Behavior: An Anthology of Classroom Observation Instruments*. Philadelphia: Research for Better Schools.

Somekh, B. (1995) The contribution of action research to development in social endeavours: a position paper on action research methodology, *British Educational Research Journal*, 21(3): 339–55.

Stake, R. (1995) *The Art of Case Study Research*. Thousand Oaks, CA: Sage.

Stanton, J. and Rogelberg, S. (2001) Using Internet/intranet web pages to collect organizational research data, *Organizational Research Methods*, 4(3): 200–17.

Stevens, S.S. (1946) On the theory of scales of measurement. *Science* 103(2684): 677–80.

Strauss, A. (1987) *Qualitative Analysis for Social Scientists*. Cambridge: Cambridge University Press.

Strauss, A.L. and Corbin, J. (1990) *Basics of Qualitative Research: Grounded Theory Procedures and Techniques*. London: Sage.

Strauss, A.L. and Corbin, J (1998) *Basics of Qualitative Research: Techniques and Procedures for Developing Grounded Theory*, 2nd edn. Thousand Oaks, CA: Sage.

Susman, G. and Evered, R. (1978) An assessment of the scientific merits of action research, *Administrative Science Quarterly*, 23(4): 582–603.

Tashakkori, A. and Teddlie, C. (1998) *Mixed Methodology: Combining Qualitative and Quantitative Approaches*. Thousand Oaks, CA: Sage.

Tashakkori, A. and Teddlie, C. (eds) (2003) *Handbook of Mixed Methods in Social and Behavioral Research*. Thousand Oaks, CA: Sage.

Tesch, R. (1993) Software for qualitative researchers: analysis needs and program capabilities, in N. Fielding and R. Lee (eds) *Using Computers in Qualitative Research*, 2nd edn. London: Sage.

Truell, A.D., Bartlett, J.E. and Alexander, M.W (2002) Response rate, speed and completeness: a comparison of Internet-based and mail surveys, *Behaviour Research Methods, Instruments and Computers*, 34(1): 46–9.

Turner, B. (1983) The use of grounded theory for the qualitative analysis of organizational behaviour, *Journal of Management Studies*, 20(3): 333–48.

van Leeuwen, T. and Jewitt, J. (eds) (2001) *Handbook of Visual Analysis*. London: Sage.

van Manen, M. (1990) *Researching Lived Experience: Human Science for an Action Sensitive Pedagogy*. London, Ontario: Althouse.

van Maanen, J. (ed.) (1995) *Representation in Ethnography*. Thousand Oaks, CA: Sage.

Webb, E.J., Campbell, D.T., Schwartz, R.D. and Sechrest, L. (1966) *Unobtrusive Measures: Non-reactive Research in the Social Sciences*. Chicago: Rand McNally.

Whyte, W.F. ([1943] 1981) *Street Corner Society: The Social Structure of an Italian Slum*, 3rd edn. Chicago: University of Chicago Press.

Winter, R. (1996) Some principles and procedures for the conduct of action research, in O. Zuber-Skerritt (ed.) *New Directions in Action Research*. London: Falmer Press.

Wittgenstein, L. (1968) *Philosophical Investigations*. Oxford: Basil Blackwell.

Woods, P. (1979) *The Divided School*. London: Routledge and Kegan Paul.

Woods, P. (1993) Managing marginality: teacher development through grounded life history, *British Educational Research Journal,* 19(5): 447–65.

Woods, P. (2006) *Successful Writing for Qualitative Researchers,* 2nd edn. London: Routledge.

Wooffitt, R. (2005) *Conversation Analysis and Discourse Analysis: A Comparative and Critical Introduction.* London: Sage.

Worthington, H. and Holloway, P. (1997) Making sense of statistics, *International Journal of Health Education,* 35(3): 76–80.

Yin, R. (1994) *Case Study Research: Design and Methods,* 2nd edn. Newbury Park, CA: Sage.

Zuber-Skerritt, O. (ed.) (1996) *New Directions in Action Research.* London: Falmer Press.

INDEX

Open up your options

 Education

 Health & Social Welfare

 Management

 Media, Film & Culture

 Psychology & Counselling

Sociology

Study Skills

for more information on our
publications visit **www.openup.co.uk**

OPEN UNIVERSITY PRESS
McGraw - Hill Education